The Bumper Book of
Cricket Extras

The Bumper Book of CRICKET EXTRAS

Marc Dawson

Foreword by
DAVID GOWER

Kangaroo Press

For Courtney and Kate

Cover design by Darian Causby showing a detail of a stamp designed for Australia Post
by Garry Emery and (inset) Greg Blewett in action.

First published in 1993 by Kangaroo Press Pty Ltd
3 Whitehall Road Kenthurst NSW 2156 Australia
P.O. Box 6125 Dural Delivery Centre NSW 2158
Typeset by G.T. Setters Pty Limited
Printed by Australian Print Group, Maryborough, Victoria 3465

ISBN 0 86417 570 1

Contents

Foreword by David Gower 7
1 A Team Effort 9
2 The Run-Scorers 18
3 Bowlers 40
4 Age 50
5 PMs and GGs 53
6 Family Connections 58
7 The One-Day Game 69
8 The Don 79
9 Captains and Captaincy 82
10 The Theatre, Film, Television and Radio 85
11 The Wicket-Keepers 90
12 Imports and Exports 96
13 Cricket and Other Sports 102
14 Duck Soup 111
15 What's in a Name? 120
16 LBW 121
17 Cricket Stamps 123
18 Births and Deaths 125
19 Music, Music, Music and Other Cricket Records 127
20 Averages 130
21 Here, There and Everywhere 136
22 Coincidentally 137
23 Literary Connections 142
24 Extra Extras 144
25 Stop Press! 150
Picture Credits 152
Bibliography 153
Index 154

Foreword by David Gower

Marc Dawson's book contains probably the most complete set of cricketing quirks and coincidences ever to be collated in one volume. This is definitely not a book for reading from cover to cover in one sitting, but very much one to nibble at frequently.

Put all these snippets of information onto computer and you have the ideal companion for any cricketing commentator or follower, especially in English, or predominantly damp, conditions. Any freak storms or flash floods can be eased away by dipping into this vast store of knowledge.

Cricket has long been a game adored by statisticians—they will find this tome irresistible, as much for the opportunity to try and catch out Marc Dawson on a matter of fact as for the knowledge contained therein.

David Gower

1 A Team Effort

Despite a total of only 86 by Middlesex at Lord's in 1899, they created history by dismissing Somerset for 35 and 44 to grab victory by an innings and 7 runs. The match was completed on the first day and remains the shortest on record, with only three hours and five minutes of play.

•

In the inaugural Australia–Sri Lanka Test, at Kandy in 1983, five of the first six in Australia's batting order were left-handers—Kepler Wessels, Graeme Wood, Graham Yallop, David Hookes and Allan Border. Greg Chappell, at number 4, was the odd man out.

•

New South Wales has twice scored over 700 in the second innings of a first-class match:

770 v South Australia at Adelaide 1920–21
761–8d v Queensland at Sydney 1929–30

•

The Pakistan–India Test series of 1954–55 was the first rubber in Test history to comprise five drawn matches. The 'feat' was repeated in the return series of 1960–61.

•

In 1974 England achieved a unique hat-trick of victories when for the third time it won a Test match after losing only two wickets. The first occasion came at the expense of South Africa at Lord's in 1924, the second against New Zealand at Leeds in 1958, the third against India at Edgbaston.

•

There were seven run outs in the Test match between Australia and Pakistan at Melbourne in 1972–73.

•

When Australia beat England 4–0 in 1989 a new record for absolute consistency was set when, for the first time in a six-Test series, the same pairs of opening batsmen and bowlers were used in every innings. Geoff Marsh and Mark Taylor opened the batting in all 11 innings and Terry Alderman and Geoff Lawson opened the bowling attack each time. By contrast England had a different pair of bowlers in each of the six Tests, and five different sets of batsmen. Only seven Australians were required to bowl during the entire series—Alderman, Lawson, Merv Hughes, Trevor Hohns, Steve Waugh, Greg Campbell and Allan Border. England used 19 bowlers.

•

Australia made a total of 3,877 runs in the six Tests in England in 1989, a new record in an Ashes series, beating the 3,757 runs scored by England in 1928–29.

•

A record number of West Australians represented Australia in Test matches during the home-and-away series in 1981–82. Seven played in eight Tests, against Pakistan and the West Indies at home, and in New Zealand—Bruce Laird, Graeme Wood, Kim Hughes, Rod Marsh, Bruce Yardley, Dennis Lillee and Terry Alderman. The record, though, for the highest representation by one state in an Australian side is nine. In the first Test against South Africa at Durban in 1921–22 there were nine players from New South Wales.

•

During the 1992–93 Test series against Sri Lanka, Australia's front-line batsmen recorded one of the worst performances of all time, being reduced, at one stage, to 4 for 9 at Moratuwa. Not since 1896 at The Oval, when the score was 4 for 7, had Australia lost so many wickets for so few runs.

GREATEST TOP-ORDER COLLAPSES IN TEST CRICKET

Score	*FOW*	*Match*
6–7	0/0/1/7/7/7	Australia v England at Manchester 1888
5–6	0/5/5/6/6	India v England at The Oval 1952
4–0	0/0/0/0	India v England at Leeds 1952
4–7	0/3/7/7	Australia v England at The Oval 1896
4–8	0/7/7/8	England v India at Bangalore 1976–77
4–9	6/6/6/9	Australia v Sri Lanka at Moratuwa 1992–93
3–0	0/0/0	Australia v England at Brisbane 1950–51
3–1	1/1/1	Australia v England at Sydney 1936–37
3–1	0/1/1	West Indies v India at Port-of-Spain 1982–83
3–1	1/1/1	New Zealand v West Indies at Bridgetown 1984–85

•

When England played the West Indies at Edgbaston in 1991, all 11 players had scored a first-class century—Graham Gooch, Hugh Morris, Michael Atherton, Graeme Hick, Allan Lamb, Mark Ramprakash, Jack Russell, Derek Pringle, Phillip DeFreitas, Chris Lewis and Richard Illingworth.

•

Three-figure scores dominated play in the 1986–87 Duleep Trophy final, with a record nine hundreds scored over the four days play. West Zone batted first and made 516 with Anshuman Gaekwad (138), Lalchand Rajput (105) and Ravi Shastri (127) all hitting centuries. South Zone's 740 included 112 from its captain Kris Srikkanth, 102 from Carlton

Saldanha and 149 from Bharat Arun. In their second innings Wests made 3 for 472, Rajput scoring his second century of the match with 109, Shrikant Kalyani an unbeaten 101, and Suresh Keshwala 124 not out.

•

In 1936-37, Australia staged one of the greatest comebacks in Test history when it became the first country to win a Test series after being two matches down. England inflicted two heavy defeats on Australia, winning the first Test by 322 runs and the second by an innings and 22, but then lost the next three. Don Bradman played a big part, scoring centuries in each of the last three games—270, 212 and 169.

•

When India made 524 for 9 declared against New Zealand at Kanpur in 1976, it was the first time in Test cricket that a total of 500 had been achieved without an individual century. All 11 batsmen reached double figures for the eighth time in Test history—Mohinder Amarnath top-scored with 70.

•

In 1884, Australia scored 551 at The Oval, becoming the first country to pass the 500-run mark in a Test match. Australia was also first to reach 100, 200 and 600 in a Test innings. Below is a breakdown of where and when each of the century totals was first achieved:

INNINGS LANDMARKS IN TEST CRICKET:
WHO GOT THERE FIRST

Total	*Country*	*Opposition*	*Match*	*Score*
100	Australia	England	Melbourne 1876-77	245
200	Australia	England	Melbourne 1876-77	245
300	England	Australia	The Oval 1880	420
400	England	Australia	The Oval 1880	420
500	Australia	England	The Oval 1884	551
600	Australia	England	Melbourne 1924-25	600
700	England	West Indies	Kingston 1929-30	849
800	England	West Indies	Kingston 1929-30	849
900	England	Australia	The Oval 1938	7d-903

•

The second and third Tests between the West Indies and England in 1973-74 contained seven players from the same English county—Dennis Amiss, John Jameson, Bob Willis, Alvin Kallicharran, Rohan Kanhai, Deryck Murray and Lance Gibbs had all played for Warwickshire.

•

During the 1982-83 Ashes series, all of England's first-innings wickets fell to catches in two successive Tests, at Brisbane and Melbourne.

•

During the five-match series against Australia in 1990-91 the West Indies used the same team for each Test, matching the record set by England against Australia in 1884-85 and equalled by South Africa against England in 1905-06.

•

Victoria, bowled out for 90 by New South Wales at Newcastle in 1982-83, came up with a record score next time around, making 7 declared for 479 after being forced to follow on. Four batsmen hit half-centuries, with both Mick Taylor and Dean Jones scoring 94.

•

In 1920-21, six totals in excess of 500 were scored in first-class matches against South Australia—802 by New South Wales at Sydney, 724 by Victoria at Melbourne, 770 by New South Wales at Adelaide, 639 by Victoria at Adelaide, and 627 and 5 declared for 512 by the MCC at Adelaide.

•

During the fourth Test at Bridgetown in 1983, all 20 West Indies and Indian batsmen were caught in the first innings. This also happened in the fifth Test against India at Perth in 1991-92, a match which contained 33 catches, a world record in Test cricket, bettering the 32 in the Leeds Test against Pakistan in 1971. Of the 166 wickets that fell in the 1991-92 series with India, a record 121 went to catches. An average of 24.2 catches was recorded in each Test, another record.

•

In 1982-83, Jammu and Kashmir celebrated Christmas by achieving its first-ever victory in the Ranji Trophy. Since entering the competition in 1959-60, Jammu and Kashmir had played 99 successive matches without success, a sequence which included 92 losses and seven draws. Its first win, in its 100th first-class match, was recorded over Services at Udhampur in the North Zone league. Eleven matches later they inflicted an innings defeat on Himachal Pradesh at Srinigar in 1985-86. In between, though, the team lost eight of its matches by an innings margin, including four in a row in 1984-85 and three out of four the previous season.

•

At Melbourne in 1990-91, England suffered one of its worst-ever collapses in Test cricket, losing six wickets for 3 runs to be all out for 150. Another famous England collapse also took place at Melbourne, in 1936-37, when on a rain-affected pitch it lost six wickets for 8 (3-68 to 9-76).

•

When New South Wales defeated Western Australia in the 1982-83 Sheffield Shield final it was their first victory in Perth since 1964-65. The next time Western Australia lost a match to the Blues at the WACA came six seasons later in 1988-89, and it brought to an end its 31-match Sheffield Shield sequence without defeat at home.

•

New Zealand began its tour of England in 1983 with a score of 9 declared for 544 in its opening first-class match, against Somerset at Taunton. Five of its batsmen scored half-centuries but none a century—Geoff Howarth top-scored with 88, while John Wright made 85 and Richard Hadlee 82. Their total was only 37 runs behind the highest score in all first-class cricket not to contain an individual century. In 1899, Nottinghamshire made 581 against Derbyshire, with Billy Gunn's 90 the highest contribution from any one batsman.

•

The 1948 Australians

The greatest number of runs in a day by one team is 721 by the 1948 Australians against Essex at Southend. Don Bradman top-scored with 187; three others also contributed centuries.

S.G. Barnes	hit wicket b R. Smith	79
W.A. Brown	c Horsfall b Bailey	153
D.G. Bradman	b P. Smith	187
K.R. Miller	b Bailey	0
R.A. Hamence	c P. Smith b R. Smith	46
S.J. Loxton	c Rist b Vigar	120
R.A. Saggers	not out	104
I.W. Johnson	st Rist b P. Smith	9
D. Ring	c Vigar b P. Smith	1
W.A. Johnston	b Vigar	9
E.R.H. Toshack	c Vigar b P. Smith	4
Extras		9
		721

•

The second week of February in 1990 would have to be one of the bleakest periods on record for English cricket. Three teams representing England were defeated within 48 hours in different parts of the world:

English XI v South Africa at Johannesburg (8–10 February)
England XI v Windward Islands at St. Lucia (8–11 February)
England 'A' v Kenya at Nairobi (11 February)

•

When Tasmania opposed Western Australia in their first-ever Sheffield Shield match, at Perth in 1977–78, it was only the second encounter between the two teams at first-class level since their inaugural meeting at Hobart in 1929–30.

•

One of the most one-sided matches of all time took place in the Ayub Zonal Tournament in Pakistan in 1964–65. Against a particularly weak team, Railways made 910 for 6 declared and then dismissed Dera Ismail Khan for 32 and 27. Four batsmen made centuries in Railway's total, the highest being 337 not out by Pervez Akhtar. Their winning margin of an innings and 851 runs is the record in first-class cricket.

•

Only two countries have played in 500 Test matches. England was first to reach the target when they took on Pakistan at Leeds in 1974, having contested the first-ever Test, at Melbourne, 97 years earlier. Australia was the next nation to achieve the 500 mark, against England at Brisbane in 1990–91, 113 years after the initial Test. Although Australia lost a greater number of matches than did England, its win record was superior, completing 204 victories against England's 190:

ENGLAND'S FIRST 500 TESTS
15 March 1877 - 25 July 1974

Opposition	*Tests*	*Won*	*Lost*	*Drawn*	*Tied*
Australia	214	70	82	62	0
South Africa	102	46	18	38	0
West Indies	66	21	19	26	0
India	48	22	6	20	0
New Zealand	45	22	0	23	0
Pakistan	25	9	1	15	0
Total	500	190	126	184	0

AUSTRALIA'S FIRST 500 TESTS
15 March 1877 - 23 November 1990

Opposition	*Tests*	*Won*	*Lost*	*Drawn*	*Tied*
England	271	102	88	81	0
West Indies	67	28	22	16	1
South Africa	53	29	11	13	0
India	45	20	8	16	1
Pakistan	34	12	9	13	0
New Zealand	26	10	6	10	0
Sri Lanka	4	3	0	1	0
Total	500	204	144	150	2

•

In 1983–84, Australia defeated Pakistan 2–0 in a five-match

Test series. Graham Yallop's aggregate of 554 runs, Geoff Lawson's bag of 24 wickets and Rod Marsh's total of 21 dismissals were all new records for a series between the two countries.

•

England's nail-biting victory over Australia by 3 runs at Melbourne in 1982–83 gave Test cricket the first instance of a match in which all 40 wickets fell and the four innings totals came within a range of 10 runs—England 284 and 294, Australia 287 and 288.

•

When Jeff Crowe and Ian Smith both scored their maiden Test hundreds (against England) at Auckland in 1983–84, New Zealand finished with eight Test century-makers in their side, the others being John Wright, Bruce Edgar, Geoff Howarth, Martin Crowe, Jeremy Coney and Richard Hadlee.

•

During a nine-month period in 1984, Australia became the first side to play six consecutive Tests against one country without a win, while at the same time failing to take a single second-innings wicket. The sequence began with five Tests against the West Indies in 1983–84, and another at home in 1984–85:

			Australia	West Indies	Result for Australia
First Test	Georgetown	2–7 March	279 & 9d–273	230 & 0–250	D
Second Test	Port-of-Spain	16–21 March	255 & 9–299	8d–468	D
Third Test	Bridgetown	30 March–4 April	429 & 97	509 & 0–21	L
Fourth Test	St John's	7–11 April	262 & 200	498	L
Fifth Test	Kingston	28 April–2 May	199 & 160	305 & 0–55	L
First Test	Perth	9–12 November	76 & 228	416	L

During the 1980s Australia created a unique record at the Sydney Cricket Ground, remaining undefeated in 11 Test matches played there. Victories were gained over every country, including two each against the West Indies and England:

		Result for Australia
1979–80	v England	6 wickets
1980–81	v India	Innings and 4 runs
1981–82	v West Indies	Drawn
1982–83	v England	Drawn
1983–84	v Pakistan	10 wickets
1984–85	v West Indies	Innings and 55 runs
1985–86	v New Zealand	4 wickets
1985–86	v India	Drawn
1986–87	v England	55 runs
1987–88	v England	Drawn
1988–89	v West Indies	7 wickets

Some of Australia's most famous victories in recent times were secured in Sydney, with spin bowlers playing a prominent role. In 1984–85, Bob Holland took 10 wickets against the seemingly invincible West Indies; Peter Taylor, on his Test debut, collected eight wickets against England in 1986–87; and Allan Border got 11 wickets against the West Indies in 1988–89.

•

During a run of nine Tests from late 1983 to mid-1984, the West Indies lost only four second-innings wickets—one to India at Madras in 1983–84, a run out to England at Lord's and two wickets in the third Test at Leeds in 1984.

•

During 1989, Australia established a new record for topping 400 in the first innings of successive Test matches the most times. Australia managed to record nine in a row to beat Pakistan's seven in 1982–83 and India's seven in 1986–87:

Score	Opposition	Test	Match	Result
401	West Indies	Fourth	Sydney 1988–89	W
515	West Indies	Fifth	Adelaide 1988–89	D
601–7d	England	First	Leeds 1989	W
528	England	Second	Lord's 1989	W
424	England	Third	Birmingham 1989	D
447	England	Fourth	Manchester 1989	W
602–6d	England	Fifth	Nottingham 1989	W
468	England	Sixth	The Oval 1989	D
521–9d	New Zealand	Only	Perth 1989–90	D

•

Bombay (651 & 8d–714) and Maharashtra (407 & 604) at Poona in 1948–49 scored the greatest number of runs in any first-class match—2,376 for the loss of 38 wickets.

•

New Zealand proved to be the dark horse in Test cricket during the 1980s, winning 28.81% of its 59 matches, second only to the West Indies, which won 53% of its 83 Tests. Both countries proved to be virtually unbeatable at home—New Zealand contested 10 Test series and lost none of them, while the West Indies played in seven home series without a loss.

NEW ZEALAND AT HOME IN THE 1980s

		Tests	Won	Lost	Drawn
v West Indies	1979–80	3	1	0	2
v India	1980–81	3	1	0	2
v Australia	1981–82	3	1	1	1
v Sri Lanka	1982–83	2	2	0	0
v England	1983–84	3	1	0	2
v Pakistan	1984–85	3	2	0	1
v Australia	1985–86	3	1	0	2
v West Indies	1986–87	3	1	1	1
v England	1987–88	3	0	0	3
v Pakistan	1988–89	2	0	0	2
Totals		28	10	2	16

•

When Tasmania was bowled out for 51 and 25 by Victoria at Hobart in 1857–58, no batsman reached double figures in either innings, a unique occurrence in Australian first-class cricket.

•

During the second Test against England at Auckland in 1991–92, three wickets fell on the same score three times, an incident that had happened only twice before in Test cricket (England v India at Leeds in 1952 and New Zealand v West Indies at Auckland in 1955–56). Following England's mini-collapse in the second innings of the match with the score on 321, New Zealand's openers were then both dismissed for nought, bringing to five the number of wickets that fell without a single run being scored.

•

Australia dismissed India for under 150 in each innings of a Test match in successive series during the late 1950s—for 136 and 136 at Calcutta in 1956–57, and 149 and 138 at Madras in 1959–60.

•

In its first Test, against India at Harare in 1992–93, Zimbabwe scored 456 in its first innings. The total is a record score for a country new to Test cricket, and surpassed, by a long way, the previous best of 245 by Australia v England at Melbourne in 1876–77.

•

An unprecedented number of Test matches (165) in the late 1950s brought with it a new record for the most individual centuries (239) in a decade. Each decade since has seen both of these records broken, with 200 Tests played for the first time, and 400 centuries scored, in the 1980s. No country has yet made 100 centuries in a decade, England top-scoring with 94 in the 1960s, and Australia 90 in the 1980s.

TEST CENTURIES BY EACH COUNTRY IN EACH DECADE

	Tests	*A*	*E*	*SA*	*WI*	*NZ*	*I*	*P*	*SL*	*100s*
1870s	3	1	0	–	–	–	–	–	–	1
1880s	29	8	11	0	–	–	–	–	–	19
1890s	32	17	20	1	–	–	–	–	–	38
1900s	41	17	20	5	–	–	–	–	–	42
1910s	29	12	14	9	–	–	–	–	–	35
1920s	51	37	51	11	0	–	–	–	–	99
1930s	89	45	74	18	15	5	3	–	–	160
1940s	44	28	34	12	15	3	11	–	–	103
1950s	165	49	58	20	58	9	31	14	–	239
1960s	186	59	94	23	50	17	32	20	–	295
1970s	198	77	76	6	68	33	50	47	–	357
1980s	267	90	79	–	75	41	69	68	19	441
Total	1,134	440	531	105	281	108	196	149	19	1,829

•

When the touring Australians played the MCC at Lord's in 1878 the total number of runs scored by both sides was only 105—a record in first-class cricket, which still stands, for a completed match. The MCC made 33 and 19, the Australians 41 and 1 for 12 in a contest that lasted a little over six hours.

•

During the 1990 English summer, three counties—Lancashire, Essex and Surrey—recorded totals of 700 in first-class matches. Two of them broke long-standing records for their highest ever totals.

	Total	*Opposition*	*Venue*	*Previous best*
Essex	6d–761	Leicestershire	Chelmsford	692 (v Somerset at Taunton 1895)
Lancashire	863	Surrey	The Oval	801 (v Somerset at Taunton 1895)

•

Australia's total of 5 declared for 513 against Sri Lanka at Hobart in 1989–90 was only the seventh time Australia had reached 500 in the second innings of a Test match, and the first since 1946–47 when 536 was made against England at Melbourne.

•

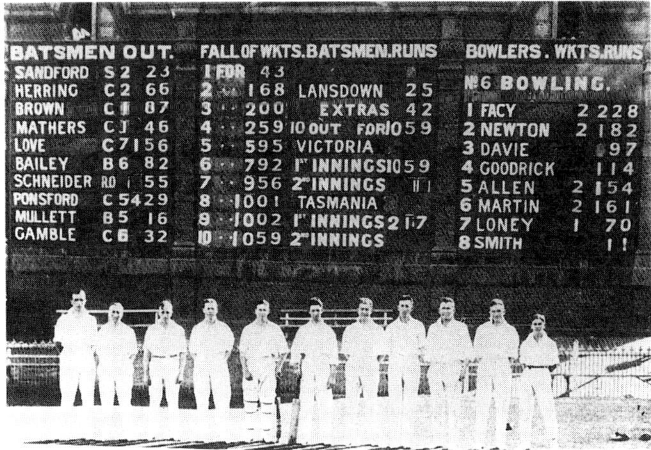

Victoria's total of 1,059, the first time 1,000 had been achieved in first-class cricket

Victoria remains the only team to score 1,000 runs in a first-class innings, and it has done so twice:

1107 v New South Wales at Melbourne 1926–27
1059 v Tasmania at Melbourne 1922–23

THE HIGHEST INNINGS TOTAL IN FIRST-CLASS CRICKET

Victoria v New South Wales, Melbourne, 1926–27

W.M. Woodfull	c Ratcliffe b Andrews	133
W.H. Ponsford	b Morgan	352
H.L. Hendry	c Morgan b Mailey	100
J. Ryder	c Kippax b Andrews	295
F.L. Morton	run out	0
H.S.B. Love	st Ratcliffe b Mailey	6
S. King	st Ratcliffe b Mailey	7
A.E. Hartkopf	c McGuirk b Mailey	61
A.E. Liddicut	b McGuirk	36
J.L. Ellis	run out	63
D.D.J. Blackie	not out	27
Extras	(b 17, lb 8, nb 2)	27
		1,107

•

In January 1930, two England teams were involved in two Test matches simultaneously, one against New Zealand at Christchurch (10–13 January), the other against the West Indies at Barbados (11–16 January). This is the only example of a country playing in two Tests at the same time, although England contested two series simultaneously in 1891–92, against Australia and South Africa.

•

During the 1925-26 Sheffield Shield season, New South Wales made the following scores in consecutive innings—554, 705, 642, 593 and 708.

•

Between 1982 and 1984, England staged 12 consecutive Test matches which saw conclusive results. This record sequence included five wins for the home team, five for the West Indies and one each for Pakistan and New Zealand.

•

When Australia made 8 for 758 against the West Indies at Kingston in 1954-55, a record five batsmen contributed centuries—Colin McDonald (127), Neil Harvey (204), Keith Miller (109), Ron Archer (128) and Richie Benaud (121). Five bowlers also made the record books by each conceding over 100 runs in the innings, also a first in Test cricket—Tom Dewdney (1-115), Frank King (2-126), Denis Atkinson (1-132), 'Collie' Smith (2-145) and Frank Worrell (1-116). (The other West Indian bowler used—Garry Sobers—took 1 for 99.)

•

When Australia played the West Indies in 1954-55, a record number of centuries (21) was scored in the five-match series. Australia made 12 hundreds, the West Indies nine:

Australia	*West Indies*
Neil Harvey 204, 133, 133	Clyde Walcott 155 & 110, 126 & 110, 108
Keith Miller 147, 137, 109	Denis Atkinson 219
Colin McDonald 127, 110	Everton Weekes 139
Ron Archer 128	Clairmonte Depeiza 122
Richie Benaud 121	'Collie' Smith 104
Ray Lindwall 118	
Arthur Morris 111	

Sixteen centuries were scored by Australia (10) and the West Indies (6) in the 1968-69 series. The fourth Test at Adelaide produced three of them, and a further 14 innings in excess of 50:

Australia	*West Indies*
Doug Walters 110 & 50	Basil Butcher 52 & 118
Ian Chappell 76 & 96	Garry Sobers 110 & 52
Bill Lawry 62 & 89	'Joey' Carew 90
Keith Stackpole 62 & 50	Rohan Kanhai 80
Graham McKenzie 59	David Holford 80
Paul Sheahan 51	

There were centuries galore in the 1990 series between England and India. A record 15 were scored in the three-match rubber, 12 of them in the first two Tests:

First Test—Lord's	*Second Test—Manchester*	*Third Test—The Oval*
Graham Gooch 333 & 123	Mohammad Azharuddin 179	Ravi Shastri 187
Allan Lamb 139	Michael Atherton 131	David Gower 157*
Mohammad Azharuddin 121	Robin Smith 121*	Kapil Dev 110
Robin Smith 100*	Sachin Tendulkar 119*	
Ravi Shastri 100	Graham Gooch 116	
	Allan Lamb 109	

England's eight centuries in successive Tests—four at Lord's and four at Manchester—is also a Test record.

•

When Middlesex met Essex at Lord's in 1981 it provided the first instance in English first-class cricket of a team made up entirely of Test players: Mike Brearley, Paul Downton, Clive Radley, Mike Gatting, Roland Butcher, Graham Barlow, John Emburey, Phil Edmonds, Mike Selvey, Jeff Thomson and Wayne Daniel.

•

During the 1921 Test series with Australia, England tried 30 players during the five Tests—two more than the previous record of 28 (by Australia v England 1884-85). Only two players, Frank Woolley and Johnny Douglas, appeared in all five matches:

George Brown (3)	'Harry' Howell (1)
Alfred Dipper (1)	Vallance Jupp (2)
Johnny Douglas (5)	Donald Knight (2)
Andy Ducat (1)	Phil Mead (2)
Jack Durston (1)	Charlie Parker (1)
John Evans (1)	'Ciss' Parkin (4)
Percy Fender (2)	Wilfred Rhodes (1)
Nigel Haig (1)	Tom Richmond (1)
Charlie Hallows (1)	Charles Russell (2)
Wally Hardinge (1)	Andy Sandham (1)
J.W. Hearne (1)	Bert Strudwick (2)
'Patsy' Hendren (2)	Lionel Tennyson (4)
John Hitch (1)	Ernest Tyldesley (3)
Jack Hobbs (1)	Jack White (1)
Percy Holmes (1)	Frank Woolley (5)

When Australia set the previous record of 28 during the 1884-85 series, England established a record of its own by keeping the same XI throughout the five-match rubber. A similar set of circumstances arose when the two sides met in 1989—England employed 29 players in the six Tests while Australia required the services of just 12.

•

In 1959-60, the South African side Border was dismissed for 16 and 18 by Natal at East London. The aggregate of 34 runs represents the lowest match total by one team in all first-class cricket.

•

During the 1978-79 season in South Africa, a combined universities team pulled off one of the most remarkable victories in the history of first-class cricket when it beat the Currie Cup champions Western Province. Set a target of 499 for victory, South African Universities got there for the loss of seven wickets to become only the fourth team in all first-class cricket to score 500 runs in the fourth innings and win the match.

FOURTH INNINGS TOTALS OF OVER 500 TO WIN A FIRST-CLASS MATCH

7-507	Cambridge University v MCC at Lord's 1896
6-506	South Australia v Queensland at Adelaide 1991-92
6-502	Middlesex v Nottinghamshire at Nottingham 1925
8-502	Players v Gentlemen at Lord's 1900
7-500	South African Universities v Western Province at Stellenbosch 1978-79

•

During 1959, India suffered eight Test losses, a record equalled by England in 1984.

•

When Australia made 75 against South Africa at Durban in 1949–50 it provided the lowest completed Test innings on record in which every batsman scored. The lowest individual score was 1 by Colin McCool; five batsmen were dismissed for 2.

•

During the six Tests at home in 1980–81, Australia won three of them within three days—two in succession against New Zealand and one against India.

•

The greatest number of wickets to fall in a day is 39 in the match between Oxford University and the MCC at Oxford in 1880.

•

During the 1950s and early '60s New South Wales had a virtual stranglehold on the Sheffield Shield, winning the cup in nine successive seasons, from 1953–54 to 1961–62 inclusive. The Blues had previously held the record for most Shield titles, winning six from 1902–03 to 1906–07.

In the English County Championship Surrey is the record-holder with seven consecutive titles from 1952 to 1958. The best performance in all first-class cricket belongs to Bombay which was the Ranji Trophy champion 15 seasons in a row, from 1958–59 to 1972–73.

•

Northamptonshire finished at the bottom of the County Championship table in three successive seasons—1936, 1937 and 1938. During that time Northants failed to bring off a single victory, and went for 99 first-class matches without a win between 1935 and 1939:

	M	*W*	*L*	*D*
1936	24	0	9	15
1937	24	0	16	8
1938	24	0	17	7

Derbyshire failed to secure a victory in a season on four occasions, the barren years being 1897, 1901, 1920 and 1924.

•

In 1928, Yorkshire finished the County Championship season undefeated for the fifth time in its history, having completed the feat in 1900, 1908, 1925 and 1926.

•

Australia staged its greatest comeback in Test history in 1992, when it beat Sri Lanka at Colombo by 16 runs after trailing by 291 on the first innings. (Australia 256 & 471; Sri Lanka 8d–547 & 164.)

Sri Lanka recorded its lowest Test score and its (then) highest in consecutive matches in 1990–91. Against India at Chandigarh it was dismissed for 82, but then made 497 in its next Test, against New Zealand at Wellington. New Zealand also made its highest score in Test cricket in this match—4 for 671, a total which was more than 100 runs better than their previous best of 7 declared for 553 at Brisbane in 1985–86. The score was also a record for the second innings in a Test match, beating Pakistan's 8 declared for 657 at Bridgetown in 1957–58. When New Zealand lost its third wicket with the score on 615, another Test record was broken. Previously the highest score at this point in a Test innings was 602 by the West Indies against Pakistan, at Kingston in 1957–58.

•

Despite Western Australia making only 159 against New South Wales at Perth in 1992–93, Justin Langer and Tim Zoehrer shared a sixth-wicket stand of exactly 100. Western Australia's score is one of the lowest completed totals on record in first-class cricket to include a century partnership.

•

England's seven-wicket victory over Sri Lanka at Lord's in 1988 brought to an end a record sequence of 18 consecutive Test matches without a win. Its previous taste of success was gained in Melbourne in 1986–87, a victory that coincided with Australia's longest sequence of Tests without a win. Australia's 55-run victory over England in the next Test at Sydney ended a run of 14 successive matches without a win since Sydney 1985–86, all of them under the captaincy of Allan Border:

Season	*Opposition*	*Venue*	*Result*
1985–86	New Zealand	Perth	L
1985–86	India	Adelaide	D
1985–86	India	Melbourne	D
1985–86	India	Sydney	D
1985–86	New Zealand	Wellington	D
1985–86	New Zealand	Christchurch	D
1985–86	New Zealand	Auckland	L
1986–87	India	Madras	T
1986–87	India	New Delhi	D
1986–87	India	Bombay	D
1986–87	England	Brisbane	L
1986–87	England	Perth	D
1986–87	England	Adelaide	D
1986–87	England	Melbourne	L

The longest sequence of Test matches without a win by any country is 44 by New Zealand, from its inaugural Test in 1929–30 against England at Christchurch to its first victory, over the West Indies at Auckland, in 1955–56.

•

TEAMS TO LOSE A TEST MATCH AFTER SCORING 500

Losing team	*Winning team*	*Margin*	*Venue and season*
Australia 586 & 166	England 325 & 437	10 runs	Sydney 1894–95
South Africa 506 & 80	Australia 348 & 327	89 runs	Melbourne 1910–11
England 519 & 257	Australia 491 & 5–287	5 wickets	Melbourne 1928–29
Australia 520 & 209	South Africa 435 & 4–297	6 wickets	Melbourne 1952–53
India 164 & 510	England 4d–550 & 4–126	6 wickets	Headingley 1967
West Indies 7d–526 & 2d–92	England 404 & 3–215	7 wickets	Port-of-Spain 1967–68
Pakistan 8d–574 & 200	Australia 5d–441 & 425	92 runs	Melbourne 1972–73
Sri Lanka 8d–547 & 164	Australia 256 & 471	16 runs	Colombo 1992–93

When Australia knocked over the West Indies by an innings at Sydney in 1984–85 it was the Caribbean team's first loss in 27 Tests since Melbourne 1981–82 and only their second in 44 matches since Christchurch 1979–80:

D,D v New Zealand 1979–80
W,D,D,D,D v England 1980
D,W,D,D v Pakistan 1980–81
W,W,D,D v England 1980–81
Loss to Australia at Melbourne 1981–82
D,W v Australia 1981–82
W,D,D,W,D v India 1982–83
W,D,W,D,W,D v India 1983–84
D,D,W,W,W v Australia 1983–84
W,W,W,W,W v England 1984
W,W,W,D v Australia 1984–85

The West Indies' run of 27 matches without defeat (17 wins and 10 draws) included a Test record 11 consecutive victories, all under the guidance of Clive Lloyd and all against Australia and England:

Season	*Opposition*	*Venue*	*Victory margin*
1983–84	Australia	Bridgetown	10 wickets
1983–84	Australia	St John's	Innings and 36 runs
1983–84	Australia	Kingston	10 wickets
1984	England	Birmingham	Innings and 180 runs
1984	England	Lord's	9 wickets
1984	England	Leeds	8 wickets
1984	England	Manchester	Innings and 64 runs
1984	England	The Oval	172 runs
1984–85	Australia	Perth	Innings and 112 runs
1984–85	Australia	Brisbane	8 wickets
1984–85	Australia	Adelaide	191 runs

Australia's most successful period came directly after the Second World War, with 25 consecutive matches without defeat (20 wins and five draws):

Season	*Opposition*	*Venue*	*Captain*	*Result*
1945–46	New Zealand	Wellington	Bill Brown	W
1946–47	England	Brisbane	Don Bradman	W
1946–47	England	Sydney	Don Bradman	W
1946–47	England	Melbourne	Don Bradman	D
1946–47	England	Adelaide	Don Bradman	D
1946–47	England	Sydney	Don Bradman	W
1947–48	India	Brisbane	Don Bradman	W
1947–48	India	Sydney	Don Bradman	D
1947–48	India	Melbourne	Don Bradman	W
1947–48	India	Adelaide	Don Bradman	W
1947–48	India	Melbourne	Don Bradman	W
1948	England	Nottingham	Don Bradman	W
1948	England	Lord's	Don Bradman	W
1948	England	Manchester	Don Bradman	D
1948	England	Leeds	Don Bradman	W
1948	England	The Oval	Don Bradman	W
1949–50	South Africa	Johannesburg	Lindsay Hassett	W
1949–50	South Africa	Cape Town	Lindsay Hassett	W
1949–50	South Africa	Durban	Lindsay Hassett	W
1949–50	South Africa	Johannesburg	Lindsay Hassett	D
1949–50	South Africa	Port Elizabeth	Lindsay Hassett	W
1950–51	England	Brisbane	Lindsay Hassett	W
1950–51	England	Melbourne	Lindsay Hassett	W
1950–51	England	Sydney	Lindsay Hassett	W
1950–51	England	Adelaide	Lindsay Hassett	W

•

Victoria won the Sheffield Shield in 1990–91 after being the wooden-spooners the previous season.

•

When New South Wales defeated the West Indies at Sydney in 1984–85, it was their first loss in a first-class match, outside Tests, in four years. In 1980–81 they lost their opening first-class match on the tour of Pakistan to a President's XI side at Rawalpindi. On the same day (19 November) that the West Indies lost to New South Wales, the touring England team recorded a loss to India's Under-25 XI at Ahmedabad. It was only their second loss in India outside Test cricket and their first innings defeat outside Tests since New South Wales beat them at Sydney in 1962–63.

•

During the 1970s more counties won the Championship than in any other decade, with different teams taking the title in seven successive seasons—Kent in 1970, Surrey in 1971, Warwickshire 1972, Hampshire 1973, Worcestershire 1974, Leicestershire 1975, Middlesex 1976—and Essex in 1979.

•

During a single week in 1925, New South Wales and Victoria made history when both sides fielded completely different teams against each other in consecutive first-class matches:

NEW SOUTH WALES v VICTORIA
(Sydney)

NSW	*Victoria*
H.O. Rock	R.E. Mayne
J.G. Morgan	W.M. Woodfull
A.T. Ratcliffe	H.S.T.L. Hendry
A.F. Kippax	A.E. Liddicut
B.M. Salmon	F.A. Tarrant
A.P. Wells	A.E.V. Hartkopf
C.V. Morrissey	K.J. Schneider
C.H.W. Lawes	C.B. Willis
A.D.A. Mayes	J.L. Ellis
J.D. Scott	D.D. Blackie
M.W. Bosely	P.H. Wallace

VICTORIA v NEW SOUTH WALES
(Melbourne)

NSW	*Victoria*
H.L. Collins	J. Ryder
W. Bardsley	W.H. Ponsford
J.M. Taylor	H.S.B. Love
T.J.E. Andrews	K.J. Millar
L.W. Gwynne	R.L. Park
C. Kelleway	J.L. Keating
A.T.E. Punch	V.S. Ransford
W.A.S. Oldfield	J.A. Atkinson
J.E.H. Hooker	H.S. Gamble
A.A. Mailey	W.J. Rayson
S.C. Everett	H. Ironmonger

•

Despite totals of 357 and 319 in the fifth Test at Kingston in 1954–55, the West Indies lost the match to Australia (8d–758) by an innings and 82 runs.

•

In consecutive Tests against England in 1978, Pakistan lost four first innings wickets for one run—at Birmingham they slumped from 5 for 125 to 9 for 126 and at Lord's they collapsed from 5 for 96 to 9 for 97.

•

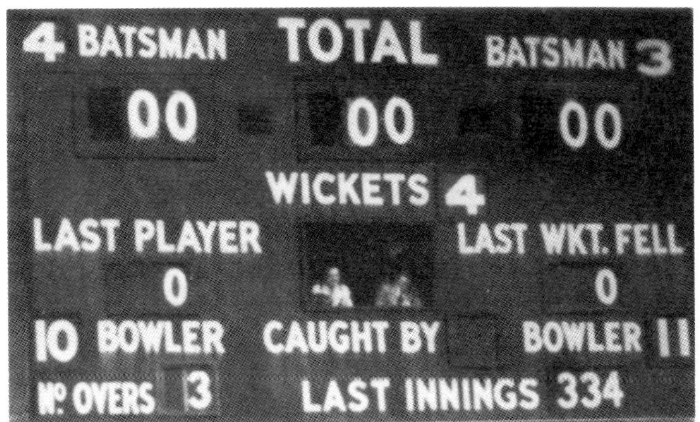

A sad and sorry tale for India at Leeds in 1952—four wickets down with no runs on the board

On the third day of the third Test at Manchester in 1952, India suffered the ignominy of being dismissed twice—for 58 and 82—a fate no other country has had to bear. In the first Test, at Leeds, India entered the record books by losing its first four wickets for no runs, and in the fourth Test at The Oval created history, losing its top five batsmen for six runs.

In Pakistan's inaugural Test match against the West Indies, at Bridgetown in 1957–58, history was created when Pakistan scored 8 declared for 657—the highest total on record by a team following on in Test cricket.

•

Warwickshire finished runners-up to Essex in the 1991 English County Championship, despite registering only four centuries during the entire season—Asif Din 100 and 140, Dominic Ostler 120 not out and Andy Moles 133. Somerset, which finished last on the table, recorded 23 hundreds, just one behind the 24 scored by the winners Essex.

•

Despite being dismissed for 258 by Derbyshire in 1991, two of Hampshire's batsmen—Chris Smith (114) and Kevan James (101)—scored hundreds. This is the lowest total in English first-class cricket to contain two individual centuries (previously 271 by Lancashire v Northamptonshire at Manchester in 1947).

•

In 1986 England hit rock bottom by losing two Test series at home for the first time in its history—India won 2–0 and New Zealand triumphed 1–0.

2 The Run-Scorers

With the exception of the SCG, every Australian cricket ground saw a century scored in its inaugural Test. Charles Bannerman began the process in 1877 at the MCG and Mark Taylor completed the cycle at the Bellerive Oval in Hobart in 1989.

Sydney's first Test, the second against England in 1881–82, produced two half-centuries, the highest knock being 67 by England's George Ulyett. The third Test of the series, also at the SCG, saw Percy McDonnell score his maiden century in first-class cricket (147) and the ground's first Test hundred. McDonnell also had the honour of scoring the first century in a Test match at the Adelaide Oval.

Ground	*First Test*	*First centurion*	*Score*
MCG	A v E 1876–77	Charles Bannerman	165*
SCG	A v E 1881–82	Percy McDonnell	147[a]
Adelaide Oval	A v E 1884–85	Percy McDonnell	124
Exhibition Ground	A v E 1928–29	'Patsy' Hendren	169
Woolloongabba	A v SA 1931–32	Don Bradman	226
WACA	E v A 1970–71	Brian Luckhurst	131
Bellerive Oval	A v SL 1989–90	Mark Taylor	108

[a]Scored in the third Test of the series

•

Frank Woolley and W.G. Grace both made 1,000 runs in a season 28 times. Between 1907 and 1938, Woolley achieved the feat in consecutive seasons in which first-class cricket was played (there were none between 1915 and 1918 because of the war), reaching the milestone of 2,000 runs on 12 occasions and 3,000 runs once.

•

Kepler Wessels is the only batsman to have scored Test centuries for different countries. He hit four hundreds in 24 Tests for Australia, and recorded his first for South Africa (118 v India at Durban) in 1992–93.

•

The fourth Test against Australia at Birmingham in 1981 was the first match since 1935 not to include an individual half-century. The highest scores came from the captains, Mike Brearley 48 and Kim Hughes 47.

•

On his Test debut in 1930–31, West Indies captain 'Jackie' Grant became the first batsman to score a not out fifty in each innings of a Test match—53* & 71* v Australia at Adelaide.

•

South African batsman Barry Richards made 205 appearances in English county cricket during the 1960s and '70s—204 times for Hampshire and once for Gloucestershire in 1965. In his first full season, for Hampshire in 1968, he scored 2,395 runs at 47.90 with five centuries and a top score of 206.

•

In 1965 the Lancashire opener David Green experienced a most unusual summer when he totalled over 2,000 runs in first-class matches, but failed to score a century. In 35 matches Green hit 2,037 runs at 32.85—on 14 occasions he passed 50 and finished with a highest score of 85 (v Warwickshire at Blackpool).

D.M. GREEN: 2,000 RUNS IN A SEASON WITHOUT A CENTURY

39, 2, 43 & 42, 0, 31 & 14, 19, 20 & 81, 12 & 5, 19 & 44*, 17 & 24, 4 & 3, 61 & 53, 39 & 69, 37 & 0, 23 & 0, 40 & 28, 35 & 28, 78 & 37, 66, 24 & 20, 53, 50 & 34, 36, 6 & 16, 64 & 32, 62 & 8, 55 & 40, 18 & 37, 15 & 85, 21 & 10, 8 & 33, 56 & 48, 46 & 19, 2 & 24, 79 & 23

•

England skipper Graham Gooch had a sorry start to the English Test season in 1990, falling for a first-ball duck to Richard Hadlee at Nottingham. That failure aside, Gooch proceeded to make the most runs in an English Test season on record. In his next 10 innings he hit 85, 37, 154 and 30 against New Zealand and 333, 123, 116, 7, 85 and 88 against India. His total for the summer was 1,058 runs at 96.18 in six Tests which beat Don Bradman's aggregate of 974 against England in 1930.

•

When Allan Border scored 106 against Sri Lanka at Moratuwa in 1992, it was his first hundred in a Test match since 1988–89. During that time, Border went 61 innings without a ton, a record sequence for an Australian batsman between centuries.

MOST CONSECUTIVE INNINGS BETWEEN CENTURIES IN TEST CRICKET

Inns	*Batsman*	*Period*	*Runs*	*HS*	*50s*
64	Syed Kirmani (I)	1979–80 to 1984–85	1,175	78	5
63	Alan Knott (E)	1971 to 1974–75	1,723	92	14
61	Allan Border (A)	1988–89 to 1992–93	2,113	91*	21
60	Richard Hadlee (NZ)	1979–80 to 1986–87	1,456	99	9
59	Ray Lindwall (A)	1946–47 to 1954–55	1,037	77	5

•

W.G. Grace scored three centuries in consecutive innings five times during his first-class career. The most impressive set was in 1876 when he hit 344 for the MCC against Kent, 177 for Gloucestershire against Nottinghamshire and an unbeaten 318 for Gloucestershire v Yorkshire—a total of 839 runs at an average of 419.50.

•

Javed Miandad

Javed Miandad was the first batsman to score a century in his first Test match and his 100th—163 v New Zealand at Lahore in 1976-77 and 145 v India, also at Lahore, in 1989-90. Javed also scored a century in his 100th Test innings—104 v New Zealand at Hyderabad in 1984-85.

•

In first-class matches the most runs by a batsman between dismissals is 709 by K.C. Ibrahim in 1947-48. Garry Sobers holds the Test record with 490 runs—365* and 125—against Pakistan in 1957-58. The Australian first-class record belongs to Bob Simpson, the English to Graeme Hick.

709	K.C. Ibrahim (Bombay 1947-48): 218*, 36*, 234*, 77*, 144
645	G.A. Hick (Worcestershire 1990): 171*, 69*, 252*, 100*, 53
545	R.B. Simpson (Western Australia 1959-60): 236*, 230*, 79

•

Australia's Clem Hill was the first batsman to score 500 runs in a Test series without the aid of a century. He set this odd record, against England in 1901-02, with the help of three successive nineties—99, 98 and 97.

•

Mohinder Amarnath scored over 900 runs on the 1982-83 tour of the West Indies, a total which included nine fifties in 10 successive first-class innings—114 v Trinidad and Tobago, 58 & 117 v West Indies, 13 v West Indies, 61 & 101* v Barbados, 91 & 80 v West Indies and 54 & 116 v West Indies.

•

Qasim Omar, who played 26 times for Pakistan, only scored three Test centuries, but two of them were double-centuries—210 v India at Faisalabad in 1984-85 and 206 v Sri Lanka at Faisalabad in 1985-86.

•

During the fifth Test against the West Indies at The Oval in 1966, Ken Higgs (63) and John Snow (59*) each scored their maiden fifty in first-class cricket, and became the first numbers 10 and 11 to score a half-century in the same Test innings. With John Murray, who hit a century batting at number 9, England's last three wickets contributed over 350 runs.

•

Of the 151 centuries scored by Geoff Boycott, 68 were unbeaten, a record in first-class cricket. Phil Mead, of Hampshire, had 50 not-out centuries, while Glenn Turner collected 38.

•

Martin Crowe, the first New Zealand batsman to score 10 Test centuries, began his international career without a single double-figure score in his first five Test innings—9, 2, 0, 9 and 0 v Australia in 1981-82. Ken Rutherford, another top-order New Zealand batsman, also experienced a bitter start to Test cricket with seven single-digit scores first-up—0, 0, 4, 0, 2, 1 and 5 v West Indies in 1984-85. Other recent specialist batsmen with poor starts to a Test career include Andrew Hilditch (3, 1, 3), Bill Athey (9, 1, 2, 1, 3, 1), Graham Gooch (0, 0, 6), Neil Fairbrother (0, 3, 1, 1), Mike Gatting (5, 6, 0) and Graeme Hick (6, 6, 0).

•

Clem Hill

During the 1980s no batsman was able to score a triple-century in a Test match. Javed Miandad, with an unbeaten knock of 280 against India in 1982–83, came the closest. Since the Second World War the only other decade without a Test match triple-century was the 1940s. By passing 250 another two times in the 1980s Javed set a new record by claiming three of the four highest individual scores during the decade.

THE TOP FIVE HITS

		The 1980s		
280*	Javed Miandad	P v I	Hyderabad	1982–83
271	Javed Miandad	P v NZ	Auckland	1988–89
268	Graham Yallop	A v P	Melbourne	1983–84
260	Javed Miandad	P v E	The Oval	1987
236*	Sunil Gavaskar	I v WI	Madras	1983–84
		The 1970s		
302	Lawrence Rowe	WI v E	Bridgetown	1973–74
291	Viv Richards	WI v E	The Oval	1976
274	Graeme Pollock	SA v A	Durban	1969–70
274	Zaheer Abbas	P v E	Birmingham	1971
262*	Dennis Amiss	E v WI	Kingston	1973–74
		The 1960s		
311	Bob Simpson	A v E	Manchester	1964
310*	John Edrich	E v NZ	Leeds	1965
307	Bob Cowper	A v E	Melbourne	1965–66
258	Seymour Nurse	WI v NZ	Christchurch	1968–69
256	Ken Barrington	E v NZ	The Oval	1964
		The 1950s		
365*	Garry Sobers	WI v P	Kingston	1957–58
337	Hanif Mohammad	P v WI	Bridgetown	1957–58
285*	Peter May	E v WI	Birmingham	1957
278	Denis Compton	E v P	Nottingham	1954
261	Frank Worrell	WI v E	Nottingham	1950
		The 1940s		
234	Sid Barnes	A v E	Sydney	1946–47
234	Don Bradman	A v E	Sydney	1946–47
208	Denis Compton	E v SA	Lord's	1947
206	Martin Donnelly	NZ v E	Lord's	1949
206	Len Hutton	E v NZ	The Oval	1949
		The 1930s		
364	Len Hutton	E v A	The Oval	1938
336*	Walter Hammond	E v NZ	Auckland	1932–33
334	Don Bradman	A v E	Leeds	1930
325	Andy Sandham	E v WI	Kingston	1929–30
304	Don Bradman	A v E	Leeds	1934
		The 1920s		
251	Walter Hammond	E v A	Sydney	1928–29
211	Jack Hobbs	E v SA	Lord's	1924
203	Herbie Collins	A v SA	Johannesburg	1921–22
201*	Jack Ryder	A v E	Adelaide	1924–25
200	Walter Hammond	E v A	Melbourne	1928–29
		The 1910s		
214*	Victor Trumper	A v SA	Adelaide	1910–11
204	Aubrey Faulkner	SA v A	Melbourne	1910–11
191	Clem Hill	A v SA	Sydney	1910–11
187	Jack Hobbs	E v SA	Cape Town	1909–10
187	Jack Hobbs	E v A	Adelaide	1911–12
		The 1900s		
287	'Tip' Foster	E v A	Sydney	1903–04
185*	Victor Trumper	A v E	Sydney	1903–04
166	Victor Trumper	A v E	Sydney	1907–08
160	Clem Hill	A v E	Adelaide	1907–08
159*	Warwick Armstrong	A v SA	Johannesburg	1902–03
		The 1890s		
201	Syd Gregory	A v E	Sydney	1894–95
188	Clem Hill	A v E	Melbourne	1897–98
178	Joe Darling	A v E	Adelaide	1897–98
175	K.S. Ranjitsinhji	E v A	Sydney	1897–98
173	Andrew Stoddart	E v A	Melbourne	1894–95
		The 1880s		
211	Billy Murdoch	A v E	The Oval	1884
170	W.G. Grace	E v A	The Oval	1886
164	Arthur Shrewsbury	E v A	Lord's	1886
153*	Billy Murdoch	A v E	The Oval	1880
152	W.G. Grace	E v A	The Oval	1880
		The 1870s		
165*	Charles Bannerman	A v E	Melbourne	1876–77
73	Alec Bannerman	A v E	Melbourne	1878–79
63	Henry Jupp	E v A	Melbourne	1876–77
62	George Ulyett	E v A	Melbourne	1876–77
52	George Ulyett	E v A	Melbourne	1876–77

•

Although out for a duck in his first innings of first-class cricket, Rod Marsh made amends in the second innings by becoming the first postwar batsman to score a century on his debut against a team touring Australia—104 for Western Australia v the 1968–69 West Indians in Perth.

•

The first eight centuries in first-class matches by Victor Trumper were 292*, 253*, 104, 300*, 208, 165 and 230.

Victor Trumper—his maiden century in first-class cricket was an innings of 292 not out against Tasmania in 1898–99, an Australian record

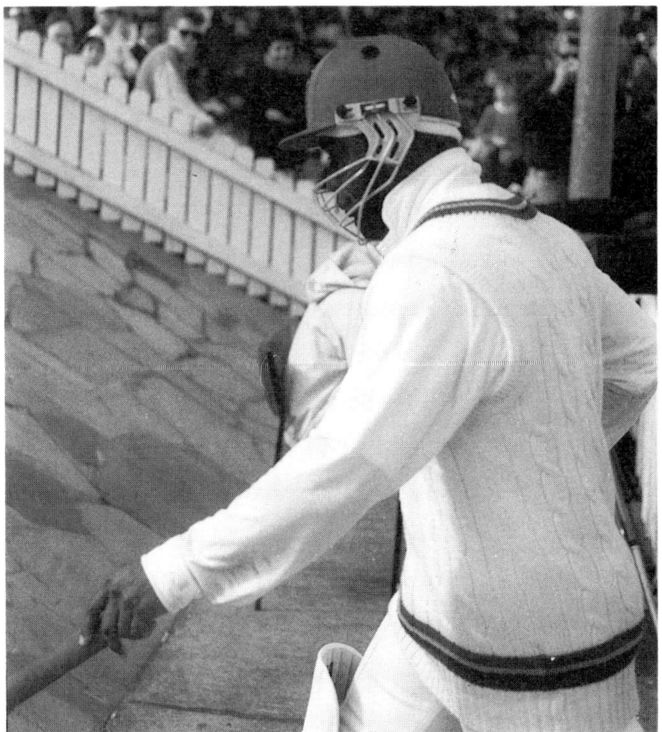
Desmond Haynes

West Indies opener Desmond Haynes was the first player to bat throughout both innings of a Test match. He was twice last man out scoring 55 and 105 against New Zealand at Dunedin in 1979–80.

•

In the five-match Test series against the West Indies in 1983–84, Australia experimented with six different sets of opening batsmen. This was a number matched and exceeded by England during the same period. In the early part of 1984, they tried seven pairs of openers, with five different combinations in consecutive innings.

Australia's six v West Indies 1983–84
Steve Smith & Kepler Wessels—Georgetown
Kepler Wessels & Wayne Phillips—Port-of-Spain
Steve Smith & Graeme Wood—Bridgetown
Wayne Phillips & Greg Ritchie—St John's
Wayne Phillips & Steve Smith—Kingston
Wayne Phillips & Greg Matthews—Kingston

In all Test cricket, the record for the greatest chopping-and-changing goes to Australia, which used a different opening pair in 10 successive Test innings between 1884–85 and 1886:

Jack Blackham & Percy McDonnell—Adelaide 1884–85
Sammy Jones & Sam Morris—Melbourne 1884–85
Sammy Jones & William Bruce—Melbourne 1884–85
Alec Bannerman & Sammy Jones—Sydney 1884–85
Alec Bannerman & George Bonnor—Sydney 1884–85
George Palmer & Tom Garrett—Sydney 1884–85
Percy McDonnell & Alec Bannerman—Sydney 1884–85
Alec Bannerman & William Bruce—Melbourne 1884–85
Alec Bannerman & Tom Garrett—Melbourne 1884–85
'Tup' Scott & Sammy Jones—Manchester 1886

•

The 1982–83 Test series against India, which Pakistan won 3–0, was dominated by the scoring feats of Mudassar Nazar, Zaheer Abbas and Javed Miandad. They each scored over 500 runs at a century average and provided the first instance of three batsmen contributing 2,000 runs in a Test series:

	T	*I*	*NO*	*R*	*HS*	*100s*	*Avge*
Zaheer Abbas	6	6	1	650	215	3	130.00
Mudassar Nazar	6	8	2	761	231	4	126.83
Javed Miandad	6	6	1	594	280*	2	118.80
Total	6	20	4	2,005	280*	9	125.31

Although the Indians were completely outplayed, they did manage to set a batting record of their own, with 12 batsmen scoring half-centuries during the series. Previously the Test record was 11, made three times by England—against Australia in 1928–29 and 1981, and against India in 1959. Five of India's 12 scores of 50 or more were converted to hundreds, Mohinder Amarnath achieving the century-mark three times:

Mohinder Amarnath	120, 109*, 103*, 78, 64, 61
Sunil Gavaskar	127*, 83, 67, 60
Ravi Shastri	128
Dilip Vengsarkar	89, 79, 58*
Sandeep Patil	85, 68
Madan Lal	54, 52*
Kapil Dev	73
Balwindersingh Sandhu	71
Syed Kirmani	66
Yashpal Sharma	63*
Gundappa Viswanath	53
Arun Lal	51

Every Pakistan batsman who scored a 50 went on to record a century. Six batsmen hit hundreds, with Mudassar Nazar completing four:

Mudassar Nazar	231, 152*, 152, 119, 50
Zaheer Abbas	215, 186, 168
Javed Miandad	280*, 126, 85
Mohsin Khan	101*, 94, 91
Imran Khan	117
Salim Malik	107

Zaheer Abbas and Javed Miandad also did well in the one-day internationals, a series of four matches won by Pakistan 3–1:

Zaheer Abbas	10, 118, 105, 113	346 runs
Javed Miandad	106*, 3*, 119*, 6*	234 runs

•

In 1932–33, Walter Hammond scored 739 runs in four consecutive innings, a Test record:

101 / 75*	v Australia at Sydney
227	v New Zealand at Christchurch
336*	v New Zealand at Auckland

•

Although W.G. Grace made over 100 hundreds in first-class cricket, only one of them was scored outside England—159* v Victoria at Melbourne in 1891–92.

•

Of the first dozen centuries scored by Mark Waugh in first-class matches for New South Wales, a record nine of them were undefeated:

101*	v Tasmania	Devonport	1987–88
114*	v Victoria	Sydney	1987–88
100*	v Victoria	Melbourne	1987–88
116	v Tasmania	Sydney	1987–88
103*	v West Indians	Sydney	1988–89
100*	v Tasmania	Devonport	1988–89
172	v South Australia	Adelaide	1989–90
100*	v Victoria	Albury	1989–90
100*	v Victoria	Melbourne	1989–90
137	v South Australia	Sydney	1989–90
198*	v Tasmania	Sydney	1989–90
229*	v Western Australia	Perth	1990–91

•

When Don Bradman hit 270, batting at number 7 against England at the MCG in 1936–37, he became the first batsman to total 1,000 runs in five consecutive Tests, a feat only Garry Sobers and Graham Gooch have been able to match.

Walter Hammond was the last batsman to score 30,000 first-class runs in a decade—31,165 during the 1930s.

•

Four batsmen were dismissed in the nineties during the New Zealand–England Test match at Christchurch in 1991–92—Robin Smith made 96, Allan Lamb 93, and Dipak Patel and John Wright 99 each.

•

Harry Rock played in only six first-class matches for New South Wales in the mid-1920s but was good enough to amass 758 runs at 94.75; in his four Shield matches 560 runs at 112.00. On his debut in 1924–25 he scored 127 and 27 not out against South Australia, and in his next match, 235 and 51 against Victoria. But so strong was the side, Rock had to be dropped to make way for players returning from Test duty.

•

BATSMEN WITH 1,000 RUNS IN FIVE CONSECUTIVE TESTS

	Scores	*Runs*	*Avge*
Graham Gooch	85, 37, 154 & 30 v NZ 1990; 333, 123, 116, 7, 85 & 88 v I 1990	1,058	105.80
Don Bradman	304, 244 & 77 v E 1934; 38, 0, 0, 82, 13 & 270 v E 1936–37	1,028	114.22
Garry Sobers	365*, 125, 109*, 14 & 27 v P 1957–58; 25, 142*, 4 & 198 v I 1958–59	1,009	168.16

In his next match, Bradman scored 26 and 212, which increased his run tally to 1,266 in six appearances—an effort which remains the Test record.

MOST RUNS IN SIX CONSECUTIVE TESTS

	Scores	*Runs*	*Avge*
Don Bradman	304, 244 & 77 v E 1934; 38, 0, 0, 82, 13, 270, 26 & 212 v E 1936–37	1,266	115.09
Graham Gooch	85, 37, 154 & 30 v NZ 1990; 333, 123, 116, 7, 85 & 88 v I 1990; 20 & 58 v A 1990–91	1,136	94.66
Garry Sobers	365*, 125, 109*, 14 & 27 v P 1957–58; 25, 142*, 4, 198 & 106* v I 1958–59	1,115	185.33
Walter Hammond	44, 28, 251, 200, 32, 119*, 177, 38 & 16 v A 1928–29; 18 & 138* v SA 1929	1,061	117.88

•

When Bob Simpson and Bill Lawry shared a first-wicket stand of 244 against England at Adelaide in 1965–66 they became the first opening pair to score centuries in the same innings three times in Test cricket. They went on to achieve the feat a fourth time in 1967–68.

•

When David Boon hit 200 against New Zealand at Perth in 1898–90, he became the fourth member of the Australian team—after Dean Jones, Mark Taylor and Allan Border—to have scored a Test match double-century.

•

Individual scores	*Opening stand*	*Opposition*	*Match*
W.M. Lawry (106); R.B. Simpson (311)	201	England	Manchester 1964
W.M. Lawry (210); R.B. Simpson (201)	382	West Indies	Bridgetown 1964–65
W.M. Lawry (119); R.B. Simpson (225)	244	England	Adelaide 1965–66
W.M. Lawry (100); R.B. Simpson (109)	191	India	Melbourne 1967–68

•

C.B. Fry (Sussex), who five times scored a century in each innings of a first-class match, holds the rather unusual record of missing out three other times by one run:

99 & 131	v Hampshire at Hove in 1898
99 & 127*	v Leicestershire at Hove in 1903
125 & 99*	v Worcestershire at Hove in 1907

•

•

Apart from scoring 1,000 runs in his first 12 months of Test cricket, Mark Taylor came close to 1,000 runs in his first Sheffield Shield season. The New South Wales opener scored 903 runs in 1985–86, and 937 runs in all first-class cricket in his first year. In 1991–92, Queensland opening batsman Matthew Hayden passed Taylor's Shield aggregate, becoming the highest run-scorer ever for a first-year player, but due to the effects of a tropical cyclone was robbed of the chance of reaching 1,000 runs in the competition. In Queensland's final match of the season, Hayden was left stranded on 57 not out against Tasmania in Brisbane, just 18 runs short of the milestone. Hayden began his career scoring a century on debut, then hit another two hundreds in his next three matches, and finished the season with a record 1,028 runs in all first-class cricket at an average of 54.11.

•

Bill Ponsford scored centuries in 10 successive first-class matches for Victoria in the late 1920s:

138	v New South Wales	Sydney	1925–26
214	v South Australia	Adelaide	1926–27
151	v Queensland	Melbourne	1926–27
352	v New South Wales	Melbourne	1926–27
108	v South Australia	Melbourne	1926–27
116	v Queensland	Brisbane	1926–27
133	v South Australia	Adelaide	1927–28
437	v Queensland	Melbourne	1927–28
202	v New South Wales	Melbourne	1927–28
336	v South Australia	Melbourne	1927–28

•

Ian Chappell came up with a unique double against Victoria in Melbourne in 1973–74, scoring two centuries which both represented over 50% of South Australia's total in each innings—141* (4d–277/51.98%) and 130 (226/57.22%).

•

Graeme Wood

Graeme Wood's score of 112 in the 1980 Centenary Test was the first instance of any batsman recording a century in a Test in his first innings at Lord's.

•

In terms of runs scored, Allan Border was the leading Test batsman of the 1980s. In 98 Tests, Border made 7,386 runs at an average of 55.11 with a top score of 205 against New Zealand at Adelaide in 1987–88. So good was Border that his tally was 1,190 runs ahead of the next batsman on the list, David Gower.

TOP FIVE BATSMEN OF THE 1980s

	Tests	*Runs*	*100s*	*Avge*
Allan Border (A)	98	7,386	20	55.11
David Gower (E)	89	6,196	12	42.43
Javed Miandad (P)	76	5,642	16	54.77
Viv Richards (WI)	79	5,113	15	49.16
Gordon Greenidge (WI)	76	5,103	12	45.97

Border made over 4,000 runs more than the next most successful Australian batsman, David Boon (3,119), who didn't make his Test debut until half-way through the decade. Kim Hughes was also one of the leading Australian batsmen of the 1980s with 3,026 runs until his last Test in 1983–84.

Border's aggregate was also a new record for a particular decade.

LEADING RUN-SCORERS IN TESTS SINCE WORLD WAR II

		Tests	*Runs*	*Avge*
1950s	Neil Harvey (A)	57	4,719	50.74
1960s	Ken Barrington (E)	75	6,397	59.78
1970s	Sunil Gavaskar (I)	60	5,647	55.91
1980s	Allan Border (A)	98	7,386	55.11

•

When England's John Emburey hit 46 against Tasmania at Hobart in 1986–87, he gained a place in the record books for passing the previous highest first-class score (44) made up entirely of boundaries. Emburey's knock comprised 10 fours and a six and came off 30 balls in 33 minutes.

•

In his first Test appearance against India, at Faisalabad in 1978–79, Zaheer Abbas missed out by just four runs in scoring a century in each innings (176 & 96). The unlikely bowler who denied him the double was Sunil Gavaskar, who took his only wicket in his 125-match Test career.

•

Going into what turned out to be his final match in first-class cricket, Geoff Boycott needed 69 runs to bring up 1,000 runs for the 1986 season. He managed to score just 61 in Yorkshire's only innings and so failed by 8 to complete 1,000 first-class runs in a season for the 24th consecutive year.

•

The first two centuries in the first-class career of Worcestershire's 'Doc' Gibbons were both scored before lunch—107 v Hampshire at Southampton (first day) and 140 v Kent at Worcester (third day) in 1928.

•

The fifth Test against Australia at St John's in 1991 marked the final appearance at home by the great Viv Richards. He was dismissed for 0 and 2, his worst-ever performance in his illustrious 121-Test match career.

In 1989, Australia's Mark Taylor became the first batsman to score 1,000 Test runs in his first year of international cricket. With 1,219 runs at 64.16 in 11 Tests, he beat the previous record of 918 runs by Sunil Gavaskar in 1971:

MARK TAYLOR'S 1,000 RUNS IN 1989

Opposition	*Scores*	*Tests*	*Months*
West Indies	25, 3, 3, 36	2	January–February
England	136, 60, 62, 27, 43, 51, 85, 37*, 219, 71, 48	6	June–August
New Zealand	9	1	November
Sri Lanka	9, 164, 23, 108	2	December

Sunil Gavaskar made 1,000 runs in a calendar year on four occasions, in 1976, 1978, 1979 and 1983. Allan Border is the only batsman to score exactly 1,000 runs, in 1986. India's Mohinder Amarnath holds the record for scoring the runs in the shortest time. He was good enough to reach the target by 3 May in 1983 and went on to complete 1,077 runs for the year in 14 Tests:

MOHINDER AMARNATH'S 1,000 RUNS IN 1983

Opposition	*Scores*	*Tests*	*Months*
Pakistan	22, 78, 61, 64, 120, 19, 103*	4	January–February
West Indies	29, 40, 58, 117, 13, 91, 80, 54, 116	5	February–May
Pakistan	4, 7	2	September
West Indies	0, 0, 1, 0, 0, 0	3	October–December

The first batsman to top the 1,000 run mark in a calendar year was Clem Hill, in 1902. The feat was not achieved again until 1947 when Denis Compton made 1,159 runs in nine Tests. Vic Richards has scored the most runs in a calendar year, 1,710 in 1976, a total which included seven centuries and five fifties:

VIV RICHARDS' 1,000 RUNS IN 1976

Opposition	*Scores*	*Tests*	*Months*
Australia	44, 2, 30, 101, 50, 98	3	January–February
India	142, 130, 20, 177, 23, 64	4	March–April
England	232, 63, 4, 135, 66, 38, 291	4	June–August

•

The highest score by a batsman obtaining his maiden first-class century is 337 not out by Pervez Akhtar for Railways v Dera Ismail Khan at Lahore in 1964–65.

•

In 1948 Vijay Hazare hit 116 and 145 in the fourth Test at Adelaide—not only was it the first instance of an Indian batsman scoring two centuries in a Test, but it was also the first time a batsman had achieved twin hundreds in any first-class match and still finished on the losing side by an innings.

•

Three batsmen finished the 1979–80 Test series between Australia and England with a top score that was one shy of a century—Graham Gooch (99), Geoff Boycott (99*) and Kim Hughes (99). David Gower had a highest score for the series of 98 not out.

•

Darren Lehmann

Darren Lehmann hit a fifty, two centuries and a double-century in successive innings for South Australia in 1989–90:

228	v New South Wales at Adelaide
80	v New Zealand at Adelaide
109	v Sri Lanka at Adelaide
128	v Victoria at Melbourne

•

Pakistan's Shoaib Mohammad hit a century in five successive Test matches against New Zealand. The first four hundreds were scored in successive innings:

163	Second Test at Wellington	1988–89
112	Third Test at Auckland	1988–89
203*	First Test at Karachi	1990–91
105	Second Test at Lahore	1990–91

The fifth—142—came up in the second innings of the third Test at Faisalabad and raised his aggregate for the series to 507, a new record between Pakistan and New Zealand.

•

Apart from a slight hiccup at Adelaide, Australia recorded a 50-run partnership in each of its innings against India in 1967–68:

99 & 0	Bob Simpson & Bill Lawry at Adelaide
191	Bob Simpson & Bill Lawry at Melbourne
76 & 116	Bill Lawry & Ian Redpath at Brisbane
61 & 111	Bill Lawry & Bob Cowper at Sydney

•

Gordon Greenidge established a remarkable record in 1990 when he scored 298 with Desmond Haynes against England at Antigua. He then shared the record for the West Indies' best opening partnerships against all their opponents in Test cricket:

298	v England with Desmond Haynes	Antigua 1989–90
296	v India with Desmond Haynes	St John's 1982–83
250*	v Australia with Desmond Haynes	Georgetown 1983–84
225	v New Zealand with Desmond Haynes	Christchurch 1979–80
182	v Pakistan with Roy Fredericks	Kingston 1976–77

•

India's Sunil Gavaskar, the first batsman to score 10,000 runs in Test cricket, marked his first Test series—against the West Indies in 1970–71—with a massive 774 runs in four Tests, at 154.80, a record for a debutant batsman. He struck a half-century in all but one of his eight innings, equalling the feat of six other batsmen in scoring seven fifties in a Test series.

S.M. GAVASKAR v WEST INDIES 1970–71

65 & 67*	Second Test at Port-of-Spain
116 & 64*	Third Test at Georgetown
1 & 117*	Fourth Test at Bridgetown
124 & 220	Fifth Test at Port-of-Spain

•

Mark Waugh's long-awaited elevation to Test cricket in 1991 ended the longest apprenticeship in first-class cricket for any Australian player since the Second World War. From the time he made his debut for New South Wales in 1985–86, Waugh amassed 7,500 runs in 100 first-class matches before his first Test. Others who've had to wait a similar time include Greg Chappell and Ken 'Slasher' Mackay. Both needed over 5,000 runs before winning their first Test cap.

•

England batsman Mark Ramprakash was dismissed in the twenties seven times in his first eight Test innings—27, 27, 24, 13, 21, 29, 25 and 25 v West Indies in 1991.

•

In 10 successive first-class innings in 1926, Ernest Tyldesley scored 144, 69, 144*, 226, 51, 131, 131, 106, 126 and 81.

•

Ken Barrington played 10 first-class innings for England and the MCC at the Adelaide Oval, and each time scored a half-century—104, 52, 52*, 63 and 132* in 1962–63 and 69, 51, 63, 60 and 102 in 1965–66.

•

The India–New Zealand Test at Delhi in 1955 saw the batsmen average over 100 runs per wicket. Overall, 1,093 runs were scored in three innings for the loss of just 10 wickets—New Zealand 2 declared for 450 and 1 for 112; India 7 declared for 531.

•

Despite a double-century against India at Leeds in 1967 Geoff Boycott was dropped for the next Test at Lord's on disciplinary grounds. His 246 not out came off 555 balls in 573 minutes, his first hundred in 341 minutes off 316 balls.

•

In 30 Test innings in England Doug Walters never scored a century. His best was 86 at Manchester in 1968.

•

The record for the most centuries in consecutive Test innings is five by the West Indian Everton Weekes:

141 v England	Kingston 1947–48
128 v India	Delhi 1948–49
194 v India	Bombay 1948–49
162 v India	Calcutta 1948–49
101 v India	Calcutta 1948–49

Weekes made 90 in his next innings at Madras, and with 56 at Bombay extended to seven the number of fifties he'd scored in successive innings—thereby establishing another world record.

•

Michael Bevan

Michael Bevan, who hit a century on his first-class debut for South Australia in 1989–90, hit five hundreds in six consecutive innings for New South Wales in 1990–91. His record run with the bat included four 100s in a row, a first by any batsman for New South Wales in first-class matches. He also became the first batsman to score centuries in consecutive matches against five different states:

106*	v Western Australia at Sydney
20 / 104	v South Australia at Adelaide
153*	v Victoria at Sydney
121	v Queensland at Sydney
136	v Tasmania at Hobart

•

Peter Kirsten

In 1980 South African batsman Peter Kirsten hit six centuries for Derbyshire in the County Championship, equalling Leslie Townsend's record set in 1933. Three of his hundreds were double-centuries, and all were unbeaten—213* v Glamorgan, 209* v Northamptonshire and 202* v Essex. He hit another two double-centuries in 1981 and the following season claimed Townsend's record by accumulating eight hundreds in the County Championship.

•

Only once in first-class cricket has a single match contained four opening partnerships of over 100—Somerset v Cambridge University at Taunton in 1980:

172 & 112 by Graham Atkinson & Roy Virgin for Somerset
198 & 137 by Roger Prideaux & Tony Lewis for Cambridge University

•

Worcestershire batsman Glenn Turner had an unusual match in 1977 against Glamorgan at Swansea. He carried his bat for 141, yet no other batsman reached double figures. His score represented 83.40% of Worcestershire's total.

G.M. Turner	not out	141
B.J.R. Jones	lbw b Nash	1
P.A. Neale	c E.W. Jones b Wilkins	3
E.J.O. Hemsley	b Cordle	3
B.L. D'Oliveira	c E.W. Jones b Cordle	0
D.N. Patel	c E.W. Jones b Nash	4
D.J. Humphries	c Llewellyn b Cordle	0
V.A. Holder	lbw b Nash	4
N. Gifford	c Llewellyn b Lloyd	7
J. Cumbes	lbw b Nash	5
A.P. Pridgeon	lbw b Cordle	0
Extras	(lb 1)	1
		169

•

Gordon Greenidge celebrated his 100th one-day international and his 100th Test by scoring a century:

102*	v Pakistan at Sharjah in 1988–89
149	v England at St John's in 1989–90

•

During the first Test against India at Lord's in 1990, Graham Gooch and Michael Atherton shared an opening partnership of 204, a stand which eclipsed England's previous best of 178 by Graeme Fowler and Tim Robinson at Madras in 1984–85. In the next Test at Manchester, they then broke their own record by scoring 225, becoming the first pair to record two successive double-century opening stands in Test cricket.

•

Up until 1988 the West Indies record partnership for the ninth wicket against Pakistan was 46 by Joel Garner and Colin Croft at Port-of-Spain in 1976–77. It was then broken in three successive innings within the space of nine days in the 1987–88 series:

56 by Jeff Dujon & Winston Benjamin	Second Test	Port-of-Spain (2nd innings)
58 by Malcolm Marshall & Winston Benjamin	Third Test	Bridgetown (1st innings)
61*by Jeff Dujon & Winston Benjamin	Third Test	Bridgetown (2nd innings)

•

Transvaal's total of 6 declared for 587 against Northern Transvaal in the 1987–88 Currie Cup included three batsmen who each scored over 150 inside 300 balls—Jimmy Cook (159), Bruce Roberts (179) and Clive Rice (150*).

•

Lindsey Jerman, who played for Essex, hit a six off the first ball he faced in first-class cricket, batting at number 11 against Surrey at Southend in 1951.

•

When New Zealand met England in the second Test at Nottingham in 1986, the top-scorers for each side were the opposing off-spin bowlers—John Bracewell (110) and John Emburey (75).

•

Heartbreak for New Zealand's Martin Crowe at Wellington in 1990–91. Going for what would have been his first triple-century in first-class cricket, he was dismissed with the last ball in the first Test against Sri Lanka for 299. It was his maiden 200 in a Test match, the highest individual Test score by a New Zealander, and his partnership of 467 with Andrew Jones (186) was a world record for any wicket in a Test match.

Earlier, Aravinda de Silva made 276, the highest score ever made by a Sri Lankan, and provides only the third instance in Test history of two separate innings of over 250 in the same match.

After his innings of 186 at Wellington, Jones reeled off another two centuries in the next Test (122 & 100*) to become the first New Zealander to score hundreds in three consecutive innings. Sri Lanka's Asanka Gurusinha also hit two centuries (119 & 102) in the second Test at Hamilton, providing only the second instance in all Test cricket of a batsman from each side performing the feat in the same match. Previously, only Denis Compton (147 & 103*) and Arthur Morris (122 & 124*) had done so, at Adelaide in 1946–47.

•

When Graeme Wood and Martin Kent opened the innings together for the first time in a Test, at The Oval in 1981, their contribution of 120 was the first century opening stand for Australia since Ian Davis and Alan Turner's 134 against Pakistan at Melbourne in 1976–77. Over 100 innings were played between these two partnerships—the highest stand was 96 by Rick Darling and Andrew Hilditch, against Pakistan at Perth in 1978–79. Australia's next most barren stretch for its openers occurred last century when 89 innings went by without a 100-run partnership.

THE MOST CONSECUTIVE INNINGS BY AUSTRALIA IN TEST CRICKET WITHOUT A CENTURY OPENING PARTNERSHIP

106	Melbourne 1976–77 to Manchester 1981
89	The Oval 1882 to The Oval 1899
67	Christchurch 1981–82 to Melbourne 1985–86
65	Manchester 1968 to Kingston 1972–73

A CENTURY OF TEST INNINGS WITHOUT A CENTURY PARTNERSHIP
Melbourne 1976–77 to Manchester 1981

6		8 & 2	
3 & 32	v P 1976–77	21 & 13	
9 & 37		1 & 13	
31 & 28*	v NZ 1976–77	32 & 20	
11 & 33	v E 1976–77	0 & 21	
25 & 5		28 & 11	v I 1979–80
4 & 0		19 & 40	v WI 1979–80
79 & 18		2 & 91	v E 1979–80
8 & 31		38 & 43	v WI 1979–80
0	v E 1977	18 & 31	v E 1979–80
24 & 0		23 & 12	v WI 1979–80
19 & 13		52 & 20	v E 1979–80
0 & 42		8 & 38	
29 & 26		1	
89 & 17	v I 1977–78	50 & 4	v P 1979–80
7 & 59		64 & 15	v E 1980
13 & 21		80 & 63*	
28 & 11		0 & 3	
23 & 9		0 & 25	v NZ 1980–81
0 & 65	v WI 1977–78	3	
2 & 0		84 & 5	
8 & 8		30 & 11	v I 1980–81
65 & 55		0 & 20	
1 & 38		62 & 2	
5 & 31		55 & 13	
18 & 8	v E 1978–79	5 & 2	
11 & 49		20 & 7	v E 1981
96 & 87	v P 1978–79		

•

When David Boon and Geoff Marsh made 217 against India at Sydney in 1985–86, it was the first century opening stand in 36 Tests, and the first 200-run stand by Australian openers in 172 Tests.

•

Rusi Surti, who appeared in 26 Tests for India during the 1960s, scored 8,000 runs and six centuries in first-class cricket, but never made it to 100 at Test level. The closest he came was at Auckland in 1968 in his final Test match. He was twice dropped on 99, but was still caught, one short of his century. He became the fourth batsman, after Norman Yardley, John Beck and Maqsood Ahmed, to end his Test career with a top score of 99.

•

Dirk Wellham

One batsman who suffered from the 'nervous nineties' syndrome more than most was Dirk Wellham during his time with Tasmania. In three seasons, Wellham made it to the nineties six times but failed to reach 100.

92	v Queensland	Brisbane 1988–89
90*	v Western Australia	Perth 1988–89
94	v South Australia	Adelaide 1988–89
90	v New South Wales	Hobart 1989–90
91	v New South Wales	Sydney 1990–91
95	v Victoria	Hobart 1990–91

•

During the calendar year of 1990 three English batsmen performed the relatively rare feat of a hundred and a double-hundred in the same first-class match. The double was also recorded during the year in Pakistan's Quaid-e-Azam Trophy.

Rizwan-uz-Zaman	139 & 217*	PIA v PACO	Lahore 1989–90
Graham Gooch	333 & 123	England v India	Lord's 1990
Graeme Hick	252* & 100*	Worcestershire v Glamorgan	Abergavenny 1990
Neil Taylor	204 & 142	Kent v Surrey	Canterbury 1990

Prior to Rizwan's double, the feat had only ever been achieved on 26 occasions in the history of first-class cricket. Graham Gooch, with 333 and 123, became the first batsman to score a triple-century and a century in the same first-class match.

•

In 1977–78 against the touring Indians, Victoria's opening batsman Paul Hibbert became the first Australian batsman to score a century (100) in a first-class match without a single boundary. India's opener Chetan Chauhan played a similar innings, scoring only two boundaries in his knock of 157.

•

Sussex batsman James Broadbridge holds the most unusual record of scoring more than half of his team's total in each innings of a first-class match on two occasions. He was the first batsman to achieve the feat, in 1825, and did it again, providing the second instance, in 1828:

63 & 92 Sussex (121 & 168) v Hampshire at Petworth 1825
20 & 14 Sussex (35 & 22) v Kent at Sevenoaks 1828

•

Graeme Labrooy, who topped Sri Lanka's bowling averages against New Zealand in 1990–91 (13 wickets at 27.46), made a name for himself with the bat in the final Test at Auckland, scoring 70 not out off 80 balls with 12 fours and two sixes. He became the first player in Test history to reach 50 without any singles—4, 6, 6, 4, 3, 2, 4, 4, 4, 4, 4, 4, 4—his 13 scoring strokes in getting there also a Test record.

•

When Lancashire's Neil Fairbrother hit 366 against Surrey in 1990, 311 runs came on the third day, with 100 runs in each session of play—100, 108 and 103.

•

One of the most unwanted records in first-class cricket was broken not once but three times within the space of a month in the Australian summer of 1989–90. During the Western Australia–Tasmania match at the WACA, former Perth batsman Greg Shipperd took 449 minutes to reach 100, the slowest-ever century in Australian first-class cricket. Three weeks later, New Zealand's Mark Greatbatch scored a match-saving 146 not out in the Test match at Perth, his century coming in 462 minutes, beating Shipperd's record by 13 minutes. However, Shipperd regained the record a few days later taking 481 minutes to score 100 against Victoria at Launceston.

•

Only one batsman—Frank Worrell—has been involved in a 500-run partnership on two occasions in first-class cricket:

574* for the 4th wicket with Clyde Walcott—Barbados v Trinidad at Port-of-Spain in 1945–46
502* for the 4th wicket with John Goddard—Barbados v Trinidad at Bridgetown in 1943–44

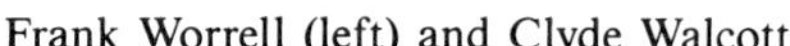

Frank Worrell (left) and Clyde Walcott

In England in 1979 no batsman was able to score 2,000 runs for the season, the first time this had happened since 1894. Roy Virgin came the closest with 1,936 runs for Northamptonshire.

•

In two successive first-class matches against Pakistan in which he batted, Dean Jones hit four centuries—116 & 121* for Australia at Adelaide in 1989–90 and 134* & 105 for Durham at Chester-le-Street in 1992.

•

During the 1956 Ashes series, no Australian batsman scored a century in the five Test matches played. The highest individual score was 97 by Richie Benaud in the second Test at Lord's. A similar thing happened to England during the five-Test series against the West Indies in 1985–86. In fact, no century was scored in the five other first-class matches on tour, the best score being 90 by David Gower in the last match, the fifth Test at St John's.

•

In 1981–82 South Australia's opening batsmen recorded eight century first-wicket stands in its 11 first-class matches. Five of them were achieved in the Sheffield Shield, which it won for the first time since 1975–76. Rick Darling and Wayne Phillips were the most effective pair with four 100-run partnerships, including two in the same match against the touring Pakistanis.

123	Rick Darling & Ian McLean	v New South Wales	Adelaide
141	Rick Darling & Kim Harris	v West Indians	Adelaide
125	Wayne Phillips & Jeff Crowe	v New South Wales	Sydney
228	Rick Darling & Wayne Phillips	v Pakistanis	Adelaide
100	Rick Darling & Wayne Phillips	v Pakistanis	Adelaide
168	Wayne Phillips & Kim Harris	v Queensland	Adelaide
163	Rick Darling & Wayne Phillips	v Tasmania	Launceston
101	Rick Darling & Wayne Phillips	v Victoria	Adelaide

The Sheffield Shield runners-up, New South Wales, were equally successful with their openers, particularly Rick McCosker and John Dyson, who in successive matches shared in four stands of 100 or more. In nine Shield matches and 10 first-class matches in the season, the Blues registered six century opening partnerships:

191	Rick McCosker & John Dyson	v South Australia	Adelaide
102	Rick McCosker & John Dyson	v West Indians	Sydney
122	Rick McCosker & John Dyson	v South Australia	Sydney
174	Rick McCosker & John Dyson	v Victoria	Sydney
219	Ian Davis & Trevor Chappell	v Tasmania	Hobart
145	Rick McCosker & Ian Davis	v Western Australia	Sydney

McCosker and Dyson also scored heavily in the 1981–82 McDonald's Cup, with a 100-run opening stand in three successive matches.

•

During his knock of 131 not out against Warwickshire at Taunton in 1982, Ian Botham on two occasions hit three successive sixes off Simon Sutcliffe. Botham was just as savage on the bowling of Paul Smith, hitting him for 30 runs off one over on his way to 100 in 52 minutes off 56 balls. His century was the fastest of the season and included 10 sixes and 12 fours.

•

In 1983 four batsmen hit a first-class century in the English County Championship in under 50 minutes.

Min. taken to 100	*Batsman*	*Match*	*Balls taken to reach 100*
35	Steve O'Shaughnessy (105)	Lancashire v Leicestershire at Manchester	54
41	Nigel Popplewell (143)	Somerset v Gloucestershire at Bath	60
46	Graeme Fowler (100)	Lancashire v Leicestershire at Manchester	67
50	Paddy Clift (100*)	Leicestershire v Sussex at Hove	58

The century by O'Shaughnessy, in only 35 minutes, equalled the then world record for the fastest century in first-class cricket, an honour shared with Percy Fender who hit a century in similar time for Surrey v Northamptonshire in 1920.

With the assistance of part-time bowlers who were brought on to expedite a declaration, both O'Shaughnessy and Fowler took full advantage of the situation and recorded a double-century opening stand in just 43 minutes—a world record in first-class cricket. O'Shaughnessy's century came off only 25 scoring strokes—another world record—and included five sixes and 17 fours, the proportion of boundaries (98) in his hundred also being a record. Fowler's hundred contained 84 runs in boundaries, including a sequence of 10 consecutive scoring strokes hit for six, which beat Mike Procter's record of eight in a county match in 1979.

•

When Australia was dismissed for 76 by Hampshire on the 1985 Ashes tour, the number-11 batsman—Wayne Phillips (who batted down the order due to injury)—made the highest individual score (15).

•

Geoff Boycott, with 48,426, has scored more runs in first-class cricket than any other living cricketer.

•

Mike Gatting's maiden double-century in Test cricket—207 at Madras in 1987—was England's 500th Test match century. His was the 31st double-century for England—of the other 469 three-figure scores, four were triple-centuries, the highest being Len Hutton's 364 against Australia at The Oval in 1938.

•

Charlie Parker of Gloucestershire played in 954 first-class innings for the county and never scored a century. His highest score was 82; his number of innings without a hundred is a record in English first-class cricket.

•

After scoring 129 on his first-class debut for Western Australia against Queensland in 1963–64, Derek Chadwick made 58 and 114 in his next match, against Victoria in Melbourne. Mark Lavender recorded a similar double for Western Australia in 1990–91, scoring 118 on his first-class debut, against Victoria at Melbourne, and 113 not out in his next match, against Queensland at Brisbane.

•

When Gordon Greenidge made 259 for Hampshire v Sussex in 1975, he reached 50, 100, 150 and 200 with sixes. All in all his innings contained 13 sixes, a new record in the County Championship.

•

Everton Weekes began the West Indies' 1955–56 tour of New Zealand with a record five centuries in his first five innings—156, 148, 123, 119* and 103.

•

Keith Medlycott

In 1984, Nick Falkner and Keith Medlycott made their first-class debuts for Surrey against Cambridge University at Banstead. The two newcomers both scored centuries (101* and 117*), a first in England, and only the fourth such occurrence anywhere in the world.

The 1947 Test series between England and South Africa contained a record number of batsmen (five) to score 500 runs—Denis Compton (753), Dudley Nourse (621), Bruce Mitchell (597), Alan Melville (569) and Bill Edrich (552).

•

Eight batsmen scored over 400 runs in the 1975–76 Test series between Australia and West Indies—Greg Chappell (702), Ian Redpath (575), Clive Lloyd (469), Ian Chappell (449), Alan Turner (439), Viv Richards (426), Alvin Kallicharran (421) and Roy Fredericks (417).

•

During his innings of 66 not out in the third Test at Bombay in 1986, Allan Border reached a unique milestone, scoring the one millionth run in Test cricket.

•

Within the space of just eight days in January 1985, Indian all-rounder Ravi Shastri found himself in the record books for vastly differing performances with the bat. In the third Test against England at Calcutta, he scored a century which took 422 minutes off 330 balls, one of the slowest hundreds on record in Test cricket. But then playing for Bombay in a Ranji Trophy match a few days later, Shastri scored an unbeaten double-century in the world record time of 113 minutes off 123 balls. His first hundred came in 71 minutes off 80 balls, his second in 42 minutes off 43 balls.

•

In Zimbabwe's inaugural Test, against India at Harare in 1992, its opening pair of Grant Flower and Kevin Arnott made history when they put on a 100-run opening partnership in the first innings. This was the first time that a country new to Test cricket had begun with a century first-wicket stand, beating the 86 by the Caribbean pair of George Challenor and 'Freddie' Martin in the West Indies' first Test, against England at Lord's in 1928.

•

On two occasions during his career Greg Chappell retired after scoring a century in a first-class match—130 for Australia v Wellington in 1976–77 and 101 against Lancashire at Manchester in 1980. He is one of only eight batsmen in the history of Australian first-class cricket to end an innings in such unusual circumstances, and the only one to do it twice.

•

During the New South Wales–Western Australia Shield match at Sydney in 1989–90, Mike Veletta carried his bat for 110 in the first innings and was out first ball in the second—an odd double, believed to be unique in Australian first-class cricket.

•

PREVIOUS INSTANCES OF TWO DEBUTANT BATSMEN FROM THE SAME SIDE SCORING CENTURIES IN THE SAME MATCH

N.L. Gooden (102) & A.G. Moyes (104)	South Australia v Western Australia	Adelaide 1912–13
O.W. Bill (115) & L.R. Leabeater (128)	New South Wales v Tasmania	Sydney 1929–30
F.E. Fontaine (118) & R.J. Lawson (119)	Victoria v Tasmania	Hobart 1930–31

During a six-week period in 1979, Gloucestershire's captain Mike Procter experienced a magic time with both bat and ball, scoring 658 runs and taking 31 wickets in just seven matches. Against Leicestershire at Bristol, he hit a century before lunch and also achieved a hat-trick. One week later, and in his next match, he took another hat-trick—all lbw—against Yorkshire at Cheltenham. Then with the bat he scored a ninety in four successive matches, all of which came in lightning time. His 100 against Northamptonshire at Bristol was reached in just 57 minutes and was the fastest century of the season:

Opposition	*Venue*	*Date*	*Score*	*Time*
Surrey	Cheltenham	18–21 August	102	100 in 76 m
Somerset	Taunton	25–28 August	93	93 in 46 m
Warwickshire	Bristol	1–4 September	92	92 in 35 m
Northamptonshire	Bristol	5–7 September	105	100 in 57 m

•

In 1986, the Warwickshire opening pair of Andy Moles and Paul Smith shared nine stands of over 50 in their first 12 innings together—a world record. Among their partnerships were four century stands, including two of over 150 in the same match—161 & 155 v Somerset at Weston-super-Mare.

•

In 1941–42, Vijay Merchant became the only batsman in first-class cricket to score 150 or more in four successive innings:

170*	Bombay v Nawanagar at Jamnagar
243*	Hindus v The Rest at Bombay
221	Hindus v Parsees at Bombay
153*	Bombay v Sind at Bombay

•

On two occasions the 'Three Ws'—Frank Worrell, Clyde Walcott and Everton Weekes—all scored centuries in the same innings of a Test match:

Fifth Test v India at Kingston in 1952–53—Worrell 237, Walcott 188, Weekes 109
Fourth Test v England at Port-of-Spain in 1953–54—Weekes 206, Worrell 167, Walcott 124

•

In 1976–77, an extraordinary set of batting records was set during a Patron Trophy match at Karachi, when two young bowlers opened the batting for Karachi Whites against Quetta and created a world record first-wicket stand of 561. Neither Waheed Mirza (324) nor Mansoor Akhtar (224*) had previously reached three figures in a first-class match. Their partnership eclipsed the long-standing record of 555 by Percy Holmes and Herbert Sutcliffe for Yorkshire against Essex in 1932.

•

When Lance Cairns scored his maiden century in first-class cricket, it was one of the fastest ever recorded. Playing for Wellington against Otago in 1979–80, Cairns raced to his century in 52 minutes, off just 45 balls. His eventual score of 110 included 98 runs in boundaries—11 fours and nine sixes.

•

Neil Harvey

In 14 Tests and 23 innings against South Africa, Neil Harvey scored 1,625 runs with one double century, seven centuries and a further five half-centuries.

•

When Javed Miandad began his Test career in 1976 with scores of 163, 25*, 25, 206 and 85 he became the first batsman to reach the milestone of 500 runs in his first five innings. India's Vinod Kambli has since matched Javed's feat, and joined a small band of players to score 500 runs in four Tests.

500 RUNS IN FIRST THREE TESTS						
	I	*NO*	*Runs*	*100s*	*50s*	*Avge*
Javed Miandad (P)	5	1	504	2	1	126.00
500 RUNS IN FIRST FOUR TESTS						
Sunil Gavaskar (I)	8	3	774	4	3	154.80
George Headley (WI)	8	0	703	4	0	87.87
Conrad Hunte (WI)	7	1	577	3	0	96.16
Vinod Kambli (I)	5	1	544	2	1	136.00
K.S. Ranjitsinhji (E)	8	2	516	2	2	86.00
Barry Richards (SA)	7	0	508	2	2	72.57

Kambli's batch of 500 runs was boosted with the inclusion of two double centuries, a feat without precedence in Test history for a player so new to the game. His scores of 224 and 227 came in successive innings and etched his name alongside Walter Hammond, who achieved the feat twice, and Don Bradman.

DOUBLE CENTURIES IN SUCCESSIVE TEST INNINGS

Walter Hammond	251	v Australia at Sydney 1928–29
	200	v Australia at Melbourne 1928–29
	227	v New Zealand at Christchurch 1932–33
	336*	v New Zealand at Auckland 1932–33
Don Bradman	304	v England at Leeds 1934
	244	v England at The Oval 1934
Vinod Kambli	224	v England at Bombay 1992–93
	227	v Zimbabwe at New Delhi 1992–93

•

During the first-class seasons 1926–27 and 1927–28, Bill Ponsford hit five 200s in only 15 innings, an Australian Record:

214 v South Australia	Adelaide	1926–27
352 v New South Wales	Melbourne	1926–27
437 v Queensland	Melbourne	1927–28
202 v New South Wales	Melbourne	1927–28
336 v South Australia	Melbourne	1927–28

•

Indian batsman Ajay Jadeja missed out by the narrowest of margins in scoring double centuries in three successive first-class matches in 1991–92. After hitting 256 for Haryana v Services and 228 v Punjab he was then out for 199 in his next match against Himachal Pradesh.

•

'Jack' Badcock, who scored 25 hundreds in first-class cricket for Tasmania and South Australia, possesses one of Test cricket's most bizarre records. In seven Test matches, Badcock only once made it into double-figures and then went on to score a century—118 against England at Melbourne in 1936–37. In his other 11 Test innings his highest score was just nine—8, 0, 2, 118, 9, 5, 0, 0, 4, 5*, 0 and 9.

•

When Graeme Hick made his record-breaking 405 not out in 1988 it was the highest individual score ever recorded during the month of May. He also became only the eighth batsman to reach 1,000 runs before the end of May in first-class matches in England.

A record number of batsmen—five—scored 3,000 runs in the English summer of 1928:

	I	*NO*	*Runs*	*HS*	*100s*	*Avge*
Frank Woolley (Kent)	59	4	3,352	198	12	60.94
'Patsy' Hendren (Middlesex)	54	7	3,311	209*	13	70.44
Phil Mead (Hampshire)	50	10	3,027	180	13	75.67
Ernest Tyldesley (Lancashire)	48	10	3,024	242	10	79.57
Herbert Sutcliffe (Yorkshire)	44	5	3,002	228	13	76.97

In 1928, 414 individual centuries were scored, a record number until 1990, when there were 428. Of that total, 32 were double-centuries, and three were triples, which equalled the record three scored in 1899 and 1934.

•

Chris Broad

When Chris Broad and Steve Windaybank shared partnerships of 126 and 89 for the first wicket—in their match for Gloucestershire v Cambridge University at Cambridge in 1979—each batsman was making his first-class debut.

•

HIGHEST FIRST-CLASS SCORE FOR EACH MONTH

	Score	*Batsman*	*Match*	*Venue*	*Season*
January	499	Hanif Mohammad	Karachi v Bahawalpur	Karachi	1958–59
February	429	Bill Ponsford	Victoria v Tasmania	Melbourne	1922–23
March	369	Don Bradman	South Australia v Tasmania	Adelaide	1935–36
April	336*	Walter Hammond	England v New Zealand	Auckland	1932–33
May	405*	Graeme Hick	Worcestershire v Somerset	Taunton	1988
June	345	Charles Macartney	Australians v Nottinghamshire	Nottingham	1921
July	424	Archie MacLaren	Lancashire v Somerset	Taunton	1895
August	364	Len Hutton	England v Australia	The Oval	1938
September	317	Ken Rutherford	New Zealanders v D.B. Close's XI	Scarborough	1986
October	359	Bob Simpson	New South Wales v Queensland	Brisbane	1963–64
November	383	Charles Gregory	New South Wales v Queensland	Brisbane	1906–07
December	443*	B.B. Nimbalkar	Maharashtra v Kathiawar	Poona	1948–49

During the 1977 season, Essex batsman Ken McEwan twice scored over 25 runs off a single over in first-class matches:

Runs	*Bowler*	*Match*
28 (4,2,6,6,4,6)	Kerry O'Keefe	Essex v Australians at Chelmsford
27 (4,6,6,6,4,1)	Mark Allbrook	Essex v Cambridge University at Cambridge

•

In the early part of his first-class career, Dean Jones had an extraordinary ability to turn centuries into major scores. His maiden century in first-class cricket was 199. His first five hundreds in Test cricket were 210, 184*, 102, 216 and 157.

•

India's record total of 7 for 676 against Sri Lanka at Kanpur in 1986–87 included three batsmen who each scored over 150—Mohammad Azharuddin (199), Sunil Gavaskar (176) and Kapil Dev (163). This was a first in postwar Test matches. The other occasion was in 1938 when Len Hutton (364), Maurice Leyland (187) and Joe Hardstaff (169*) were the batsmen in England's score of 7 declared for 903 against Australia at The Oval.

•

In the third Test against India at Bombay in 1992–93, England's number-11, Phil Tufnell, scored 2 not out in each innings. His first knock lasted a record 81 minutes and 40 deliveries. Colin Croft, the West Indies' last man in at Brisbane in 1979–80, scored 2 not out in 80 minutes off 73 balls.

•

Gordon Greenidge and Desmond Haynes came within four runs of a 300-run opening partnership against India at St John's in 1982–83. Their stand ended when Greenidge retired, with his score on 154, to be with his critically ill daughter, who died two days after the Test match finished. Greenidge became the first batsman in Test history to end his innings 'retired not out'.

•

During the 1970s only one batsman was able to score a double-century in a Test match against Australia. It happened in only the second Test of the decade, at Durban in 1969–70, when Graeme Pollock hit 274. No other batsman was able to repeat the feat for the next 10 years and 85 Test matches, until Pakistan's wicket-keeper Taslim Arif made 210 not out at Faisalabad in 1979–80.

In all Test cricket, the record is held by England, which went for 103 successive Test matches between 1894–95 and 1924–25 without conceding a double century.

•

Jim Gill experienced the highs and lows of batting in his only first-class match with both a century (106) and a duck v MCC at Dublin in 1948.

•

Despite scoring close to 5,000 runs in Test cricket, Ian Redpath only ever hit two sixes, and collected them both in the same innings of his penultimate Test, against the West Indies at Adelaide in 1975–76.

•

On each occasion Australia has toured the West Indies, at least one of its batsmen has scored a century on his first-class debut in the Caribbean in the opening match:

Arthur Morris	157	v Jamaica	Kingston	1954–55
Bob Simpson	111	v Jamaica	Kingston	1964–65
Bob Cowper	121	v Jamaica	Kingston	1964–65
Norman O'Neill	125	v Jamaica	Kingston	1964–65
Greg Chappell	106	v Jamaica	Kingston	1972–73
Graeme Wood	122	v Leeward Islands	Basseterre	1977–78
Kepler Wessels	126*	v Leeward Islands	Basseterre	1983–84
Mark Taylor	101	v President's XI	Basseterre	1990–91

The centuries by Simpson, Cowper and O'Neill against Jamaica in 1964–65 all came in the same innings, which also included an unbeaten knock of 89 by Brian Booth. Kepler Wessels backed up his century in 1983–84 with 86 in the second innings, falling 14 runs short of becoming the first Australian to register two centuries in the same first-class match in the West Indies, a feat which was realised in the next match by Steve Smith (105 & 116 v Guyana at Georgetown). In doing so, Smith became the first Australian tourist to score a century in each innings on his first-class debut anywhere overseas.

Australian batsman Bob Cowper who scored a century in his first match in the West Indies

•

Frank Woolley, who with 58,969 is second on the list of the greatest run-getters of all time, made every score between 0 and 111 during his first-class career. His highest innings was 305 not out for the MCC v Tasmania at Hobart in 1911–12.

One of the best-ever starts to a Test career, in terms of double-figure scores, was made by Australian opener Colin McDonald who made his Test debut in 1951-52. No bowler was able to dismiss him for less than 10 in his first 23 Test innings:

32 & 62 v West Indies 1951-52
27, 17, 82, 23, 67, 154, 15, 41 & 11 v South Africa 1952-53
48, 29, 72 & 37 v England 1954-55
50, 7*, 110, 61, 31, 46, 17 & 127 v West Indies 1954-55

•

Michael Atherton

With a partnership of 203 at Adelaide in 1990-91, Graham Gooch and Michael Atherton became the first England pair to compile three double-century opening stands in Test matches. In a mere eight months, their first 16 innings in partnership produced a further three half-century stands and another two which exceeded 150. The three double-century partnerships came within the space of just 10 innings, an accomplishment which beat by a considerable margin the previous record time. Bill Lawry and Bob Simpson shared three 200-run stands in 24 Test innings; the first three by Gordon Greenidge and Desmond Haynes came in the space of 37 innings.

•

On Australia's 1969-70 tour of South Africa, Ian Redpath went on a six-hitting spree during the match with Orange Free State at Bloemfontein. Facing an over from Neil Rosendorff, he hit four consecutive sixes and a couple of boundaries, for a record number of runs by an Australian batsman in first-class cricket.

John Langridge, who made 34,380 runs for Sussex, scored the most centuries (76) in first-class cricket without ever playing in a Test match. He scored over 2,000 runs in a season 10 times, and made eight double centuries with a highest score of 250 not out against Glamorgan in 1933.

•

Gordon Greenidge and Desmond Haynes, the first pair to open 100 Test match innings together, were also the first pair to score more than 15 century opening partnerships. Their 16th 100-run stand, which gave them the record previously held by Jack Hobbs and Herbert Sutcliffe, was 129 against Australia at Bridgetown in 1991:

Series	*Opposition*	*T*	*I*	*R*	*Highest stand*	*100s*	*50s*	*Avge*
1977-78	Australia	2	3	234	131	1	1	78.00
1979-80	Australia	3	6	197	68	0	1	39.40
1979-80	New Zealand	3	6	329	225	1	1	54.83
1980	England	5	6	169	83	0	1	28.16
1980-81	England	4	5	320	168	2	0	64.00
1981-82	Australia	2	4	85	37	0	0	21.25
1982-83	India	5	7	567	296	1	2	94.50
1983-84	India	6	10	291	50	0	1	29.10
1983-84	Australia	5	8	684	250*	3	1	136.80
1984	England	5	8	295	106	1	2	36.87
1984-85	Australia	5	8	189	83	0	1	23.62
1984-85	New Zealand	4	7	220	82	0	2	44.00
1985-86	England	5	6	325	79*	0	4	65.00
1986-87	Pakistan	3	5	116	49	0	0	23.20
1986-87	New Zealand	3	6	245	150	1	0	49.00
1987-88	India	3	6	247	114	1	2	41.16
1987-88	Pakistan	2	4	42	21	0	0	10.50
1988	England	3	5	247	131	1	1	49.40
1988-89	Australia	5	10	447	135	1	2	44.70
1988-89	India	4	7	221	84	0	1	31.57
1989-90	England	4	7	506	298	1	2	72.28
1990-91	Pakistan	3	5	91	47	0	0	18.20
1990-91	Australia	5	9	416	129	2	1	59.42
Total		89	148	6,483	298	16	26	47.32

•

The first Test series contested by India and New Zealand in 1955-56 included no fewer than four double centuries, two of which were scored by Vinoo Mankad. Polly Umrigar reached 223 in the first Test at Hyderabad, a score equalled by Mankad in the second Test at Bombay. New Zealand's opening batsman Bert Sutcliffe made an unbeaten 230 in the next match at Delhi and Mankad recorded India's then-highest score of 231 in the fifth Test at Madras, sharing with Pankaj Roy a Test record first-wicket partnership of 413.

•

Lawrence Rowe's score of 302 against England at Bridgetown in 1973-74 was his 11th century in first-class cricket, but his first at a venue other than Sabina Park in Kingston. In 1971-72 he hit four centuries in a row at Kingston, including two hundreds (214 & 100*) on his Test debut.

•

MOST RUNS OFF ONE OVER BY AUSTRALIANS IN FIRST-CLASS CRICKET

Runs	*Batsman*	*Bowler*	*Match*
32 (6,6,6,6,4,4)	Ian Redpath	Neil Rosendorff	Australians v OFS at Bloemfontein 1969-70
30 (6,4,4,6,4,6)	Tom Moody	Adrian Tucker	Western Australia v NSW at Sydney 1990-91
28 (6,6,6,6,0,4)	David Hookes	Dennis Lillie	South Australia v Queensland at Adelaide 1981-82

Glenn Turner had a liking for Lancaster Park in Christchurch. He hit three centuries and a ninety in four successive Test innings on the ground during the mid-1970s—101 & 110* v Australia in 1973–74, 98 v England in 1974–75 and 117 v India in 1975–76.

•

Sanath Jayasuriya

On Sri Lanka's 'B' tour of Pakistan in 1988–89, Sanath Jayasuriya hit two unbeaten double centuries in successive first-class innings—203* at Lahore and 207* at Karachi.

•

During the 1991 English County Championship, the prolific Somerset opener Jimmy Cook became the first batsman to score 2,000 runs in a season for the third successive year. In 1989 Cook amassed 2,173 Championship runs in his first season, a record previously held by Barry Richards who scored 2,039 runs for Hampshire in 1968. The 1990 Championship brought Cook 2,432 runs, his aggregate for his first two seasons of 4,605 also being a record in the competition. In 1991 he also became the first player to score a century in his initial first-class match as captain of Somerset. His score of 209 not out against the touring Sri Lankans at Taunton was the highest innings by any batsman on his county captaincy debut. In his three seasons with Somerset, Cook scored 7,604 runs at first-class level, at an average of 72.42.

•

In 1989 two Indian batsmen—Venkat Raman and Arjan Kripal Singh—made history by both scoring triple centuries in the same innings of a first-class match. Raman hit 313 and Singh an unbeaten 302 for Tamil Nadu against Goa at Panaji in the 1988–89 Ranji Trophy. Prior to their effort, the nearest example to two triple-hundreds in an innings was Bill Ponsford's 352 and Jack Ryder's 295 in the Victorian total of 1,107 against New South Wales at Melbourne in 1926–27.

•

When Mark Taylor made 101 against Pakistan in 1989–90, he became the first Australian to score centuries in his first Test on three Australian grounds—the Gabba, Bellerive and the MCG—and in his first appearance against three countries—England, Sri Lanka and Pakistan.

•

Joe Solomon, of British Guiana, began his first-class career in fine style scoring a century in his first three innings—114* v Jamaica and 108 v Barbados in 1956–7, and 121 v Pakistanis in 1957–58.

•

Denis Compton hit a record 18 hundreds in 1947. His aggregate for the season of 3,816 runs—and 4,962 runs for the calendar year—are also records:

BATSMEN WITH 4,000 RUNS IN A CALENDAR YEAR

	Runs	*Inns*	*Avge*	*Year*
Denis Compton	4,962	69	85.55	1947
Walter Hammond	4,445	69	71.69	1933
Don Bradman	4,368	52	97.06	1930
Herbert Sutcliffe	4,340	62	80.37	1932
Len Hutton	4,167	69	69.45	1948
Bill Edrich	4,103	69	68.38	1947
Martin Crowe	4,045	60	79.31	1987

Bill Edrich and Denis Compton, who both scored over 4,000 first-class runs in 1947

On three successive tours, New Zealand's Martin Crowe scored a century in the state match against South Australia. But, not to be outdone, local bastman Glenn Bishop also scored a hundred each time:

1985–86	Martin Crowe	242*
	Glenn Bishop	202
1987–88	Martin Crowe	144
	Glen Bishop	123
1989–90	Martin Crowe	143
	Glenn Bishop	173

•

David Hookes

One of the fastest centuries in first-class cricket in terms of both time taken and of balls received was the 107 scored by David Hookes against Victoria at Adelaide in 1982–83. His hundred came in 43 minutes off 34 balls.

•

Dean Jones began the 1991–92 Sheffield Shield season in irresistible form with three double centuries in just five innings. In Victoria's first match of the season, Jones scored 243 not out against Tasmania in Melbourne, 68 and 144 against New South Wales in Sydney, 214 off South Australia at the MCG and 204 against Western Australia at the WACA. While Jones' performance was one of the best starts to a season since the Second World War it fell well short of Bill Ponsford's deeds for Victoria in 1927–28. In his first five innings, Ponsford scored 1,146 runs at 229.20 with innings of 133, 437, 202, 38 and 336.

•

In 1968–69, Ian Chappell emulated Don Bradman's hitherto unique achievement of scoring 1,000 runs in first-class matches against a team touring Australia. Bradman set the pace in 1931–32 against the South Africans and Chappell scored his 1,000 against the West Indies. Bill Lawry came close with 979 runs against the England tourists of 1965–66.

BATSMEN WITH 1,000 FIRST-CLASS RUNS AGAINST TOURING TEAMS

	Team and season	*I*	*NO*	*Runs*	*HS*	*Avge*
Don Bradman	South Africans 1931–32	8	1	1,190	299*	170.00
Ian Chappell	West Indians 1968–69	12	1	1,062	188*	96.54

•

When S. Nazir Ali scored 52 for the Indians against Yorkshire in 1932, the visitors' total of only 66 became the lowest in all first-class cricket to include a half-century. Ali's innings represented 78.70% of his team's total.

•

In the first Test match of them all, at Melbourne in 1877, Charles Bannerman scored 67.34% of Australia's first innings—165 not out out of 245. Other batsmen to monopolise the scoring in a Test match to such an extent include Gordon Greenidge, Asanka Gurusinha, John Reid and Seymour Nurse:

63.50%	Gordon Greenidge	134(211)	West Indies v England at Manchester 1976
63.41%	Asanka Gurusinha	52*(82)	Sri Lanka v India at Chandigarh 1990–91
62.89%	John Reid	100(159)	New Zealand v England at Christchurch 1962–63
61.87%	Seymour Nurse	258(417)	West Indies v New Zealand at Christchurch 1968–69

•

David Hookes was the first batsman to score 10,000 runs in first-class cricket for one state, recording the milestone for South Australia in 1991–92. Later in the season, in his last home match for the Croweaters, Hookes became the leading run-scorer in the Sheffield Shield, a record previously held by John Inverarity.

•

Mudassar Nazar, who made over 1,000 first-class runs on Pakistan's 1983–84 tour of Australia, hit five centuries in five matches outside the Tests. In successive matches against state sides, Mudassar scored 104 & 28* against Queensland, 93 & 71 against South Australia, 113 & 2 against Western Australia, 34 & 139 against New South Wales, and 103 & 123 against Victoria.

•

During his 108-match Test career, only once did Geoff Boycott not open the batting for England. On the 1973–74 tour of the West Indies, he went in at number 4 in the third Test at Bridgetown and scored 10 and 13.

Tim Robinson

England's Tim Robinson made over 400 runs in each of his first two Test series, but made just 72 in his third. In 1984–85 Robinson came second in the averages in his debut series against India with 444 runs at 63.42. He followed that with 490 runs at 61.25 against Australia in 1985, but failed dismally in his third series, scoring just 72 runs in eight innings against the West Indies in 1985–86. With nearly 1,000 runs in his first year of Test cricket, Robinson went on to score four hundreds in 29 matches, the lowest of which was 148.

•

Kepler Wessels was the first South African-born batsman to score a century on his Test debut—162 for Australia v England at Brisbane in 1982–83. And he marked his first Test match for South Africa with a pair of fifties—59 & 74 v West Indies at Bridgetown in 1991–92.

•

On his Test debut for Sri Lanka at Kandy in 1983–84, Mudalige Amerasinghe top-scored with an innings of 34 batting at number 11. It was in this same match, against New Zealand, that Sri Lanka was bowled out for 97, the lowest total in Test history to include an individual half-century—51 by Arjuna Ranatunga.

•

Belinda Haggett, who made 126 against England at Worcester in 1987, was the first Australian woman to score a century on her Test debut.

•

During the 1988–89 seasons in Australia and New Zealand, four instances of 300-run first-wicket partnerships were recorded, two in successive innings by Geoff Marsh and Mike Veletta for Western Australia, and two in successive matches by Wellington batsmen in the Shell Trophy:

374	Geoff Marsh (209) & Mike Veletta (166*)—Western Australia v Tamil Nadu at Perth
310	Geoff Marsh (223) & Mike Veletta (157)—Western Australia v Tasmania at Hobart
333	Bruce Edgar (147*) & Andrew Jones (177)—Wellington v Auckland at Wellington
310	Bruce Edgar (140) & Bert Vance (254*)—Wellington v Northern Districts at Wellington

The partnership of 374 against Tamil Nadu was a record for Western Australia until the next season when Veletta (150) and Marsh (355*) put on a massive 431 against South Australia at Perth. It was the highest opening stand in the Sheffield Shield and the seventh-highest in all first-class cricket, Marsh and Veletta becoming the first opening pair to record three triple-century opening stands in Australian first-class cricket.

Mike Veletta, the first Australian batsman to take part in three triple-century first wicket partnerships

Former New Zealand opener Bruce Edgar, who took part in two 300-run stands in successive matches for Wellington in 1988–89

In 1989 Gamini Wickremasinghe, a Sri Lankan wicket-keeper, christened Australia's 31st cricket ground with one of the country's slowest-ever batting performances. Playing against Victoria in 1989–90 at the City Oval in Sale, the 24-year-old Sri Lankan spent 111 minutes without scoring a run, beating the South African Bruce Mitchell, who occupied the crease scoreless for 90 minutes at Brisbane in 1931–32. Wickremasinghe was only 20 minutes off equalling the world record of 131 minutes, set by Shoaib Mohammad for Karachi Blues v Lahore City Whites in 1983–84. All up, the Sri Lankan took 175 mintues to score 13, a snail-like performance on par with Paul Nicholls' 4 runs in 114 minutes for Western Australia v South Australia at Adelaide in 1971–72.

•

Opening the batting for Victoria in a Sheffield Shield match in 1991–92, Darrin Ramshaw came close to emulating the batting exploits of England's Trevor Bailey, who in 1958–59 took a world-record 357 minutes to score a half-century against Australia at Brisbane. Ramshaw spent 316 minutes to reach 50 against New South Wales at Sydney, an effort which gave him the record for the slowest fifty by an Australian, and the slowest fifty in all first-class cricket outside Test matches.

•

In scoring 155 against Central Districts in 1990–91, Otago's Ken Rutherford became only the second batsman in the history of first-class cricket to score a half-century entirely in boundaries (10 fours and two sixes). Previously, only Rod Marsh had performed the feat, for Western Australia against the touring West Indians at Perth in 1975–76.

•

New South Wales batsman Arthur Morris enjoyed a remarkable experience of scoring a century on his first-class debut in four different countries—Australia, England, South Africa and the West Indies:

148 / 111	New South Wales v Queensland	Brisbane 1940–41
138	Australians v Worcestershire	Worcester 1948
153	Australians v Natal	Durban 1949–50
157	Australians v Jamaica	Kingston 1954–55

•

During a run of 10 consecutive Test innings in the early 1970s, Geoff Boycott passed 50 nine times. Graham Gooch scored 10 fifties in 12 innings in the early 1990s.

G. Boycott: 70, 50, 77, 142*, 12, 76*, 58 & 119* v Australia 1970–71; 121* & 112 v Pakistan 1971
G.A. Gooch: 333, 123, 116, 7, 85 & 88 v India 1990; 20, 58, 59, 54, 87 & 117 v Australia 1990–91

Outside Test cricket, Graeme Hick scored 12 fifties in 13 first-class innings for Worcestershire in 1990.

•

The only batsman to score 800 runs in a Test series without the aid of a double-century is Clyde Walcott. He made 827 runs in the five-match series against Australia in 1954–55 with a top score of 155.

•

Two bowlers on India's 1946 tour of England hit the headlines and made the record books with a once-in-a-lifetime performance in the match against Surrey at The Oval. Batting at numbers 10 and 11, Chandu Sarwate (124*) and Shute Banerjee (121) both hit centuries and recorded a partnership of 249 for the last wicket.

Chandu Sarwate and Shute Banerjee—the only numbers 10 and 11 to score centuries in the same innings of a first-class match

•

With 680 runs against England in 1946–47, Don Bradman became the first Australian batsman to score 500 runs in back-to-back Test series at home. Only two others have been able to match Bradman—Greg Chappell and David Boon.

500 RUNS IN SUCCESSIVE TEST SERIES IN AUSTRALIA

	M	I	NO	Runs	HS	100s	50s	Avge
Don Bradman								
England 1936–37	5	9	0	810	270	3	1	90.00
England 1946–47	5	8	1	680	234	2	3	97.14
India 1947–48	5	6	2	715	201	4	1	178.75
Greg Chappell								
England 1974–75	6	11	0	608	144	2	5	55.27
West Indies 1975–76	6	11	5	702	182*	3	3	117.00
David Boon								
England 1990–91	5	9	2	530	121	1	3	75.71
India 1991–92	5	9	2	556	135	3	1	79.43

•

During the 1986–87 Ranji Trophy semi-final against Karnataka, Delhi's score of 3 declared for 711 included a record three double-century partnerships:

234	First wicket	Manoj Prabhakar & Manu Nayyar
215	Second wicket	Manoj Prabhakar & Krishna Bhaskar Pillai
261*	Fourth wicket	Krishna Bhaskar Pillai & Raman Lamba

In the same season there were some big partnerships in the Duleep Trophy, with an opening stand of over 150 in the three innings of the final played in Bombay—256 by Anshuman Gaekwad and Lalchand Rajput and 201 by Rajput and Chandra Pandit for West Zone, and 179 by Kris Srikkanth and Carlton Saldanha for South Zone.

•

Ian Botham's two centuries against Australia in 1981 both came in under 100 deliveries—his first, in the third Test at Leeds, was scored off 87 balls; his second, at Manchester, off 86 balls.

•

During the three-match series against the West Indies in 1990–91, Pakistan tried, without success, four different sets of opening batsmen. In six innings the best stand was 15 by Ramiz Raja and Shoaib Mohammad; the others were 2, 1, 0, 2 and 0.

•

Three West Indies batsmen were dismissed in the nineties during the second Test against England at Port-of-Spain in 1934–35—George Headley for 93, Derek Sealy (92) and Learie Constantine (90).

Ramiz Raja

3 Bowlers

In a County Championship match against Middlesex at Coventry in 1982, Gladstone Small of Warwickshire sent down an 18-ball over after being no-balled 11 times for over-stepping the crease and called for one wide. Three matches later, Small was no-balled 28 times during a spell of 12 overs against Worcestershire at Birmingham.

•

Australia's Bob Massie, the first bowler to take 16 wickets on Test debut, is one of the very few to have captured as many as 20 wickets in the space of three consecutive Test innings. This he did with 8 for 84, 8 for 53 and 4 for 43 against England in 1972—his first three innings in Test cricket. Jim Laker is the only bowler with 25 wickets in three consecutive innings—6–55, 9–37 and 10–53 against Australia in 1956. Outside Test cricket, Gloucestershire's Charlie Parker is the winner, with 26 wickets (9–44, 8–12 and 9–118) in three innings in 1925.

•

During the 1983–84 season, Central Districts bowler Peter Visser performed the first hat-trick in New Zealand domestic cricket in four years. Another hat-trick was taken a few days later, when Steve Maguiness took five wickets for Wellington against Northern Districts. Maguiness was in the news again for performances achieved in his next match, taking 7 for 17 against Canterbury at Rangiora in 1984–85 and top-scoring with 43 batting at number 11.

•

South African off-spinner Hugh Tayfield bowled 137 bowls without conceding a single run in the third Test against England at Durban in 1956–57. Although he took only one wicket, his analysis of 24–17–21–1 is a record. In the second innings he claimed 8 for 69, the best return by a South African in Tests until his 9 for 113 in the next Test at Johannesburg.

•

Surrey fast bowler Tom Richardson reached the milestones of 1,000 and 2,000 wickets in 134 and 327 matches respectively—both achievements are records in first-class cricket.

•

When the West Indies rattled up its record Test score of 3 declared for 790 at Kingston in 1957–58, three of the opposition's bowlers finished the innings with over 100 runs against their names. Two of them—Khan Mohammad and Fazal Mahmood—created history by each conceding 200 runs. This was the first time a pair of bowlers had conceded as many runs in the same Test match, let alone the same innings.

•

When Glamorgan met Yorkshire at Swansea in 1965, two of their leading spinners, Jim Pressdee and Don Shepherd, each took nine wickets in an innings—a unique occurrence in first-class cricket. Their analyses bore a remarkable resemblance, with Pressdee claiming 9 for 43 and Shepherd 9 for 48—both sent down 12 maidens.

	O	*M*	*R*	*W*
Jim Pressdee	23.3	12	43	9
	26	8	73	1
Don Shepherd	23	12	33	0
	27.5	12	48	9

Pressdee's performance was his best in first-class cricket and Shepherd missed out by one run, having returned an analysis of 9 for 47 against Northamptonshire in 1954.

•

During the calendar year of 1982, Imran Khan took 62 wickets, average 13.29, in just nine Tests. He twice claimed 10 wickets in a match, including a career-best 14 for 116 against Sri Lanka at Lahore.

•

Although he made only one appearance in first-class cricket, William Brown made his mark in the game by taking 15 wickets. On his debut against Victoria at Hobart in 1857–58, Brown captained Tasmania taking 7 for 42 and 8 for 31, a record performance in Australian first-class cricket.

•

William Caesar, who made his first-class debut for Surrey in 1922 as a specialist bowler, had to wait 24 years for his first wicket. Following his unsuccessful debut with Surrey, Caesar had to wait for his next match for his first wickets, when he took a career-best 4 for 59 for Somerset v Leicestershire at Melton Mowbray in 1946.

•

Opening the attack in the three-Test series against Australia in 1986–87, Kapil Dev failed to take a single wicket—0–52 & 0–5 at Madras, 0–27 at New Delhi and 0–16 & 0–24 at Bombay.

•

When Johnny Briggs dismissed Australia's wicket-keeper Affie Jarvis at Sydney in 1894–95, he became the first bowler to take 100 Test wickets. In the same match, but a few days later, Australia's Charlie Turner also took his 100th Test wicket, achieving the milestone in eight fewer Tests than Briggs.

•

Clarrie Grimmett

Clarrie Grimmett took 10 wickets in his last two Tests for Australia—10 for 110 at Johannesburg and 13 for 173 at Durban in 1935–36. His penultimate Test contained his best figures—7 for 40— and his 200th Test wicket. He was the first bowler to reach the milestone, and got there in record time (36 Tests).

TEST WICKET-TAKING MILESTONES

100 wickets	Johnny Briggs	England v Australia	Sydney 1894–95
200 wickets	Clarrie Grimmett	Australia v South Africa	Johannesburg 1935–36
300 wickets	Fred Trueman	England v Australia	The Oval 1964
400 wickets	Richard Hadlee	New Zealand v India	Christchurch 1989–90

It is a major milestone, significant in the history of world cricket. It was like a mountain and now it has been climbed.

—Richard Hadlee on becoming the first bowler to take 400 Test wickets

•

Mick Malone marked his only Test match for Australia, the fifth against England at The Oval in 1977, by taking a five-wicket haul (5–63) in the first innings.

•

Sri Lanka's Roger Wijesuriya must surely have one of the worst records of all time in Test match cricket. In 1982 he became the first player to take no wickets for 100 runs and make a duck in his first Test, and the first to concede more than 100 runs without a wicket in his first two Test innings. His career bowling average at Test level is 294.00.

•

In the 1989 Ashes series, Terry Alderman took five wickets in an innings six times, one off the record by Sydney Barnes (England v South Africa, 1913–14). Others to achieve the feat five times in a series include Alan Davidson against the West Indies in 1960–61 and Alec Bedser against Australia in 1953. Rodney Hogg took five in an innings five times in his first Test series, against England in 1978–79, and Richard Hadlee did it five times in only three Tests in Australia in 1985–86.

S.F. BARNES' FIVE WICKETS IN AN INNINGS IN SEVEN OUT OF EIGHT INNINGS

v South Africa, 1913–14

19.4–1–57–5 & 25–11–48–5	First Test	Durban
26.5–9–56–8 & 38.4–7–103–9	Second Test	Johannesburg
(16–3–26–3) & 38–8–102–5	Third Test	Johannesburg
29.5–7–56–7 & 32–10–88–7	Fourth Test	Durban

•

Victorian leggie Shane Warne gained selection for an Australian B team tour of Zimbabwe in 1991 having taken only one wicket in first-class cricket. He won his first Test cap, against India at the SCG in 1991–92, and made the record books by becoming the first Australian bowler to concede 150 runs on his Test debut (1–150).

•

On his Test debut for India in 1988, leg-spinner Narendra Hirwani took 16 wickets for 136 against the West Indies at Madras—the best return by a bowler in his first match. He also became the first bowler on debut to take 10 wickets in succession in a Test, matching the feat of Jim Laker during his 19-wicket haul against Australia at Manchester in 1956.

Hirwani had further success against New Zealand 10 months later when he took 15 wickets in his next two Tests, at Bangalore and Bombay. Never before had a bowler gained as many wickets in his first three Test appearances; his 24 wickets after two Tests is also a record. After five matches Hirwani had 37 wickets to his name, eight off the all-time record of 45 by Australian fast bowler Charlie Turner.

•

The best haul of first-class wickets in a decade is 2,058 by the English spinner 'Tich' Freeman in the 1920s, a record that's likely to remain his for all time. The only fast bowler to lead the field in a particular decade was Malcolm Marshall with 1,188 wickets in the 1980s.

	Bowler	*Wickets*
1920s	'Tich' Freeman	2,058
1930s	Hedley Verity	1,956
1940s	Tom Goddard	700
1950s	Tony Lock	1,639
1960s	Fred Titmus	1,279
1970s	Bishen Bedi	1,231
1980s	Malcolm Marshall	1,188

•

The relatively rare feat of 10 wickets in a bowler's first first-class match was achieved by two debutants when New South Wales met Victoria at Melbourne in 1855-56—Gideon Elliot took 10 for 34 for Victoria while John McKone took 10 for 36 for the visitors.

•

England's Graham Gooch was dismissed six times in nine innings by Rodney Hogg in the 1978-79 series. Craig McDermott also accounted for Gooch six times in nine innings during the 1985 series.

•

Clarrie Grimmett, Australia's prized spinner throughout the 1920s and '30s, bowled around 73,000 balls in first-class cricket. It has been said he was no-balled only once during that time.

•

The Indian pace bowler Nirode Chowdhury, who possesses a Test career average of 205.00, took 11, 9 and 10 wickets in his first three appearances in first-class cricket, in 1941-42.

•

During the early 1990s England achieved three successive Test wins, each of them against a different country. And it was their spinner Phil Tufnell who was instrumental in bowling England to victory, taking five wickets in an innings each time—6 for 25 against the West Indies at The Oval in 1991, 5 for 94 against Sri Lanka at Lord's in 1991 and 7 for 47 against New Zealand at Christchurch in 1991-92.

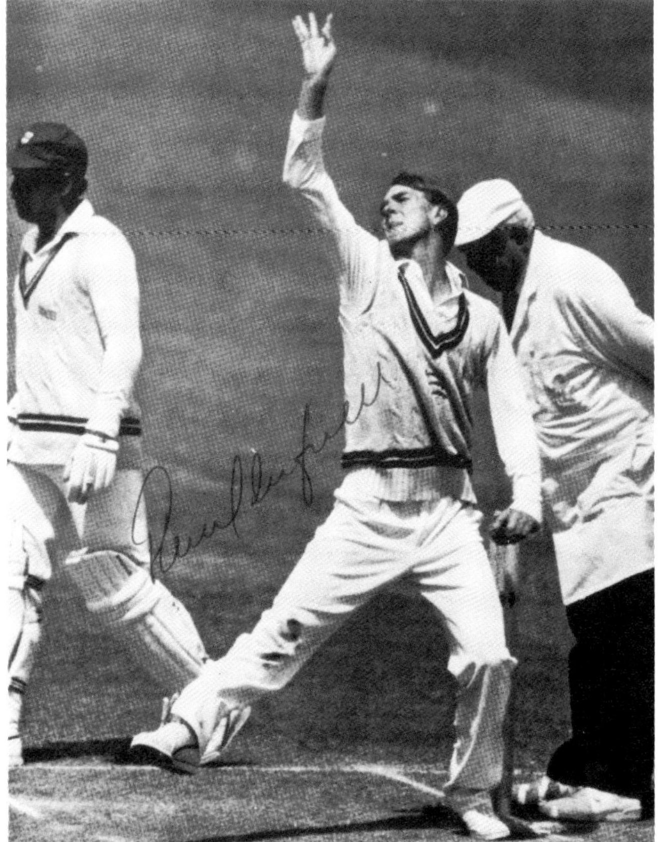

Phil Tufnell

On his first-class debut for South Australia in 1902-03, Harry Hay performed a unique bowling double by taking nine wickets in an innings and a hat-trick. His feats were achieved against an England XI at Unley Oval in Adelaide, and witnessed by John Quilty, one of the umpires, who as a player in 1881-82 had the distinction of being the only other debutant bowler in Australian first-class cricket to take nine wickets in an innings (9-55 v Victoria at Adelaide).

•

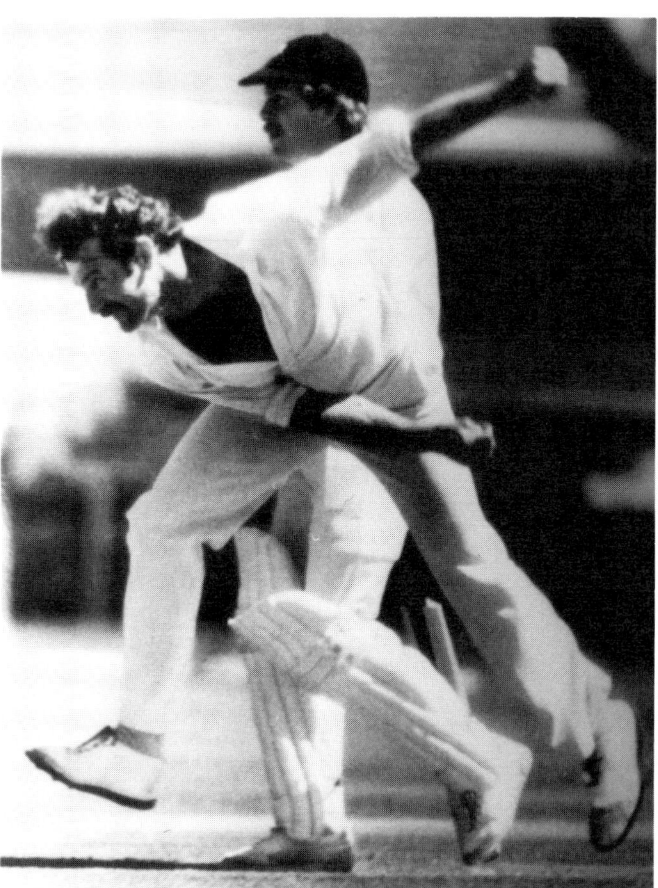

Dennis Lillee

In the calendar year of 1981, Dennis Lillee took a record 85 Test wickets. In just 13 appearances, Lillee became the first bowler to exceed 80 wickets in 12 months of Test cricket, beating Kapil Dev's 74 wickets in 1979.

D.K. LILLEE: 85 TEST WICKETS IN 1981

India	21 w	(3 Tests)
England	39 w	(6 Tests)
Pakistan	15 w	(3 Tests)
West Indies	10 w	(1 Test)

Lillee's opening partner in 10 of his 13 Tests during 1981, Terry Alderman, also passed the milestone of 50 Test wickets, becoming the first bowler to achieve the feat in the calendar year of his Test debut.

T.M. ALDERMAN: 54 TEST WICKETS IN 1981

England	42 w	(6 Tests)
Pakistan	8 w	(3 Tests)
West Indies	4 w	(1 Test)

Jack Lee of Leicestershire took his only wicket in first-class cricket with his first delivery in his only match, against Glamorgan at Cardiff in 1947.

•

When Waqar Younis took 5 for 46 against the West Indies at Faisalabad in 1990, it was his fifth five-wicket haul in his last six Test innings. The second wicket he picked up at Faisalabad boosted his career total to 50 in 10 matches—the fastest in Pakistan Test history, eclipsing Khan Mohammad's record of 50 in 11 Tests during the 1950s. Waqar collected the last 43 of his 50 wickets in just five Tests, with 29 at 10.86 in the three-match series against New Zealand in 1990-91.

WAQAR YOUNIS: 43 WICKETS IN FIVE TESTS

4-40 & 3-39 v New Zealand at Karachi 1990-91
3-20 & 7-86 v New Zealand at Lahore 1990-91
7-76 & 5-54 v New Zealand at Faisalabad 1990-91
5-76 & 4-44 v West Indies at Karachi 1990-91
5-46 & 0-41 v West Indies at Faisalabad 1990-91

•

During the 1976-77 season, Dennis Lillee took 10 wickets in a Test match three times against a different country—10-135 v Pakistan at Melbourne, 11-123 v New Zealand at Auckland and 11-165 v England at Melbourne.

•

The milestone of 250 wickets in a season has been realised only 12 times in first-class cricket. 'Tich' Freeman performed the feat on six occasions, and in consecutive seasons.

A.P. FREEMAN: 250 WICKETS IN A SEASON

Season	*O*	*M*	*R*	*W*	*Avge*
1928	1,976.1	423	5,489	304	18.05
1933	2,039	651	4,549	298	15.26
1931	1,618	360	4,307	276	15.60
1930	1,914.3	472	4,632	275	16.84
1929	1,670.5	381	4,879	267	18.27
1932	1,565.5	404	4,149	253	16.39

•

In 1989 Kapil Dev became the first bowler to appear in 100 Tests. It was during this match, against Pakistan at Karachi in 1989-90, that he took his 350th wicket, the fourth bowler to do so.

•

South Australia's Colin Miller recorded one of the greatest spells of bowling in Australian first-class cricket, with six wickets in 10 balls against New South Wales at Sydney in 1990-91. The only other comparable performance in recent times was Dennis Lillee's five wickets in nine balls against a World XI at Perth in 1971-72.

When Sussex bowler Tony Pigott took a hat-trick against Surrey at Hove in 1978, he gained his first wickets in first-class cricket.

•

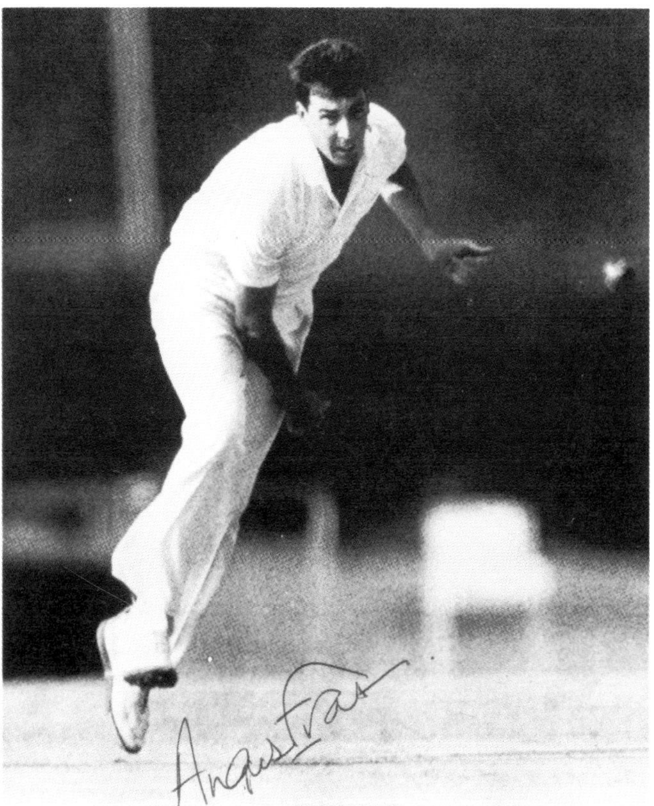

Angus Fraser

England fast bowler Angus Fraser made only one appearance in first-class cricket for Middlesex in 1985, but put his mark on the match—against Glamorgan at Cardiff—by taking three wickets in four balls.

•

Fast bowler Wayne Holdsworth ended the 1992-93 season on a high note, capturing 39 wickets in his last five games. The New South Wales quick took five wickets in an innings four times, and in three successive appearances bettered his best bowling performance in first-class cricket—7-81 v South Australia at Sydney, 7-52 v Victoria at Melbourne and 7-41 in the Shield final against Queensland at the SCG.

•

South African Test batsman 'Jackie' McGlew had the curious experience of gaining a hat-trick in a first-class match, yet had a best bowling return in his first-class career of 2 for 4. His hat-trick, for Natal against Transvaal at Durban in 1963-64, was spread over two innings.

•

BEST SPELLS OF WICKET-TAKING BY AUSTRALIANS IN FIRST-CLASS CRICKET

9 wickets in 44 balls	Tim Wall	South Australia v New South Wales	Sydney 1932-33
7 wickets in 28 balls	'Tibby' Cotter	Australians v Worcestershire	Worcester 1905
6 wickets in 10 balls	Colin Miller	South Australia v New South Wales	Sydney 1990-91
5 wickets in 9 balls	Dennis Lillee	Australia v World XI	Perth 1971-72

During South Australia's Sheffield Shield clash with New South Wales at Adelaide in 1990–91, Tim May sent down 52 overs, a stint which included 79 successive scoreless deliveries.

•

Of the 431 overs bowled in the Australia–West Indies Test at Sydney in 1988–89, 279 of them were spin, a record number in a Test match in Australia for nearly 60 years.

For Australia, the only fast bowler to take a wicket was Merv Hughes, while for the West Indies Viv Richards was the only spinner to take a wicket.

•

> **I don't care what money I get, man. It's the buzz of playing for Australia that's got me.**
>
> **–Greg Matthews**

In 1989–90, Western Australia's Ken MacLeay became the first bowler who had never played Test cricket to take 200 wickets in the Sheffield Shield.

•

Although Steve Watkin took only five wickets on his Test debut, at Leeds in 1991, all of his victims were top-order batsmen none of whom reached double-figures—Desmond Haynes 7, Jeff Dujon 6, Carl Hooper 5, Viv Richards 3 and Gus Logie 3.

•

Bob Willis bowled exactly 1,000 balls in the five-match Test series against Australia in 1977.

•

Ian Snook, an opening batsman for Central Districts in New Zealand, made the record books while bowling in a match against England at Palmerston North in 1983–84. He was given the ball for one over and was hit for 32 runs (4,6,6,4,6,6) by Ian Botham. Snook's bowling analysis of 1-0-32-0 is one of the most expensive in all first-class cricket.

•

Terry Alderman marked his debut in both first-class and Test cricket by taking five wickets in an innings:

5–65	Western Australia v New South Wales at Sydney	1974–75
5–62	Australia v England at Nottingham	1981

Only three other Australians had previously achieved this double, the previous one being Victoria's Jack Saunders in 1901–02.

•

Derek Underwood took five wickets in five successive Test innings against New Zealand, and grabbed a bag of 10 three times in four Tests between 1969 and 1971:

4–38 & 7–32 (11–70)	Lord's 1969
1–44 & 0–5 (1–49)	Nottingham 1969
6–41 & 6–60 (12–101)	The Oval 1969
6–12 & 6–85 (12–97)	Christchurch 1970–71
5–108 & 0–0 (5–108)	Auckland 1970–71

For the first and only time in first-class cricket, all 22 players bowled in the match between A.E.R. Gilligan's XI and the Australians at Hastings in 1964.

•

Devon Malcolm

After beginning his Test match career with an innings return of 1 for 166, England fast bowler Devon Malcolm improved his figures in his next four innings. His third Test match, against the West Indies in 1989–90, saw him take 10 for 137, his first 10-wicket haul in first-class cricket.

1–166	v Australia at Nottingham	1989
1–49 & 4–77	v West Indies at Kingston	1989–90
4–60 & 6–77	v West Indies at Port-of-Spain	1989–90

•

Vernon Royle, Francis MacKinnon and Tom Emmett went down in history in 1879 when their dismissals at Sydney by Fred Spofforth constituted the first hat-trick in Test cricket. Playing in only his second Test match, Spofforth also became the first bowler to take 10 wickets in a match, a feat he achieved a further three times, and which has only been matched by two others—Tom Richardson and Dennis Lillee—in Anglo-Australian Tests.

MOST 10 WICKET HAULS IN AUSTRALIA-ENGLAND TESTS

F.R. Spofforth (Australia)	
14–90 (7–46 & 7–44)	The Oval 1882
13–110 (6–48 & 7–62)	Melbourne 1878–79
11–117 (4–73 & 7–44)	Sydney 1882–83
10–144 (4–54 & 6–90)	Sydney 1884–85
T. Richardson (England)	
13–244 (7–168 & 6–76)	Manchester 1896
11–173 (6–39 & 5–134)	Lord's 1896
10–156 (5–49 & 5–107)	Manchester 1893
10–204 (8–94 & 2–110)	Sydney 1897–98

D.K. Lillee (Australia)	
11-138 (6-60 & 5-78)	Melbourne 1979-80
11-159 (7-89 & 4-70)	The Oval 1981
11-165 (6-26 & 5-139)	Melbourne 1976-77
10-181 (5-58 & 5-123)	The Oval 1972

Fred Spofforth

•

Ian Botham celebrated his recall to the England Test squad in 1991 by recording his best analysis in county cricket in his 18-year career. He took 7 for 54 for Worcestershire against Warwickshire, a performance which bettered his 7 for 61 against Glamorgan at Cardiff in 1978 when playing for Somerset. Earlier in the season, on his comeback to the one-day international arena, he took 4 for 45 against the West Indies at Edgbaston, his best figures for England, in his 99th match.

•

Eric Hollies, the Warwickshire and England leg-break bowler, ended his first-class career with more wickets than runs. From 1932 to 1957, Hollies collected 2,323 wickets but with the bat managed only 1,673 runs at an average of 5.01. Others to complete this odd career double include Bill Bowes (1,638 w; 1529 r), B.S. Chandrasekhar (1,063 w; 600 r), Charles Marriot (711 w; 574 r) and Jim Higgs (399 w; 384 r).

•

In 1965-66, three Australian bowlers celebrated their first-class debuts by taking a wicket with their first ball, in each case against the touring England side:

Bowler	*Batsman*	*Match*
B.A. Rothwell	R.W. Barber	New South Wales v MCC
A.R. Frost	G. Boycott	South Australia v MCC
K.R. Flint	P.H. Parfitt	Tasmania v MCC

•

Although Arthur Coningham, Matthew Henderson, Horace Smith and Tyrell Johnson only appeared in a single Test match each, they all put their names in the record books by claiming a wicket with their first ball in Test cricket.

WICKET WITH FIRST BALL IN TEST CRICKET

Bowler	*Batsman*	*Test*
Arthur Coningham	Archie MacLaren	A v E Melbourne 1894-95
'Bill' Bradley	Frank Laver	E v A Manchester 1899
Ted Arnold	Victor Trumper	E v A Sydney 1903-04
George Macauley	George Hearne	E v SA Cape Town 1922-23
Maurice Tate	'Fred' Susskind	E v SA Birmingham 1924
Matthew Henderson	Eddie Dawson	NZ v E Christchurch 1929-30
Horace Smith	Eddie Paynter	NZ v E Christchurch 1932-33
Tyrell Johnson	Walter Keeton	WI v E The Oval 1939
Dick Howarth	Dennis Dyer	E v SA The Oval 1947
Intikhab Alam	Colin McDonald	P v A Karachi 1959-60
Richard Illingworth	Phil Simmons	E v WI Nottingham 1991

•

Two bowlers—Tony Penberthy and Peter McPhee—share the distinction of dismissing Australia's Mark Taylor with their first delivery in first-class cricket:

A.L. Penberthy	Northamptonshire v Australians	Northampton 1989
P.T. McPhee	Tasmania v New South Wales	Hobart 1990-91

•

Kapil Dev, the first bowler to reach the milestone of 400 wickets and 4,000 runs in Test cricket, was also the first bowler to take 200 wickets in one-day internationals.

•

The very first ball delivered in a first-class match in England in 1981 resulted in a wicket. On 22 April, Essex bowler John Lever dismissed Cambridge batsman Peter Mills lbw.

•

David Hookes, famous for his deeds with the bat, took 15 wickets (7-46 & 8-35) in a club match for West Torrens against Glenelg in 1981-82.

•

Talat Ali, who opened the batting for Pakistan in the three-Test series against New Zealand in 1978-79, was dismissed in each of his five innings by Richard Hadlee.

•

England's Geoff Arnold twice took a wicket with the first ball of a Test match. In 1974 he dismissed Sunil Gavaskar with his first delivery in the third Test at Birmingham, and repeated the dose a few months later claiming John Morrison's wicket in similar fashion at Christchurch.

•

Victorian fast bowler Gideon Elliot holds the world record for the best figures in first-class cricket in terms of most wickets for the fewest runs. When Tasmania was dismissed for 33 at Launceston in 1857-58, Elliot's figures were 19-17-2-9.

•

Of the 1,165 wickets taken by England bowler David Brown in first-class cricket, the most unusual one came a few months after his 40th birthday in 1982. He made history during a County Championship match with Lancashire at Southport, becoming the first player in English cricket to take a wicket when bowling as a substitute. When Gladstone Small was put on stand-by for England, Brown in his capacity as Warwickshire manager filled in—he bowled 13 overs for 47, taking the wicket of wicket-keeper Chris Scott.

•

Alec Bedser took 11 wickets in each of his first two Tests—11 for 145 against India at Lord's in 1946, and 11 for 93 against India at Manchester.

•

J.J. Ferris holds the unique record of taking nine wickets on his Test debut for two countries. In his first Test for Australia, at Sydney in 1886-87, he claimed 9 for 103, bowling unchanged with Charlie Turner dismissing England for 45. Altogether, Ferris took 48 wickets in eight Tests for Australia, and then grabbed 13 for 91 in his one Test for England at Cape Town in 1891-92.

Albert Trott came close to repeating this feat, taking 8 for 43 in the second innings of his Test debut against England at Adelaide in 1894-95, and 9 for 110 in his first Test for England, against South Africa at Johannesburg in 1898-99.

•

New Zealand's Kenyan-born all-rounder Dipak Patel went three years and eight Tests before taking his first Test wicket. After bowling without success on his Test debut in 1987, he then bowled in another six innings before gaining the wicket of Ian Healy at Perth in 1989-90. At the end of the 1990-91 series against Pakistan, Patel had taken only one wicket in 11 innings for a world Test record average of 349.00!

•

The first West Indies bowler to take nine wickets in a Test innings was a spinner, Jack Noreiga, who captured 9 for 95 against India at Port-of-Spain in 1970-71. Recruited as a fill-in for Lance Gibbs, he took 17 wickets in four Tests in the series, but was never picked again.

•

During 'Tich' Freeman's golden summer of 1931, in which he claimed 276 wickets, the Kent bowler took 10 wickets in an innings for the third consecutive season, a feat unmatched in first-class cricket:

42-9-131-10	v Lancashire	Maidstone	1929
30.4-8-53-10	v Essex	Southend	1930
36.1-9-79-10	v Lancashire	Manchester	1931

•

In 1931-32 South Australian spinner Clarrie Grimmett took 77 wickets, completing his fourth haul of 50 wickets in consecutive seasons. For the fifth successive season, Grimmett was the country's leading wicket-taker. Both feats are records in Australian first-class cricket.

Season	*Wkts*	*Avge*	*BB*
1927-28	42	27.40	8-57
1928-29	71	34.25	6-109
1929-30	82	23.69	7-136
1930-31	74	19.14	7-87
1931-32	77	19.93	7-83

•

The Indian opening fast bowler Madan Lal had a barren time with the ball in late 1983 when in five Tests, against Pakistan and the West Indies, he failed to take a wicket in eight consecutive innings:

0-61 & 0-1 and 0-44 v Pakistan
0-50, 0-59 & 0-15 and 0-29 & 0-8 v West Indies

•

Basil Butcher played in 44 Tests for the West Indies and only ever took five wickets, but they all came in the same innings —5 for 34 against England at Port-of-Spain in 1967-68.

•

Malcolm Marshall was the only bowler to take 300 Test wickets during the 1980s. From 63 Tests he had 323 victims at 19.91. Next on the list were Richard Hadlee with 289 wickets in 53 Tests, Kapil Dev 272 in 80 Tests, Ian Botham 258 from 75 and Imran Khan 256 wickets in 54 Tests.

Geoff Lawson—Australia's leading Test wicket-taker during the 1980s

The leading Australian bowlers of the decade were Geoff Lawson (180 wickets in 46 Tests) and Dennis Lillee (171 in 36). The top spinner of the 1980s was Pakistan's Abdul Qadir, who took 216 wickets at 32.31 in 57 Tests.

Marshall's tally was a new landmark in Test cricket; never before had 300 wickets been achieved in a decade. In the 1970s, Derek Underwood was the leader with 202 wickets in 59 Tests and Graham McKenzie took 238 wickets in 54 Tests during the '60s.

•

Waqar Younis began the 1991 season with Surrey by taking 11 wickets in his first two matches—11 for 122 (5–57 & 6–65) against Lancashire at The Oval and 11 for 136 (6–66 & 5–70) against Hampshire at Bournemouth. In his first 14 appearances in the County Championship, Waqar took five wickets in an innings 10 times.

•

Derek Shackleton took 100 wickets in 20 consecutive seasons, from 1949 to 1968 inclusive.

•

During the same Test match, against Pakistan at Calcutta in 1979–80, India's Kapil Dev took his 100th Test wicket and scored his 1,000th Test run. At the time he was the youngest, at 21, to complete the double, and the first to secure both parts of the double in the same match. In 1990 John Bracewell repeated the feat, during the third Test against England at Edgbaston, becoming only the second New Zealander, after Richard Hadlee, to achieve the Test double.

•

Francis Fee only appeared five times at first-class level, but twice took 10 wickets in a match. On his first-class debut for Ireland in 1956, he took 14 for 100 against the MCC, and 12 for 60 (including an innings haul of 9–26) in his next match against Scotland in 1957.

•

Surrey's Don Adams gained his only wicket in first-class cricket by bowling W.G. Grace. His prized scalp came in his only first-class match, against London County at Crystal Palace in 1902.

•

Charles Eady, famous for scoring 566 for Break-o'-Day v Wellington at Hobart in 1901–02, also excelled with the ball in club cricket, taking 10 for 42 for South Hobart against East Hobart in 1905–06.

•

Ewan Chatfield's 50th wicket for New Zealand was taken 10 years after making his Test debut.

•

Both Dennis Lillee and Richard Hadlee bowed out of Test cricket with the world record for most wickets, and a dismissal with their final delivery. Lillee's last Test, against Pakistan at Sydney in 1983–84, saw him take 4 for 65 and 4 for 88 to boost his then world-record tally to 355. He took the last four wickets of the match, including Abdul Qadir's with his last ball. Richard Hadlee also took eight wickets in his final match, against England at Birmingham in 1990, including Devon Malcolm with his last delivery—his 431st Test wicket.

•

Over a quarter of the 431 wickets secured by Richard Hadlee in Tests were opening batsmen. While 25.52% of his victims were openers, just 11.60% were numbers 10 and 11.

	A	*E*	*I*	*P*	*W.I.*	*S.L.*	*Total*
1	15	9	10	6	6	6	52
2	14	12	12	9	7	4	58
3	14	12	8	2	7	4	47
4	11	3	5	5	3	4	31
5	11	9	5	4	5	5	39
6	8	4	6	7	6	4	35
7	15	12	5	4	3	–	39
8	13	11	5	7	3	5	44
9	13	9	4	4	3	3	36
10	7	9	5	1	6	1	29
11	8	7	1	2	2	1	21
Total	129	97	66	51	51	37	431

•

Terry Alderman took his only wicket in the 1991 Test series against the West Indies with his final delivery on the tour.

•

Tom Moody's 10-wicket haul against Victoria at Perth in 1990–91 included a career-best return of 7 for 43, the best figures by any bowler in first-class cricket during the season.

•

When Eddie Hemmings took all 10 wickets against a West Indies XI at Kingston in 1982, he became the first bowler to concede over 150 runs in getting there. Representing an International XI, Hemmings took 10 for 175, the most expensive analysis since 'Tich' Freeman's 10 for 131 at Maidstone in 1929.

Eddie Hemmings

In 1987–88, Ranjie Nanan took 20 wickets with his off-spin for Trinidad and Tobago, and became in the process the first bowler to pass the milestone of 200 wickets in West Indian domestic cricket.

•

Alec Bedser took the wicket of Australia's Arthur Morris on 18 occasions in 20 Tests between 1946 and 1953. Bedser also enjoyed a run of success against Don Bradman, dismissing him in five consecutive Test innings—Sydney 1946–47 to Lord's 1948.

•

In only his second Test match, at Wellington in 1982–83, Sri Lanka's Rumesh Ratnayake made a name for himself with a fiery spell of bowling that resulted in New Zealand opener John Wright hospitalised with a broken nose. While Wright was led from the field, his face covered in a towel, Ratnayake fainted at the sight of blood and had to be revived with smelling salts.

•

On the 1899 tour of England, New South Wales spin bowler Bill Howell created history when he took all 10 wickets against Surrey in his first match. His analysis of 10 for 28 in 23.2 overs was backed up with 5 for 29 in the second innings.

•

During the 1988 NatWest Bank Trophy Michael Holding became the second bowler to capture eight wickets in an innings in both Test and one-day cricket, the other being England slow bowler Derek Underwood.

EIGHT WICKETS IN AN INNINGS IN BOTH TEST AND LIMITED-OVERS CRICKET

M.A. Holding
Test: 8–92 for West Indies v England at The Oval 1976
One-Day: 8–21 for Derbyshire v Sussex at Hove 1988
D.L. Underwood
Test: 8–51 for England v Pakistan at Lord's 1974
One-Day: 8–31 for Kent v Scotland at Edinburgh 1987

•

Edwin Evans, a New South Wales and Australian fast bowler, began his career by taking five wickets in an innings a record 11 times in his first 10 matches. He took his 100th wicket in just 14 matches, and only once along the way did he fail to record a five-wicket haul in any of his matches.

•

In 1991–92 India used four fast bowlers in the third Test against Australia at the SCG. This was the first time the team had gone into a Test without a specialist spinner.

•

Max Walker is the only bowler to have taken 400 wickets in Australian first-class cricket without achieving 10 wickets in a match.

•

Courtney Walsh (above) and Merv Hughes (below), who both claimed a hat-trick in the 1988–89 Test series against the West Indies

During the 1988–89 Australia-West Indies Test series, two fast bowlers—Courtney Walsh and Merv Hughes—took hat-tricks. Both of them were spread over two innings and both came in consecutive matches, a unique occurrence in the history of Test cricket. Walsh's hat-trick was taken in the first Test at Brisbane, Hughes' in the second at Perth.

In an unofficial Test match against New Zealand at Dunedin in 1935–36, the MCC's captain Johnny Human sent down a single over which, in the hope of gaining a breakthrough, consisted of six wides, each of which was hit for four. Although he went for 24 runs, at the end of the match his bowling analysis read 1-1-0-0.

•

When England made 4 declared for 653 at Lord's in 1990 and India replied with 454, four of the five bowlers on each side conceded over 100 runs—Manoj Prabhakar 1-187, Sanjeev Sharma 1-122, Kapil Dev 1-120, Narendra Hirwani 1-102, Eddie Hemmings 2-109, Chris Lewis 1-108, Devon Malcolm 1-106 and Angus Fraser 5-104.

•

The best bowling performances both for and against an England team in Australia were recorded in the same match. When South Australia played Lord Hawke's England XI at Unley in 1902–03, George Thompson took 9 for 85, while Harry Hay, on debut, took 9 for 67 in the second innings for South Australia.

Wasim Akram took four wickets in five balls in the third Test against the West Indies at Lahore in 1990–91. He was only the third bowler in Test history to achieve the feat, after Maurice Allom in 1929–30 and Chris Old in 1978.

•

West Indies spinner Lance Gibbs is the only slow bowler to have reached the milestone of 300 Test wickets.

•

J.S. Rao, who claimed a hat-trick on his first-class debut, for Services, took two more in the same innings in his next match:

v Jammu and Kashmir	Delhi 1963–64
v Northern Punjab v Northern Punjab	Amritsar 1963–64

•

Joel Garner had the better of Kepler Wessels during 1984, dismissing the Australian opener six times in seven Test innings for scores of 4, 4, 4, 13, 0 and 0.

4 Age

The oldest player in the history of first-class cricket is a former governor of Bombay, the Raja Maharaj Singh, who was 72 when he played in a first-class match he himself organised against a Commonwealth XI at Bombay in 1950–51. Coincidentally, it was during the same season, and again in India, that the youngest cricketer appeared in first-class cricket—it is believed Esmail Baporia was only 11 years 261 days when he made his first-class debut for Gujarat v Baroda at Ahmedabad.

•

The oldest Test player is Wilfred Rhodes, who was 52 on the final day of his last Test. The oldest Test debutant was James Southerton—he was 49 when he appeared in the first-ever Test, at Melbourne in 1877.

OLDEST AUSTRALIAN PLAYERS ON TEST DEBUT

Years	*Days*	*Player*	*Opposition*	*Venue*	*Season*
46	253	Don Blackie	England	Sydney	1928–29
46	237	Bert Ironmonger	England	Brisbane	1928–29
38	35	Bob Holland	West Indies	Brisbane	1984–85

•

In 1989, India introduced its youngest player to Test cricket in Sachin Tendulkar, who was 16 years 205 days on the day of his Test debut against Pakistan at Karachi. In his next match, at Faisalabad, he became the youngest batsman in Test history to score a half-century (59). He later became the second youngest to record a century with 119 not out against England at Manchester in 1990, at the age of 17 years 112 days. Only Pakistan's Mushtaq Mohammad had scored a Test hundred at an earlier age (17 years 82 days—101 v India at Delhi in 1960–61). At the age of 18 years 256 days, Tendulkar became the youngest batsman to score a Test century in Australia when he made 148 not out at Sydney in 1991–92.

At 15 years 231 days Tendulkar was the youngest batsman in the history of the Ranji Trophy to score a century—100 not out on his first-class debut for Bombay against Gujarat in 1988–89. His rise to first-class ranks followed a world-record partnership of 664 with Vinod Kambli in a schools match against St Xavier's in Bombay in 1987–88.

SHARADASHRAM VIDYAMANDIR

A. Ranade	c N. Dias b Sanghani	42
R. Mulye	c Bahutule b Sanghani	18
V. Kambli	not out	349
S. Tendulkar	not out	326
Extras	(b 5 lb 3 w 5)	13
	(2 wkts dec.)	748

•

When the Nawab of Pataudi Jnr took over the captaincy of India against the West Indies in 1961–62, he was only 21, and the youngest member of the team.

•

John Marshall made his first-class debut for Tasmania in 1850–51 at the age of 55.

•

Archie MacLaren was over 50 when he made 200 not out in his last first-class innings (MCC v New Zealand XI at Wellington in 1922–23).

•

When Graham McKenzie took 2 for 34 for the ACB Chairman's XI against India in Perth in 1991–92, he was over the age of 50. Dennis Lillee, who took 1 for 26 in the same match, was 42.

•

The oldest player to score two centuries in a first-class match is Dinkar Deodhar, who at the age of 52 made 105 and 141 for Maharashtra against Nawanagar at Poona in 1944–45. 'Dave' Nourse is the oldest to score a double century—219 not out for Western Province against Natal in 1932–33, a month short of his 55th birthday. The youngest to perform the feat is Pakistan's Ijaz Ahmed. He was just 16 years and 96 days when he made 201 not out for PACO v Karachi in 1984–85.

•

The youngest Australian batsman to score 1,000 first-class runs in a season is Darren Lehmann. He was 20 years and 32 days when he passed the milestone for South Australia in 1989–90, beating Doug Walter's record which had stood since 1965–66.

•

Aftab Baloch was only 20 when he made 428 for Sind v Baluchistan at Karachi in 1972–73.

•

Dhruv Pandove, who was killed in a car accident in 1992 at the age of 18, was the youngest Indian ever to score a first-class century and the youngest to reach 1,000 runs in the Ranji Trophy. He made his first-class debut at the age of 13 and scored 94; he then hit 137 in his third match, for Punjab, at the age of 14 years 294 days.

•

SOME OVER FORTIES FACTS

Most First-class runs since turning 40

Jack Hobbs—26,441
Frank Woolley—25,963
'Patsy' Hendren—24,039

Most Tests since turning 40

Bob Taylor (England) 30
Jack Hobbs (England) 27
'Patsy' Hendren (England) 23
Tom Graveney (England) 18
Clarrie Grimmett (Australia) 16

Jack Hobbs—the scorer of the most first-class runs after the age of 40

•

In 1920-21 Warwick Armstrong became the first Australian batsman to score over 400 runs in a single first-class match—157 not out and 245 for Victoria v South Australia in Melbourne. He performed the feat, only the second instance in all first-class cricket, at the age of 41.

•

When Gordon Greenidge scored 226 against Australia at Bridgetown in 1990-91 he became the fifth-oldest batsman to register a double century in Test cricket.

When England played its first Test matches in the West Indies in 1929-30, five of the touring party were over 40: Wilfred Rhodes (52), George Gunn (50), Ewart Astill (42), Nigel Haig (42) and 'Patsy' Hendren (41).

•

When Aaqib Javed made his Test debut in 1988-89 he became the second-youngest Test cricketer on record at 16 years and 189 days. Aaqib had made his first-class debut for Lahore in 1984-85, aged just 12. Alim-ud-Din, an Indian Test cricketer, made his debut for Rajasthan in the Ranji Trophy in 1942-43 at the age of 12 years 73 days—three days younger than Aaqib Javed. In 1970-71 another 12-year-old, Qasim Feroze, made his first-class debut for Bahawalpur.

•

Warwick Armstrong scored three centuries against England in 1920-21 when over the age of 40, an achievement matched by Charles Macartney in the 1926 Ashes series.

•

Three teenagers—Waqar Younis, Moin Khan and Zahid Fazal—played for Pakistan in two Tests against the West Indies in 1990-91.

•

Of the 1,424 first-class wickets to the credit of Clarrie Grimmett, 99% were taken after his 30th birthday. Sixty per cent of 'Tich' Freeman's 3,776 wickets were taken when he was over the age of 40.

•

When Pakistan fast bowler Wasim Akram took 5 for 56 and 5 for 72 at Dunedin in 1984-85 he became the youngest, at 18, to claim five wickets in each innings of a Test match.

•

Ray Illingworth was made captain of Yorkshire in 1982 at the age of 50. Others who captained county sides in their fifties include W.G. Grace and Bob Wyatt.

•

William Lillywhite opened the bowling in a first-class match for Sussex in 1853 at the age of 61.

•

The most junior player to appear in Australian first-class cricket was Len Junor, who was 15 years and 265 days old on his debut for Victoria against Western Australia at Melbourne in 1929-30. The youngest in English first-class cricket was Charles Young; he was 15 years 131 days on his debut for Hampshire in 1867.

•

Eric Rowan	42 years 7 days	236	South Africa v England at Leeds	1951
Jack Hobbs	41 years 196 days	211	England v South Africa at Lord's	1924
'Patsy' Hendren	41 years	205*	England v West Indies at Port-of-Spain	1929-30
Dudley Nourse	40 years 208 days	208	South Africa v England at Nottingham	1951
Gordon Greenidge	39 years 355 days	226	West Indies v Australia at Bridgetown	1990-91

In his first full season of first-class cricket—1986—Graeme Hick passed 2,000 runs for Worcestershire, the first player to achieve the feat before his 21st birthday.

•

Graeme Hick

At the age of just 22, Graeme Hick had already amassed 10,000 runs and 35 centuries in first-class cricket. Only a very few batsmen have been able to attain either milestone under the age of 30—Don Bradman did so by the age of 23 and W.G. Grace achieved both legs of the double when he was 25.

YOUNGEST BATSMEN TO SCORE 10,000 FIRST-CLASS RUNS

Graeme Hick	22	W.G. Grace	25
Don Bradman	23	Frank Woolley	25
Len Hutton	23	Phil Mead	25
Colin Cowdrey	23	Tom Graveney	25
Walter Hammond	24	Barry Richards	25
Glenn Turner	24	Viv Richards	25

In 1990 Hick became the youngest batsman to score 10,000 first-class runs for Worcestershire, and the youngest to score 50 first-class centuries, and in 1993 the youngest to reach 20,000 first-class runs.

•

When Pakistan's Salim Malik scored a century on his Test debut—100 not out against Sri Lanka at Karachi in 1981-82—he became, at the age of 18 years 328 days, the youngest batsman to achieve the feat.

•

Mushtaq Mohammad, who made his Test debut for Pakistan at the age of 15, marked his first-class debut when 13, by taking 5 for 28 and scoring 87.

When Bob Simpson made his one-day international debut in 1978, against the West Indies at St John's, he was 42 years and 19 days old. At the time the Australian captain was the oldest cricketer to make his debut in a one-day international, a record he held until 1985, when Norman Gifford played in his first match, a week away from his 45th birthday, against Australia at Sharjah.

•

The South Africa-India Test at Durban in 1992-93 saw the unique selection of two debutants over the age of 39. Omar Henry was 40 years and 295 days old on the first day of the Test, while team-mate Jimmy Cook was 39 years and 105 days old.

•

Two 40-year-olds played in the 1992 World Cup—South Africa's Omar Henry was 40, while Zimbabwe's John Traicos was 44.

•

In his first season of first-class cricket, Brian Close became the youngest player to achieve the 1,000 run-100 wicket double. Close was only 18 when he scored 1,098 runs and captured 113 wickets in his debut season for Yorkshire in 1949.

Brian Close, who made his England Test debut at the age of 18

5 PMs and GGs

Prime Ministers

At least three first-class cricketers have gone on to obtain one of the highest offices in the land, that of prime minister. The first to do so was Francis Bell, who played for Wellington in the mid-1870s and was prime minister of New Zealand for a brief period in 1925. Sir Alec Douglas-Home who, as Lord Dunglass, represented Middlesex, was Britain's prime minister following the resignation of Harold MacMillan in 1963, whie Ratu Sir Kamisese Mara, a fast bowler, became Fiji's PM in 1970 when the island was granted independence. His deputy prime minister, Ratu Sir Edward Cakobau, was also a first-class cricketer of some note, having played for Fiji and Auckland.

•

Grantley Adams, prime minister of the West Indies Federation from 1958 to 1962, had earlier played representative cricket for Barbados.

•

Maurice Bonham-Carter, who played first-class cricket for Oxford and Kent, was private secretary to British prime minister Herbert Asquith between 1910 and 1916.

•

The Duke of Wellington, who was prime minister from 1828 to 1830, issued an order in 1841 that a cricket ground be built at all military barracks. As the Hon. Captain Wellesley, he often played cricket and appeared for an All-Ireland XI against The Garrison at Dublin in 1792, a match considered one of the first major cricket fixtures staged in Ireland.

•

Winston Churchill was a fag at Harrow to a future England captain, F.S. Jackson.

•

Mark Faber, who made over 1,000 runs for Sussex in 1975, was a grandson of Harold Macmillan.

•

A nephew of Sir Alec Douglas-Home, Andrew Douglas-Home played first-class cricket with Oxford University in 1970.

•

George Kemp-Welch, who captained Cambridge and also played for Warwickshire, was the son-in-law of British prime minister Stanley Baldwin.

•

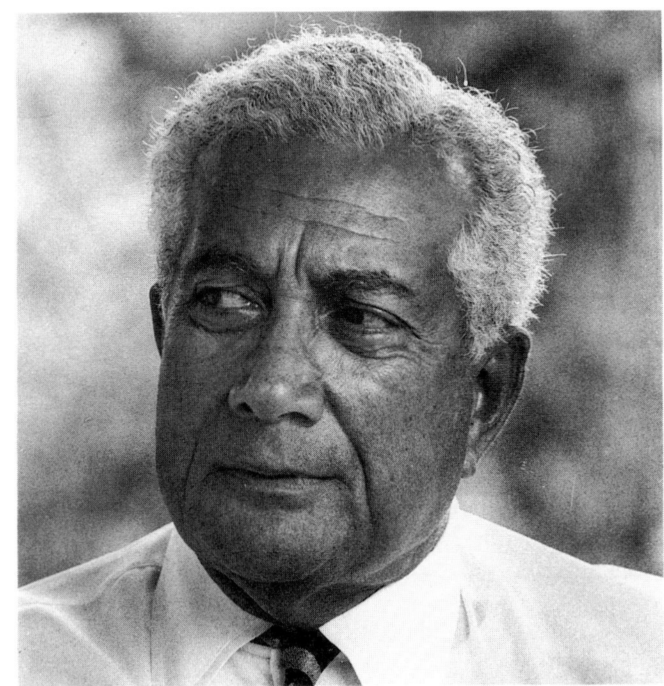

Two cricketing Prime Ministers—Sir Alec Douglas-Home and Ratu Sir Kamisese Mara

Sir Robert Menzies was president of the Kent County Cricket Club in 1968.

•

Bob Hawke, considered a fairly talented right-handed batsman, played first-grade cricket in both Perth and Canberra. While studying at the Australian National University, Hawke represented the ACT, once scoring 78 against a Newcastle side. Earlier, he'd been 12th man in a few matches for Colin Cowdrey's Oxford University team in 1954—this was the closest Hawke came to playing first-class cricket.

•

Greg Chappell, Michael Holding, Bob Hawke, Kim Hughes and Neil Bulger at a function following the Prime Minister's XI-West Indies match at Manuka Oval in 1983-84.

One of the first duties undertaken by Bob Hawke when he became prime minister in 1983 was to resurrect the Prime Minister's XI cricket match in Canberra against touring sides, a fixture started by Bob Menzies in 1951-52.

Bob Menzies with captains Peter May and Ian Johnson at the Prime Minister's XI-MCC match at Manuka Oval in 1958-59

A future Australian prime minister, Harold Holt, was one of three members of federal parliament chosen by Bob Menzies to play in the inaugural PM's XI match against the touring West Indians in 1951-52. Although Holt, the then immigration minister pulled out due to illness, the other two MPs did play—the Social Services Minister, Athol Townley, and Bill Falkinder.

PRIME MINISTER'S XI v WEST INDIES 1951-52

Played at Manuka Oval, Canberra, 22 October 1951

Result: Match Drawn

PRIME MINISTER'S XI		
J.H.B. Fingleton	c Weekes b Trim	0
A.L. Hassett	c Stollmeyer b Ferguson	29
M.P. Donnelly	hit wkt b Gomez	72
R.N. Harvey	b Ferguson	22
T. Freebody	b Ferguson	2
S.J.E. Loxton	c Goddard b Gomez	57
I.W. Johnson	c Rickards b Ferguson	14
I. McLellan	b Ferguson	1
A. Townley	c Goddard b Ferguson	14
W.J. O'Reilly	c Worrell b Gomez	7
W. Falkinder	b Ferguson	2
K. Gibb	not out	0
Extras		9
		229

1/0 2/94 3/131 4/131 5/138 6/180 7/183 8/219 9/221 10/228

West Indies	*O*	*M*	*R*	*W*
Worrell	5	0	39	0
Trim	4	0	16	1
Gomez	13	0	71	3
Ferguson	11.1	0	94	7

WEST INDIES		
J.B. Stollmeyer	b Hassett	36
A.F. Rae	lbw b O'Reilly	46
K.R. Rickards	not out	23
C.L. Walcott	not out	37
	(2 wkts)	142

1/78 2/88

Prime Minister's XI	*O*	*M*	*R*	*W*
Falkinder	3	0	16	0
Harvey	5	0	35	0
Loxton	2	0	3	0
O'Reilly	4	0	23	1
Hassett	4	0	30	1
Johnson	2	0	14	0
Townley	2	0	12	0
Donnelly	1	0	9	0

•

The Nehru Cup one-day international series, played in 1989, was staged to celebrate the centenary of the birth of India's first prime minister after independence, Jawaharlal Nehru.

•

In 1988, Bob Hawke captained a PM's XI match in Sydney against an Aboriginal Cricket Association XI, a fixture held to raise money for its tour of England later in the year. The Aboriginal XI won the match by seven wickets against a PM's side that included eight former Test players—Ian Chappell, Gary Cosier, Ian Davis, Graeme Thomas, Rod Marsh, Dennis Lillee, Max Walker and Len Pascoe. Marsh top-scored with 46, Bob Hawke was out for a duck. On their return from England, another match was arranged, and again the Aboriginal Cricket Association won, this time by three wickets. For the Prime Minister's XI, Clive Lloyd top-scored with 63, Bob Hawke contributed 2.

•

When he was 12 years old, future England prime minister, John Major, was named 'Best Young Cricketer of the Year' by the *London Evening Standard* newspaper.

•

Britain's cricket-mad Prime Minister John Major

Cricket is not just a game—it is a heritage, a thing of grace. It can have a great future provided, on-the-field and off, all those who love it play up and play the game.

—John Major

•

Australians will alway fight for those 22 yards. Lord's and its traditions belong to Australians just as much as to England.

—John Curtin, Prime Minister of Australia, 1941–45

•

Cricket was declared Canada's national sport in 1867 by the country's prime minister Sir John MacDonald.

•

India's 1984–85 tour of Pakistan was abandoned after the assassination of the Indian prime minister Mrs Indira Gandhi. A Test match and a one-day international had yet to be played, and at the time, the second one-day match was in progress at Sialkot. Dilip Vengsarkar was unbeaten on 94 when the match was called off.

•

A serious mistake, contrary to the spirit of the game.

—Australian prime minister Malcolm Fraser

An act of cowardice.

—New Zealand prime minister Robert Muldoon

Trans-Tasman reaction to the infamous Trevor Chappell underarm delivery in the final of the 1980–81 World Series Cup at the MCG.

•

As part of the Commonwealth Heads of Government Meeting in 1991, a special cricket match was held in Zimbabwe to raise money for various charities. Before a crowd of some 3,000, British PM John Major and Australia's Bob Hawke opened the batting, scoring 5 and 21 respectively. Other PMs to play in the match included Pakistan's Nawaz Sharif, who hit three sixes in a knock of 31, and Kennedy Simmonds of St Kitts-Nevis; Grenada's prime minister Nicholas Brathwaite was an umpire.

•

Alfred Lyttelton, who played for Middlesex, Worcestershire and England, was the brother-in-law of British prime minister Arthur Balfour. Alfred's brother, Spencer Lyttelton, who represented Cambridge and Eton, was chief private secretary to Prime Minister William Gladstone from 1892 to 1894.

•

Don Bradman's last big match was for the Prime Minister's XI against England in 1962–63. Batting with Don Chipp, Bradman was bowled by Brian Statham for 3.

•

Don Bradman at Manuka Oval for the Prime Minister's XI match in 1962–63

Timoci Bavadra, Fiji's ousted prime minister in the military coup of 1987, was a top-grade cricketer and a cricket administrator.

•

Oh God, if there be cricket in heaven, let there also be rain.

—Sir Alec Douglas-Home

•

Michael Manley, prime minister of Jamaica, on and off, between 1972 and 1992, was an accomplished freelance author and journalist, who wrote *A History of West Indies Cricket*, published in 1988.

•

In a match between federal and state parliaments in Melbourne in 1920–21, Australia's prime minister of the day, Billy Hughes took 4 for 45, and could have taken a hat-trick had it not been for two successive dropped catches off his bowling.

•

Sir Robert Menzies wrote a poem about Australian Test cricketer Sam Loxton:

LOOK OUT FOR SAM

Look out for Sam, O gentle stumper,
For Sam will bowl a fearful bumper,
And follow through with great displeasure
And clock the batsman, for good measure.

•

Bob Hawke found himself in the casualty section of a Canberra hospital in 1984 after being hit in the face by a cricket ball during a Prime Minister's XI–Parliamentary Press Gallery match. With 27 runs beside his name, Hawke went for a wild hook off the bowling of Melbourne *Herald* journalist Gary O'Neill. He mistimed the shot, the ball hit the top of his bat and went onto his face, shattering his glasses and blackening his right eye. Away from the match for just a short time receiving treatment, he returned to the ground with a patch over his damaged eye, to see his team take victory by six runs.

•

If I had my way I'd certainly introduce cricket into China and the Soviet Union. I think that if we could make them play cricket, we'd have a much more likely chance of a peaceful world.

—Bob Hawke, 1984

During his reign as prime minister, Bob Hawke staged nine international PM's XI matches. In that time, only two bowlers took five wickets in an innings, and both were locals. ACT captain Greg Irvine was the first with 5 for 42 against New Zealand in 1987–88; the second was former Canberra bowler Greg Rowell who took 6 for 27 in Hawke's last match, against the touring Indians in 1991–92.

•

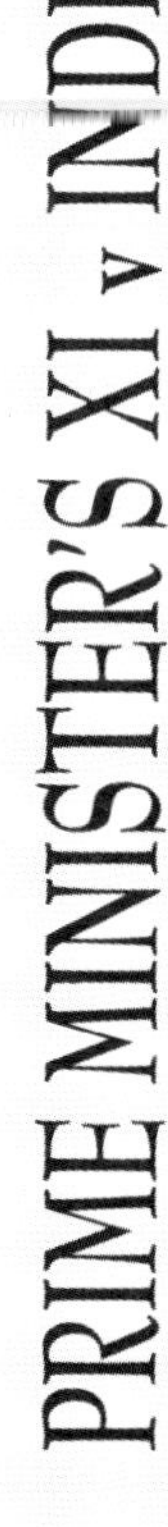

$2.50
PRIME MINISTER'S XI v INDIA
17th December, 1991 — Manuka Oval

Australia's Prime Minister, Paul Keating, with the 1992–93 PM's XI Man of the Match, Dean Jones.

There will be no ducking of bouncers, no playing for time. The bowling's going to get hit all around the ground.

—Margaret Thatcher launching her campaign in 1990 to remain party leader and prime minister of Great Britain

Australia has a terrible job playing the game at the moment and I think they have decided to abandon their mother country where cricket came from.

—New Zealand prime minister Jim Bolger after a parliamentary speech by Australian PM Paul Keating in 1992, in which he claimed England had deserted Australia during World War II.

You know you've always had my admiration and support and I'm very pleased for you on this memorable day.

—Paul Keating to Allan Border on becoming the highest run-scorer in Test cricket history in 1993

Governors-General

Freeman Thomas, who represented Sussex and Cambridge, was governor-general of Canada, 1924–31.

•

Charles Lennox, later the Duke of Richmond, played first-class cricket for Sussex and the MCC, and like Freeman Thomas, was also a Canadian governor-general.

•

Ratu Sir George Cakobau, appointed governor-general of Fiji in 1973, was vice-captain of the national cricket team which toured New Zealand in 1947–48. He finished the series as Fiji's most successful all-rounder capturing 24 wickets at 24.00 and averaging 21.00 with the bat. In 1987, two years before his death, the ICC decided to approve first-class status for five matches on the tour. The 75-year-old Sir George therefore became the oldest player in history to be awarded first-class ranking.

•

Arthur Somers, who made his first-class debut for the MCC in 1906 and then played for Worcestershire, succeeded Lord Baden-Powell as Chief Scout and later became Governor of Victoria and acting governor-general of Australia.

Viscount Cobham, New Zealand's governor-general (1957–62), batting for his first-class XI against the MCC at Auckland in 1960–61. As Charles Lyttelton, he captained Worcestershire between 1936 and 1939.

When the MCC played Wellington in 1935–36, a future governor-general appeared on each side. Charles Lyttelton, playing for the tourists, was New Zealand's governor-general from 1957 to 1962, while Denis Blundell, who took eight wickets in the match for Wellington, held the post between 1972 and 1977.

•

Lord Forster Lepe, who played first-class cricket for Hampshire and Oxford, was Australia's seventh governor-general, 1920–25.

6 Family Connections

An unusual family double in England in 1988—Lance Cairns and his son Chris both played first-class cricket during the season. Chris Cairns made two appearances in the County Championship for Nottinghamshire, while his father played in Michael Parkinson's World XI against the MCC at Scarborough.

•

It was a gathering of the clans when New Zealand took on England in the first and second Tests of 1983. Five of the New Zealanders, including Jeff and Martin Crowe, had brothers who had also played Test cricket. The others were Geoff Howarth (Hedley Howarth), Richard Hadlee (Dayle) and Brendon Bracewell (John).

•

When Greg Chappell made 112 at Manchester in 1977 it was the 10th time a Chappell had scored a century in a Test match against England. The feat of brothers scoring a total of 10 hundreds against a particular country is unique to Greg and Ian Chappell. They repeated the achievement in 1979, completing 10 Test tons against the West Indies.

13 TEST CENTURIES v ENGLAND

Greg Chappell (9)		*Ian Chappell (4)*	
108	Perth 1970–71	111	Melbourne 1970–71
131	Lord's 1972	104	Adelaide 1970–71
113	The Oval 1972	118	The Oval 1972
144	Sydney 1974–75	192	The Oval 1975
102	Melbourne 1974–75		
112	Manchester 1977		
114	Melbourne 1979–80		
117	Perth 1982–83		
115	Adelaide 1982–83		

10 TEST CENTURIES v WEST INDIES

Greg Chappell (5)		*Ian Chappell (5)*	
106	Bridgetown 1972–73	117	Brisbane 1968–69
123	Brisbane 1975–76	165	Melbourne 1968–69
109*	Brisbane 1975–76	106*	Bridgetown 1972–73
182*	Sydney 1975–76	109	Georgetown 1972–73
124	Brisbane 1979–80	156	Perth 1975–76

•

In 1978–79 Pranab Roy scored a century (105 for Bengal v Assam) on his first-class debut, as his father Pankaj Roy had done in his first match in 1946–47 (112* for Bengal v United Provinces).

•

George Downton and his Test-playing son Paul both kept wicket for Kent—George in 1948 and Paul between 1977 and 1979.

•

Len Hutton and his son, Richard, both opened the batting on their Test debuts for England. Len Hutton failed in both innings scoring 0 and 1 against New Zealand at Lord's in 1937, while his son made an unbeaten 58, sharing a 117-run opening stand with Brian Luckhurst against Pakistan, also at Lord's, in 1971.

•

A pair of cousins and a pair of brothers formed a unique batting line-up for South Australia in 1973–74. Opening the innings against Queensland at Brisbane, John Causby was joined by his cousin Barry Causby, who was making his first-class debut. They were followed by Trevor and Ian Chappell—their brother, Greg, in his first season with Queensland, also played in this match.

•

Paul Downton

Jonathan Agnew's first cousin, Mary Duggan, was a former captain of the England women's Test side in the 1960s.

•

Tony Greig and his younger brother Ian began their Test careers with identical bowling figures:

A.W. Greig 4-53 v Australia	Manchester	1972
I.A. Greig 4-53 v Pakistan	Birmingham	1982

•

Terry Alderman and Denise Emerson are the only brother and sister to play Test cricket for Australia.

•

Viv Richard's father, Malcolm, played for Antigua, as did his brother Mervyn and half-brother Donald.

•

Nazar Mohammad and Mudassar Nazar provide the only instance of a father and son both carrying their bats for a century in a Test match:

Nazar Mohammad	124* v India at Lucknow in 1952-53
Mudassar Nazar	152* v India at Lahore in 1982-83

•

Ricky Ponting, who in 1992-93 became the youngest batsman to score a century in each innings of a Sheffield Shield match, is a nephew of the former Australian fast bowler Greg Campbell.

•

No fewer than six of Clem Hill's brothers also played first-class cricket. Arthur, Henry, Les, Percival and Roland played for South Australia, while Stanley represented South Australia and New South Wales.

•

Tom Longfield, the father-in-law of Ted Dexter, captained Bengal to a 178-run victory over Punjab in the 1938-39 final of the Ranji Trophy.

•

The Australian father-and-son combination of Colin and Russell McCool both played county cricket for Somerset.

•

When Chris Cairns made his Test debut in 1989-90, a period of only four years had elapsed since his father, Lance, played in his last Test (v Australia, 1985-86). This beat by some six years the record for a gap between a father and son playing Test cricket; previously held by Colin Cowdrey, whose last Test came in 1974-75, and Chris Cowdrey who made his Test debut in 1984-85.

•

In the Indian Under-25 v Pakistan match at Bombay in 1986-87, local batsman Sanjay Manjrekar and Pakistan's Shoaib Mohammad both scored centuries. Both batsmen are the sons of famous Test cricketers, Vijay Manjrekar and Hanif Mohammad. When Pakistan next met India, in 1989-90, the two cricketing sons went one step further by posting double centuries in the third Test at Lahore, providing the first example of sons each scoring 200 in the same Test.

•

During the 1930s, some of the best opening partnerships for Somerset were recorded by the brothers Jack and Frank Lee. They took part in eight century stands, and were the first brothers to crack 200 in county cricket, performing the feat twice:

234 v Essex at Leyton in 1932
213 v Surrey at Weston in 1934

•

David Graveney, who went on an unofficial tour of South Africa in 1989-90, is the son of former Gloucestershire captain Ken Graveney, and nephew of Tom Graveney who played in 79 Tests for England.

•

A Test trial match at Bradford in 1950 was marked by the selection of both Eric and Alec Bedser—one appearing for each team. This was the first time twins had opposed each other in a first-class match.

•

In 1971 brothers David and John Steele both scored centuries in the same first-class match, but for opposing sides. This was a first in English first-class cricket, a feat they repeated in 1973:

J.F. Steele 123	Leicestershire	Leicester 1971
D.S. Steele 107*	Northamptonshire	
J.F. Steele 118	Leicestershire	Northampton 1973
D.S. Steele 116	Northamptonshire	

In the match at Leicester, John Steele dismissed David, and their cousin, Brian Crump, turned out for Northamptonshire.

•

During the 1991 Sunday League tournament, Glamorgan's Alan Butcher and his son Mark became the first father and son to play against each other in English cricket, when Surrey played host to Glamorgan at The Oval.

•

As a pair, Ian and Greg Chappell are Australia's most successful batsmen in terms of high-scoring partnerships in Test cricket. Together they staged 12 100-run partnerships, three more than Bill Lawry and Bob Simpson. The Chappells recorded six against the West Indies, four against England and two against New Zealand, their most famous stand being 264 for the third wicket at Wellington in 1973-74.

•

Three English Test cricketers—Frank Woolley, Jim Langridge and Harry Lee—had brothers who became Test umpires—Claude Woolley, John Langridge and Frank Lee.

Frank and Claude Woolley, both all-rounders, each scored a double century and claimed a hat-trick during their first-class careers. Frank made nine 200s, seven for Kent and two for the MCC, one of which was his highest score—an unbeaten 305 against Tasmania in 1911–12. His hat-trick was taken in 1919, for Kent v Surrey at Blackheath. Claude's one double century was an undefeated 204 for Northamptonshire against Worcestershire in 1921; his hat-trick was claimed the previous season while bowling against Essex at Northampton.

•

When John Hearne took a hat-trick for Middlesex in 1911, he became the sixth member of the family to perform the feat in first-class cricket. Brothers George and Alec and cousin Walter each took a hat-trick for Kent, while Tom, an uncle, and Jack, a distant cousin of John, did so for Middlesex.

THE HEARNE FAMILY HAT-TRICKS

J.T. Hearne (4)	Middlesex v Kent	Tonbridge	1896
	England v Australia	Leeds	1899
	Middlesex v Essex	Lord's	1902
	Middlesex v Warwickshire	Lord's	1912
A. Hearne (2)	MCC v Yorkshire	Lord's	1888
	Kent v Gloucestershire	Clifton	1900
J.W. Hearne (2)	Middlesex v Essex	Lord's	1911
	Middlesex v Essex	Leyton	1922
T. Hearne (1)	Middlesex v Kent	Islington	1868
G.G. Hearne (1)	Kent v Lancashire	Manchester	1875
W. Hearne (1)	Kent v Lancashire	Tonbridge	1894

•

At Canterbury in 1986, former England Test opener Brian Luckhurst and his son, Tim, fielded as substitutes for Kent in the County Championship match against Hampshire.

•

Australian Test batsmen Mike Veletta and Graeme Wood are brothers-in-law. Other Test players similarly related include Sunil Gavaskar and Gundappa Viswanath, Sarfraz Nawaz and Younis Ahmed, and Majid Khan and Javed Burki. Some of the famous cousins of Test cricket are Lance Gibbs and Clive Lloyd, Bruce Reid and John Reid, Imran Khan and Majid Khan, and Garry Sobers and David Holford.

•

Brothers-in-law Gavaskar and Viswanath both scored 1,000 Test runs for India in the calendar year of 1979.

•

Apart from playing first-class cricket for Cambridge University in 1958/59, and gaining notoriety through broadcasting, Henry Blofeld has another famous link with the game—an uncle, the Hon. F.S.G. Calthorpe, is a former England Test captain.

•

Gordon Greenidge's wife, Anita, is a cousin of West Indies fast bowler Andy Roberts.

•

Colin and Chris Cowdrey

Zaheer Abbas, Sarfraz Nawaz, Mohammad Nazir, Wasim Bari and Younis Ahmed all share the unusual distinction of having played in a Test match with Hanif Mohammad, and in a Test with his son Shoaib. Others to have played with both father and son in Test cricket include Jack Blackham (who appeared with Ned and Syd Gregory), Wilfred Rhodes (Fred and Maurice Tate) and Pat Pocock (Colin and Chris Cowdrey).

•

Victor Trumper's son, Victor junior, played six first-class matches for New South Wales in the early 1940s. On his debut, against Queensland at Brisbane in 1940–41, Trumper clean bowled openers Bill Brown and Geoff Cook in his first over.

•

Mohammad Saeed, who appeared in a series of unofficial Tests against the West Indies in 1948–49, played first-class cricket with both his son, Yawar Saeed, and son-in-law, Fazal Mahmood, for Punjab in 1954–55.

•

Apart from the famous English brothers, another set of Bedser twins, similarly christened, also played cricket. Both were all-round sportsmen; Alec played first-class cricket for Border in the Currie Cup in South Africa in 1971–72.

Only two Pakistan batsmen have scored a first-class double-century in the West Indies. They are Hanif Mohammad (337 v West Indies at Bridgetown in 1957–58) and his son Shoaib (208* v West Indies XI at Georgetown in 1987–88). When Shoaib made 203 not out against India at Lahore in 1989, they became the first father and son to score double-centuries in Test cricket.

•

During the 1989–90 Sheffield Shield, Steve and Mark Waugh both came within a few runs of each scoring their maiden double-century in first-class cricket. Steve hit a career-best 196 against Tasmania in Hobart, while Mark was left stranded on 198 not out, also against Tasmania, in Sydney. Mark eventually became the first Waugh to crack the 200-mark, with an innings of 204 a few months later, for Essex v Gloucestershire at Ilford.

•

The fraternal feats of the Waugh twins reached dizzy heights the following season, when both brothers scored a double-century in the same Sheffield Shield match, against Western Australia at Perth. Batting together, Mark finished on 229 not out and Steve was unbeaten on 216, their unbroken partnership of 464 being the world record for the fifth wicket.

THE WAUGH TWINS' 464-RUN PARTNERSHIP v WESTERN AUSTRALIA
Milestones

- Their partnership was the first 400-run stand for New South Wales in first-class cricket. The previous best was 397 for the fifth wicket by Warren Bardsley and Charles Kelleway against South Australia at Sydney in 1920–21.
- It was the highest partnership for any wicket in Australia, eclipsing 462* for the fourth wicket by the South Australian pair of David Hookes and Wayne Phillips against Tasmania in Adelaide in 1986–87.
- It was also a world record for the fifth wicket, beating 405 by Don Bradman and Sid Barnes in the second Test against England at Sydney in 1946–47.
- Their partnership was also a record by brothers in first-class cricket—previously 303* for the fourth wicket by Colin and Alan Wells (Sussex v Kent at Hove 1987). The previous best by Australian brothers was 303 by Ian and Greg Chappell, against Barbados at Bridgetown in 1972–73.
- They became the first brothers to score double centuries in the same first-class match, let alone the same innings.
- Both brothers made their highest scores in first-class cricket, and both scored their first double century in a first-class match in Australia. Mark's previous best was 207 not out for Essex v Yorkshire in 1990; Steve's highest was 196 for New South Wales v Tasmania in 1989–90.

•

The Waughs did another double act the following season, in an FAI Cup match at North Sydney, steering New South Wales to a 100-run victory over Victoria. They came together with the score at 2 for 9 and put on a record third-wicket stand of 240 in 157 minutes off 247 balls. Steve scored 126, an innings laced with 17 fours and a six, while Mark made 112 with 11 fours and two sixes. On top of their centuries, both took two wickets—Mark finished with an analysis of 6–1–26–2; Steve's was remarkably similar 6–1–30–2.

THE WAUGH TWINS' 240-RUN PARTNERSHIP v VICTORIA

- Their partnership of 240 was a record for the third wicket, beating the 172-run stand by Western Australia's Greg Shipperd and Rob Langer against Tasmania at Perth in 1981–82.

The Waugh twins—Steve and Mark

- It was the first double-century partnership by brothers in limited-overs cricket, and the highest in Australia since Ian and Greg Chappell's third-wicket stand of 111 for South Australia v Victoria at Adelaide in 1971–72.
- Both scored their maiden hundreds in the competition, and both broke the record by any state batsman for the highest score against Victoria, previously 111 not out by Rick McCosker for New South Wales at Sydney in 1981–82.
- They became the first brothers to score centuries in the 174-match history of domestic limited-overs cricket in Australia.

•

During the 1992 World Cup, both Mark and Steve recorded their highest scores in the competition in the match against Zimbabwe at Hobart. In an exhilarating display, Mark hit 66 not out off 39 balls, Steve made 55 from 43. Batting together, they put on a partnership of 113 off 69 deliveries, and at one stage carried Australia's score from 200 to 250 off just four overs.

•

During the 1988 English season, the Waugh twins became the first brothers to score centuries in the Sunday League one-day competition:

S.R. Waugh	109*	Somerset v Northamptonshire	Taunton
M.E. Waugh	103	Essex v Nottinghamshire	Colchester

Mark made history by becoming the first batsman to score a century on his League debut, while Steve's hundred for Somerset was the 300th century in the Sunday competition.

•

Steve and Mark Waugh are the only pair of twins to score centuries in the same innings of a first-class match, a feat they first achieved for New South Wales v Victoria at Sydney in 1987–88—Steve made 170 and Mark an unbeaten 114. They also did it three times against Western Australia in successive innings:

Mark	*Steve*	*Partnership*	*Venue*	*Season*
229*	216*	464*	Perth	1990–91
136	115	98	Perth	1991–92
163	113	204	Perth	1991–92

•

In 1989 the Waugh brothers became the first twins to score centuries in the same first-class match, but for opposing sides—Steve made 100 not out for the touring Australians, while Mark also scored an undefeated 100 for Essex, at Chelmsford.

•

When Mark Waugh made his first-class debut for New South Wales at Hobart in 1985–86, he and Steve became the first twins to play together in a first-class match in Australia. When Mark made his Australian debut in the World Series Cup match against Pakistan at Adelaide in 1988–89 it signalled the first appearance of twin brothers in any international cricket match.

When Mark made his Test debut at Adelaide in 1990–91, they became the first twin brothers to play Test cricket, and the 11th set of brothers to have appeared in a Test match for Australia. When Mark and Steve were selected to play for Australia in the third Test against the West Indies at Port-of-Spain in 1991, it was the first example of twin brothers in the same Test team.

•

Dean Waugh, the younger brother of Steve and Mark, broke a long-standing record held by Garry Sobers when playing club cricket in England in 1989. His innings of 153 for Astley Bridge in the Bolton League's Hamer Cup was a new record for the competition, beating Sobers' 142 not out for the Little Lever club in 1961. It also formed part of a unique family hat-trick for the Waughs in 1989—all three brothers had scores of over 150 while playing in England. Apart from Dean's record knock of 153, Mark scored 165 for Essex against Leicestershire, while Steve made 177 not out and 152 not out in successive Tests at Headingly and Lord's.

•

When Western Australia played South Australia at Perth in 1926–27, Frank and Dick Bryant made their first-class debuts and joined their brother, Bill, in the starting 11. This was only the second time in Australian first-class cricket that three brothers had played in the same match, after Clem, Stanley and Les Hill, who last appeared for South Australia in 1910–11, against New South Wales in Sydney. It was in this match that Clem with 156, and Les 123, both scored centuries in the same innings. Frank (115) and Dick Bryant (103) were the second set of brothers to achieve the feat, at Melbourne in 1933–34.

•

Jeff Dujon's father, Leroy, was an opening batsman for Jamaica during the 1940s.

•

Giff Vivian and his son, Graham, both made their Test debuts for New Zealand when under the age of 21.

•

K.S. Duleepsinhji had an uncle and a nephew who also played Test cricket—K.S. Ranjitsinhji represented England in 15 Tests, while Duleep's nephew K.S. Indrajitsinhji played four times for India during the 1960s.

•

In 1991–92, one of the great names of South African cricket resurfaced when Graeme Pollock's sons, Anthony and Andrew, both made their first-class debuts for Transvaal B, while Peter Pollock's son, Shaun, made his debut for Natal B.

•

Richard Blaker, who played for Kent, had twin daughters—Barbara and Joan—who both represented England.

•

The three Hadlee brothers—Dayle, Barry and Richard—played together on two occasions for New Zealand, both times in one-day internationals against England in 1975—at Dunedin and in a World Cup match at Nottingham.

•

George Gilbert, the first captain of New South Wales and the first bowler to achieve a hat-trick in Australian first-class cricket, was a cousin of W.G. Grace.

•

Richard Hadlee's wife, Karen, represented New Zealand in the Women's World Cup one-day international series played in India in 1977–78.

•

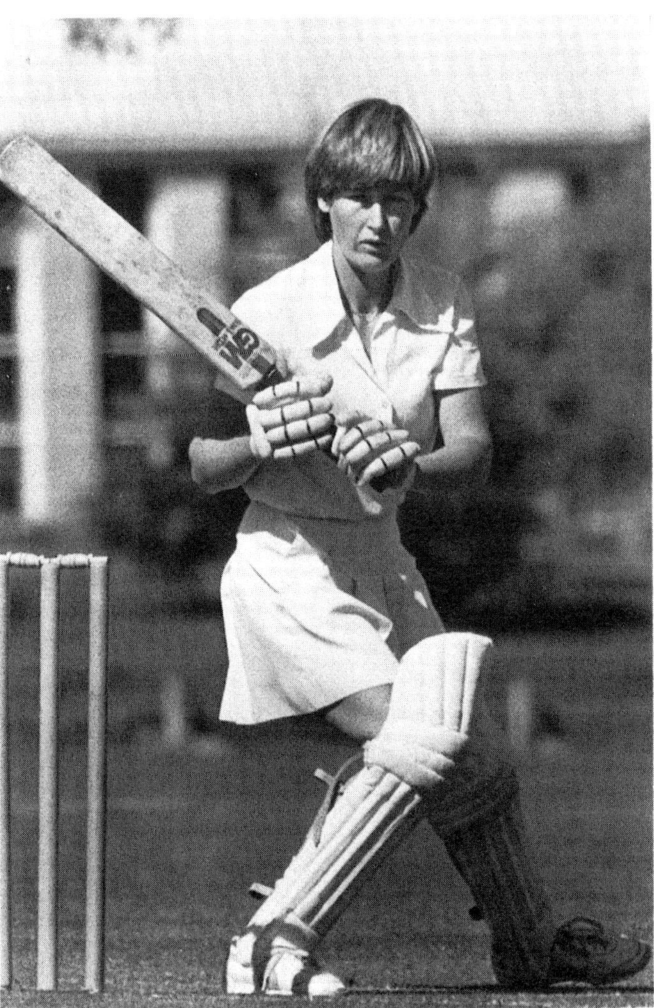

Karen Hadlee

Robin Smith, the South African-born Test batsman, scored a century (100*) on his first-class debut for Hampshire in 1983. His brother, Chris, opened the innings in this match, against Lancashire at Bournemouth, and also scored a century (100).

•

Shakoor Rana, the Pakistani umpire famous for his little chat with Mike Gatting in 1987, has two Test-playing brothers—Shafqat Rana played five Tests in six years during the 1960s and '70s, while Azmat Rana appeared once for Pakistan, against Australia in 1980.

•

Ian Chappell was the first batsman to score a century in the World Series Cricket Super Tests, while Greg was the first bowler to take five wickets in an innings. They both achieved the feats in the same match, against the West Indies at Football Park in Adelaide in 1977–78—Ian captaining the Australian XI scored 141, while Greg took 5 for 20 off 12 overs.

•

The 1954–55 Quaid-e-Azam Trophy final included an unprecedented fraternal feat when the Mohammad brothers, Wazir (118), Hanif (109) and Raees (110), all scored centuries in the same innings for Karachi versus Services. In a 1961–62 semi-final of the Quaid-e-Azam Trophy, all five of the Mohammad brethren took to the field—Hanif, Mushtaq and Raees for Karachi Whites and Sadiq and Wazir for Karachi Blues.

•

'Dave' Nourse was the first batsman to reach the milestones of 2,000 and 3,000 runs in the South African Currie Cup competition. His son, Dudley, was the first to score 4,000 runs.

•

The first twins to appear together in first-class cricket were Alfred and Arthur Payne for Oxford University in 1854. The first twins to play alongside each other in Test cricket were the New Zealand pair of Elizabeth and Rosemary Signal, who both appeared in the first women's Test against England at Leeds in 1984.

•

C.B. Fry's son, S. Fry, and grandson, C.A. Fry, also played first-class cricket.

•

The Langridge brothers—James and John—both scored over 2,000 runs for Sussex in 1937.

•

An unusual dismissal in a county match between Middlesex and Somerset at Lord's in 1933:

H.W. Lee	c F.S. Lee	b J.W. Lee	82

Harry, Frank and Jack were brothers.

•

Ajay Jadeja, who made his Test debut for India in 1992–93, is a great grand-nephew of K.S. Ranjitsinhji.

•

When Laurence Walsh made his first-class debut for South Australia in 1930–31, he and his brother Norman became the first pair of twins to play first-class cricket in Australia. Norman Walsh also played for South Australia in the 1920s. The Nagels—Lisle and Vernon—were the next twins to play first-class cricket; between them they played in 19 matches for Victoria during the 1930s.

•

Apart from his cousin John Reid who played for New Zealand, two of Bruce Reid's aunts, Betty and Dawn Newman, played cricket for Australia.

Bruce Reid

•

William Cooper and Paul Sheahan are the only great-grandfather and great-grandson to play Test cricket.

•

When New Zealand played England in the first Test at Wellington in 1983–84, more than half of their players were the sons of former first-class cricketers:

Son	*Father*
John Wright	G.T. Wright (Canterbury)
Bruce Edgar	A.J. Edgar (Wellington)
Martin Crowe	D.W. Crowe (Wellington/Canterbury)
Jeff Crowe	D.W. Crowe (Wellington/Canterbury)
Richard Hadlee	W.A. Hadlee (Canterbury/Otago/New Zealand)
Martin Snedden	W.N. Snedden (Auckland)

Five of their number had brothers with first-class or Test experience—Geoff Howarth, Jeremy Coney, Richard Hadlee and Martin and Jeff Crowe and then there was Lance Cairns, the father of a future New Zealand Test cricketer, Chris Cairns.

•

George (left) and G.V. Gunn—the only father and son to score a century in the same innings of a first-class match

George Gunn (183) and G.V. Gunn (100*) provide the only instance in first-class cricket of a father and son scoring a century in the same innings of a match—Nottinghamshire v Warwickshire at Birmingham in 1931.

•

In 1903, George Gunn's brother John and their uncle Billy shared a record third-wicket stand of 369 for Nottinghamshire against Leicestershire at Trent Bridge.

•

Ralston Otto, who in 1983–84 hit a then-record 572 runs in a season in the West Indies, is a cousin of Curtly Ambrose.

•

Malcolm Jardine, Frank Mann and Horace Brearley all played for Middlesex and each had a son who captained England—Douglas Jardine, George Mann and Mike Brearley.

•

Dean Headley, grandson of the West Indies legend George Headley and son of Ron, also a West Indies Test player, took the wicket of Ashley Metcalfe with his first ball on his County Championship debut for Middlesex in 1991 (5–46 v Yorkshire at Lord's).

•

During the 1990–91 Test series against the West Indies, the Pakistani pair of Shoaib Mohammad and Salim Malik recorded a fourth-wicket partnership of 174 in the first Test at Karachi. This was a new record for the series, previously held by Shoaib's uncle Wazir Mohammad and his father Hanif Mohammad (154 at Port-of-Spain in 1957–58).

•

Derek Pringle's father, Don, played for East Africa in the 1975 World Cup.

•

One of the most unusual occurrences in the history of first-class cricket took place at Derby in 1922, when the father-and-son combination of Bill and Bob Bestwick bowled to another father and son, Warwickshire's Willie and Bernard Quaife.

•

Andrew Snedden and Colin Snedden, the grandfather and uncle of pace bowler Martin Snedden, also played first-class cricket for New Zealand.

•

The third Test between New Zealand and South Africa at Auckland in 1963–64 was the last time that two pairs of brothers represented one country in a Test match. Graeme and Peter Pollock and Tony and David Pithey.

Peter and Graeme Pollock

•

South Africa's 94-run victory over England at Nottingham in 1965 was due in part to the feats of the brothers Pollock—Graeme scored 125 and 59, while Peter took five wickets in each innings for a match return of 10 for 87.

•

When Bobby Parks played as a substitute for England against New Zealand at Lord's in 1986, he followed his father Jim Parks and grandfather James Parks in appearing in a Test match. This is the closest three generations of one family have come to playing Test cricket.

•

In 1964 Jonathan Townsend made his first-class debut for Oxford, an event which heralded the first instance of a fourth generation family playing first-class cricket in England. His father, David Townsend, played three Tests in 1934–35. His grandfather, Charlie Townsend, played in two Test matches in 1899, while his great-grandfather, Frank Townsend, played for Gloucestershire. Two of his great-uncles, Arthur Townsend and Frank Norton Townsend, also represented Gloucestershire.

•

Sohail Mohammad, the son of former Pakistan Test cricketer Mushtaq Mohammad, Gary Butcher, son of former England batsman Alan, and Andrew Jones, son of ex-county cricketer Alan, all appeared in the same Glamorgan second XI side which took on a Kent seconds team in 1992.

•

Peter Roebuck

Apart from his Test-playing brother Mervyn, Neil Harvey had two other brothers who also represented Victoria—'Mick' Harvey, who later became a Test umpire, and Ray Harvey.

•

During the third Test at Bridgetown in 1984–85, Jeff Crowe established a new fielding record for New Zealand with four catches in the West Indies first innings total of 336. Brother Martin equalled the feat with four catches in the following Test at Kingston.

•

Claude Rock and his son, Harry, both scored a century on their first-class debuts in Australia.

C.W. Rock	102	Tasmania v Victoria at East Melbourne 1888–89
H.O. Rock	127	New South Wales v South Australia at Sydney 1924–25

Norman Rock, Harry's uncle, also played first-class cricket, and on his debut for Tasmania in 1890–91 took a first innings wicket haul of 5 for 21 against Victoria.

•

Both the mother and sister of former Somerset batsman Peter Roebuck played cricket for Oxford University. His younger brother, Paul, played for Cambridge and Gloucestershire.

•

The Bedser twins, Alec and Eric, both made over 450 appearances in first-class cricket.

•

Graham McKenzie's father, Eric, and uncle Doug McKenzie also played for Western Australia.

•

In 1913 J.T. Tyldesley (129) and his brother G.E. (109) made hundreds in the same innings for Lancashire v Leicestershire and repeated the feat in their next match, scoring 210 and 110 against Surrey.

•

When Pakistan's Sadiq Mohammad made his Test debut in 1969 against New Zealand at Karachi, he played alongside two of his brothers, Hanif and Mushtaq. This was the third—after the Graces and Hearnes—and last occasion that three brothers have played together in the same Test.

•

Steve and Mark Waugh are the only twins to each score 10 or more centuries in first-class cricket. The Bedsers come closest to matching this feat—Eric made 10 hundreds and Alec one. But with the ball the Bedsers accomplishments are unequalled amongst twins in first-class cricket. They remain alone in each taking 500 wickets.

The Surrey twins—Eric and Alec Bedser

	Career	*Wkts*	*Avge*	*Best bowling*
A.V. Bedser	1939–60	1,924	20.41	8–18 Surrey v Nottinghamshire—The Oval 1952 8–18 Surrey v Warwickshire—The Oval 1953
E.A. Bedser	1939–61	833	24.95	7–33 Surrey v Leicestershire—The Oval 1955

In England, three sets of seven brothers have played first-class cricket—the Walkers of Middlesex and Southgate; the Studds of Middlesex, Hampshire and Cambridge; and the Fosters of Worcestershire. Two of the Studds, George and Charles, played for England, while one of the Fosters, 'Tip', hit a record-breaking 287 on his Test debut, against Australia at Sydney in 1903–04.

•

During his final Test match, at Edgbaston in 1991, Richard Hadlee helped his family reach the milestone of 500 Test wickets. His tally of 431, together with brother Dayle's 71, gave the Hadlees a record total of 502 Test wickets.

•

In the two-Test series against New Zealand in 1982–83, Sri Lanka's innings were opened by Sidath and Mithra Wettimuny, equalling the fraternal feat of E.M. and W.G. Grace in 1880 and Hanif and Sadiq Mohammad in 1969.

•

Larry Gomes, who represented the West Indies in Tests 60 times, had a brother, Sheldon, who scored five first-class centuries for Trinidad and Tobago.

•

Jahangir Khan, who appeared in four Test matches for India in the 1930s, was the father of Majid Khan and the uncle of Javed Burki and Imran Khan, all of whom captained Pakistan.

•

When George A. Hearne made his Test debut for South Africa in 1922, he contributed to a family record by becoming the sixth member of the family to play Test cricket. At Cape Town in 1892, the Hearnes had already established the record for the most members of one family to appear together in a single Test—Alec and George G. Hearne (England) and Frank Hearne (South Africa) were brothers, John Hearne (England) was their cousin.

•

In 1981 Trevor Chappell made his international debut and became the fourth member of his family to appear in a Test match, after his brothers, Ian and Greg, and their grandfather Vic Richardson. Although between them they appeared in 184 Tests and scored over 13,000 Test runs, Australia's biggest and perhaps most famous cricketing family are the Gregorys. Seven of them played for New South Wales, four for Australia.

Richard Hadlee's non-appearance, due to injury, in the one-off Test against Australia at Perth in 1989–90 broke a long-standing family record. For the first time in 43 years of Test cricket against Australia, New Zealand was without the services of one of the Hadlees, be it father Walter or sons Dayle and Richard.

•

Rachael Heyhoe Flint, the first woman to hit a six in a Test match, is married to a former first-class cricketer—Derrick Flint of Nottinghamshire. His father, B. Flint, and uncle, W.A. Flint, also played for Notts.

•

Graham Saville, who played in over 100 matches for Essex during the 1960s and '70s, is a cousin of Graham Gooch.

•

During the Oxford–Cambridge University match at Lord's in 1982, history was made when Jonathon Varey took the wicket of his twin brother David.

•

Former England captain Peter May is the son-in-law of the late England captain Harold Gilligan.

•

Jack Gregory

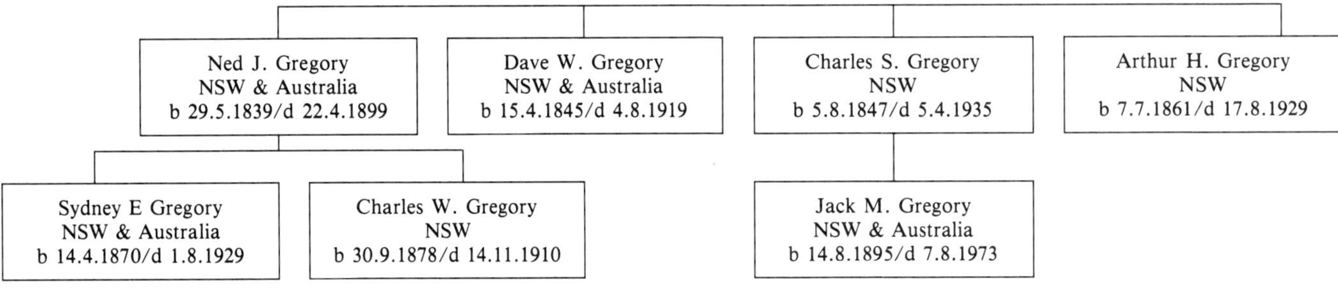

BROTHERLY LOVE

The most tests, the most runs, the most wickets and the most catches

Most Test matches—the Mohammads

	M	*I*	*NO*	*Runs*	*HS*	*100s*	*Avge*	*Wkts*	*BB*	*Avge*
Mushtaq	57	100	7	3,643	201	10	39.17	79	5-28	29.22
Hanif	55	97	8	3,915	337	12	43.98	1	1-1	95.00
Sadiq	41	74	2	2,597	166	5	35.81	0	-	-
Wazir	20	33	4	801	189	2	27.62	0	-	-
Total	173	304	21	10,956	337	29	36.64	80	5-28	62.11

Most runs and most catches—the Chappells

	M	*I*	*NO*	*Runs*	*HS*	*100s*	*Avge*	*Ct*
Greg	87	151	19	7,110	247*	24	53.86	122
Ian	75	136	10	5,345	196	14	42.42	105
Trevor	3	6	1	79	27	-	15.80	2
Total	165	293	30	12,534	247*	38	37.36	229

Most wickets—the Hadlees

	M	*Balls*	*Runs*	*W*	*BB*	*5wi*	*10wm*	*Avge*
Richard	86	21,918	9,611	431	9-52	36	9	22.29
Dayle	26	4,883	2,389	71	4-30	-	-	33.64
Total	112	26,801	12,000	502	9-52	36	9	27.96

•

Roger Prideaux—who played in three Tests in 1968—and his wife Ruth Westbrook provide the only example of a married couple playing cricket for England.

•

In 1914, when Northamptonshire played Somerset, twin brothers opened the batting for each county—an occurrence without parallel in first-class cricket. Billy Denton and his identical twin Jack opened for Northants, while Albert and Arthur Rippon went in first for Somerset.

•

Tom Lowry, New Zealand's first Test captain, had two sisters who both married cricketers, both of whom were captains—England's Percy Chapman, and Reg Bettington who captained New South Wales and Oxford University.

•

When the Australian Imperial Forces team played New South Wales at Sydney in 1919-20, two sets of brothers were included in the match, one from each family on each side. Bill Trenerry and Cyril Docker played for the AIF, while Keith Docker and Ted Trenerry represented New South Wales. In the AIF's second innings Bill Trenerry was bowled by Ted, and in the New South Wales second dig, Keith Docker was dismissed by Cyril.

Another brother in the Docker family—Phillip—played for New South Wales, as did Cyril, while two uncles—Albert and Ernest Docker—also turned out for the Blues.

•

The father-and-son combination of Frank and George Mann both captained England in all 12 Tests they played in. In 1922-23, Frank led England to a series win over South Africa, a feat also achieved by George in 1948-49.

Nelma Grout, the daughter of former Test wicket-keeper Wally Grout, is a qualified cricket umpire.

Nelma Grout

Kynaston, Charles and George Studd, who in successive years (1882/83/84) captained Cambridge University

In 1970 a former captain of Cambridge University, Peter Studd, became London's lord mayor, a post previously held by his great uncle, Kynaston Studd, who had also captained Cambridge. Kynaston was lord mayor in 1928–29, and was the brother of George and Charles Studd, both of whom played for Cambridge, Middlesex and England.

Apart from the seven Gregorys who played first-class cricket for New South Wales, five female members of the family also represented the state. In 1910 when New South Wales met Victoria, the NSW side included three sisters and two nieces. One of the sisters, Nellie Donnan, was the daughter of Ned Gregory and the wife of another Australian Test player, Harry Donnan; she later became the first president of the New South Wales Women's Cricket Association.

•

Ian Healy's brother, Ken, made his first-class debut, for Queensland, in 1990–91.

•

Grant and Andy Flower provide the only example of brothers scoring half-centuries in the same innings of a Test match in which they both made their Test debuts (Zimbabwe v India at Harare in 1992–93).

•

When Victoria played New South Wales at Melbourne in 1894–95 and dismissed them for 194 in the second innings, the Trott brothers—Harry and Albert—were involved, with either wickets, catches or run outs, in all 10 dismissals.

•

When Sussex took on Warwickshire in 1939, they included three sets of brothers in the XI—Jim and John Langridge, Charles and Jack Oakes, and James and Harry Parkes.

•

In 1875 the rather appropriately named Rowland Brotherhood made his first-class debut for Gloucestershire. He was one of eleven brothers who regularly played together as a team.

7 The One-Day Game

In 1963 Lancashire batsman Peter Marner scored the first century in a domestic limited-overs match in England. His 121, against Leicestershire at Manchester, marked the beginning of the Gillette Cup competition.

• Australia's first one-day hundred was scored by Victoria's Bill Lawry in 1972–73, against South Australia at Adelaide.

• Majid Khan has the distinction of scoring the first one-day century for Queensland and the first hundred in a one-day international for Pakistan, both in 1974.

• Dennis Amiss completed the first hundred in a one-day international—103 against Australia at Manchster in 1972.

• In the same match that Peter Marner scored his historic 121, team-mate Brian Statham took 5 for 28, the first five-wicket haul in one-day cricket.

• The first bag-of-five in Australia was achieved by Queensland's Ian King in 1969–70.

• Dennis Lillee, with 5 for 34 against Pakistan in the 1975 World Cup, was the first bowler to take five wickets in a one-day international.

• India's Kapil Dev possesses the unique record of being the first to take five wickets and the first to score a century for his country in one-day internationals—5 for 43 against Australia at Nottingham and an unbeaten 175 against Zimbabwe at Tunbridge Wells, both performances in the 1983 World Cup.

John Edrich, who scored the first half-century in one-day international cricket

	First match	*Result*	*Man of the Match*
Australia	England at Melbourne 1970–71	Australia by 5 wickets	John Edrich (82)
England	Australia at Melbourne 1970–71	Australia by 5 wickets	John Edrich (82)
New Zealand	Pakistan at Christchurch 1972–73	New Zealand by 22 runs	Mark Burgess (47) & Sarfraz Nawaz (4–64)
Pakistan	New Zealand at Christchurch 1972–73	New Zealand by 22 runs	Mark Burgess (47) & Sarfraz Nawaz (4–64)
West Indies	England at Leeds 1973	England by 1 wicket	Mike Denness (66)
India	England at Leeds 1974	England by 4 wickets	John Edrich (90)
East Africa	New Zealand at Birmingham 1975	New Zealand by 181 runs	Glenn Turner (171*)
Sri Lanka	West Indies at Manchester 1975	West Indies by 9 wickets	Bernard Julien (4–20)
Canada	Pakistan at Leeds 1979	Pakistan by 8 wickets	Sadiq Mohammad (57*)
Zimbabwe	Australia at Nottingham 1983	Zimbabwe by 13 runs	Duncan Fletcher (69* & 4–42)
Bangladesh	Pakistan at Colombo 1985-86	Pakistan by 7 wickets	Wasim Akram (4–19)
South Africa	India at Calcutta 1991-92	India by 3 wickets	Sachin Tendulkar (62) & Allan Donald (5–29)

THE FIRST CENTURIES STATE-BY-STATE IN DOMESTIC LIMITED-OVERS CRICKET

	Batsman	*Score*	*Opposition*	*Venue*	*Season*
Victoria	Bill Lawry	108*	South Australia	Adelaide	1972–73
Queensland	Majid Khan	115	South Australia	Adelaide	1973–74
New South Wales	Ron Crippin	112	Western Australia	Sydney	1973–74
South Australia	Rick Darling	101*	Tasmania	Hobart	1977–78
Western Australia	Graeme Wood	108*	Tasmania	Perth	1977–78
Tasmania	Gary Goodman	100	Queensland	Brisbane	1978–79

THE FIRST FIVE-WICKET HAULS STATE-BY-STATE IN DOMESTIC LIMITED-OVERS CRICKET

	Bowler	*Analysis*	*Opposition*	*Venue*	*Season*
Queensland	Ian King	5–33	New South Wales	Sydney	1969–70
Victoria	Graeme Watson	5–20	Western Australia	Melbourne	1969–70
New South Wales	Len Pascoe	5–28	Western Australia	Sydney	1979–80
Western Australia	David Boyd	5–15	Victoria	Perth	1982–83
South Australia	Rod McCurdy	5–23	Western Australia	Adelaide	1984–85
Tasmania	Mark Hill	5–29	Queensland	Brisbane	1985–86
FIRST TO TAKE SIX WICKETS					
	Jeff Thomson (Q)	6–18	South Australia	Brisbane	1978–79
FIRST TO TAKE SEVEN WICKETS					
	Carl Rackemann (Q)	7–34	South Australia	Adelaide	1988–89

•

The scorecard for the first-ever one-day international, between Australia and England at Melbourne in 1970–71:

ENGLAND

G. Boycott	c Lawry b Thomson	8
J.H. Edrich	c Walters b Mallett	82
K.W.R. Fletcher	c G.S. Chappell b Mallett	24
B.L. D'Oliveira	run out	17
J.H. Hampshire	c McKenzie b Mallett	10
M.C. Cowdrey	c Marsh b Stackpole	1
R. Illingworth	b Stackpole	1
A.P.E. Knott	b McKenzie	24
J.A. Snow	b Stackpole	2
K. Shuttleworth	c Redpath b McKenzie	7
P. Lever	not out	4
Extras	(b1, lb 9)	10
	(39.4 overs)	190

1/21 2/37 3/124 4/144 5/148 6/152 7/156 8/171 9/183

Australia	*O*	*M*	*R*	*W*
McKenzie	7.4	0	22	2
Thomson	8	2	22	1
Connolly	8	0	62	0
Mallett	8	1	34	3
Stackpole	8	0	40	3

AUSTRALIA

W.M. Lawry	c Knott b Illingworth	27
K.R. Stackpole	c and b Shuttleworth	13
I.M. Chappell	st Knott b Illingworth	60
K.D. Walters	c Knott b D'Oliveira	41
I.R. Redpath	b Illingworth	12
G.S. Chappell	not out	22
R.W. Marsh	not out	10
A.A. Mallett		
G.D. McKenzie		
A.N. Connolly		
A.L. Thomson		
Extras	(lb 4, w 1, nb 1)	6
	(5 wkts, 34.6 overs)	191

1/19 2/51 3/117 4/158 5/165

England	*O*	*M*	*R*	*W*
Snow	8	0	38	0
Shuttleworth	7	0	29	1
Lever	5.6	0	30	0
Illingworth	8	1	50	3
D'Oliveira	6	1	38	1

•

In World Series Cup matches, New Zealand all-rounder Lance Cairns had a career batting strike-rate of 112.94.

•

In 1981–82, the New South Wales opening pair of Rick McCosker and John Dyson opened the batting for the Blues in three McDonald's Cup matches, and each time recorded a century partnership:

169	McCosker 111* & Dyson 78	v Victoria at Sydney
253	McCosker 164 & Dyson 100	v South Australia at Sydney
118	McCosker 67 & Dyson 101	v Western Australia at Perth

•

When Western Australia beat Tasmania at Perth in 1991–92, they provided the first instance of a 10-wicket victory in the history of domestic one-day cricket in Australia. Dismissing the visitors for just 121, Geoff Marsh (44*) and Tom Moody (69*) knocked off the required number of runs in an unbeaten first-wicket stand of 125. This was the fourth 100-run opening partnership involving Geoff Marsh in five consecutive FAI Cup matches, following three the previous season with Mark McPhee:

125	Marsh 110 & McPhee 59	v South Australia	Perth 1990–91
71	Marsh 53 & McPhee 41	v Victoria	Perth 1990–91
171	Marsh 82 & McPhee 89*	v South Australia	Perth 1990–91
114	Marsh 91* & McPhee 58	v New South Wales	Perth 1990–91
125*	Marsh 44* & Moody 69*	v Tasmania	Perth 1991–92

•

During the 1989 Nehru Cup tournament, India's Mohinder Amarnath became only the second player in a one-day international to be dismissed 'obstructing the field'. In 1985–86 Amarnath made history when he was given out 'handled the ball' in a World Series Cup match against Australia in Melbourne.

•

When Tony Dodemaide made his one-day international debut in 1987–88, his haul of 5 for 21 against Sri Lanka at Perth was the best return by a bowler in his first match. He was the 10th bowler to take four wickets on debut, and only the second to take five, after Sri Lanka's Uvaisul Karnain (5–26 v New Zealand at Moratuwa in 1983–84).

•

When Australia made 3 for 332 against Sri Lanka at Sharjah in 1990, Simon O'Donnell hit 74 off only 29 balls. His 50 came off just 18 balls, the fastest one-day half-century on record.

•

Roy Dias

Sri Lanka's Roy Dias was the first batsman to score back-to-back hundreds in one-day internationals—102 and 121 against India in 1982–83.

•

In 1980–81 Greg Chappell became the first batsman to score 500 runs in a season in the World Series Cup. In 14 matches he made 686 runs, with a top score of 138 not out against New Zealand at Sydney.

•

The 1984–85 season saw a record three batsmen top the 500-run mark in World Series Cup matches—Viv Richards (651), Allan Border (590) and Desmond Haynes (513).

•

The first three centuries by Dean Jones in one-day internationals were all scored within the space of 18 days in 1986–87:

104 v England at Perth	scored on successive days
121 v Pakistan at Perth	
101 v England at Brisbane	

Jones had to wait another three years before he made his fourth hundred, 107 against New Zealand at Christchurch in 1989–90, and just one week for his fifth—102* v New Zealand at Auckland.

•

On the 1989 England tour, Australia made 300-plus in three of its first four one-day matches:

3-326 (55 overs) v League Cricket Conference at Birmingham
6-314 (50 overs) v Lavinia, Duchess of Norfolk's XI at Arundel
4-309 (55 overs) v MCC at Lord's

David Boon and Geoff Marsh began with a partnership of 277 in the match against the MCC, a record opening stand in limited-overs cricket.

In 1986 Australia's opening pair of Geoff Marsh and David Boon compiled five half-century partnerships in six successive one-day internationals against India. The sequence contained three stands in excess of 100 and included a new record in one-day international cricket of 212, at Jaipur:

MARSH AND BOON OPENING STANDS VERSUS INDIA IN 1986

Stand	*Marsh*	*Boon*	*Venue*	*Season*
152	125	83	Sydney	1985–86
50	25	27	Adelaide	1985–86
146	74	76	Melbourne	1985–86
69	36	50	Sydney	1985–86
51	9	44	Melbourne	1985–86
212	104	111	Jaipur	1986–87

•

In the 1987 World Cup, the Indian batsman Navjot Sidhu scored four consecutive half-centuries in what were his first innings in one-day international cricket. He began with 73 on debut against Australia and finished the series with 254 runs at 63.50.

•

New Zealand all-rounder Shane Thomson marked his one-day international debut against India at Dunedin in 1990 by taking 3 for 19 off six overs, including the wicket of Mohammad Azharuddin with his first ball.

•

Kepler Wessels, Wayne Phillips and Rod McCurdy were all run out in the Australia–West Indies clash at Adelaide in 1984–85. Graeme Wood, sometimes referred to as 'the Kamikaze Kid', was involved in all three.

•

During the 1986 ICC Trophy, Papua New-Guinea produced some tall totals, passing 350 on three occasions. At Cannock they established an ICC record of 9 for 455 against Gibraltar, who were dismissed for a mere 86.

•

India's Chetan Charma was the first player to score a century and take a hat-trick in one-day international cricket. In 1987 he became the first bowler to take three-in-three in the World Cup, against New Zealand at Nagpur. He made an unbeaten century (101*) against England in 1989 to complete a memorable double.

•

In a one-day festival match at Jesmond in 1990, Gordon Greenidge, captaining a World XI side, took the wickets of Bruce French and Tim Munton of the England XI with his only two deliveries (0.2–0–0–2).

•

In the five-match series against Pakistan in 1988–89, Andrew Jones was the leading run-getter on either side, hitting a half-century in each game—55* at Dunedin, 62* at Christchurch, 67 at Wellington, 82 at Auckland and 63* at Hamilton. His half-century at Hamilton was his 15th in 28 one-day internationals and his sixth in succession.

•

In 1983–84, Desmond Haynes hit three centuries, all unbeaten in the four-match series against Australia—133* at Berbice, 102* at Castries and 104* at Kingston. His series average was 340.00.

•

When the West Indies lost to Australia at Kingston in 1991, it was their first defeat at home in a one-day international since 1985–86 when England secured a win at Port-of-Spain. In between the two losses, the West Indies enjoyed 16 successive victories with two 5–0 series wins, over Pakistan in 1987–88, and against India in 1988–89. Australia's 4–1 victory in 1990–91 was the West Indies' first-ever series loss on home soil in one-day internationals.

•

Worcestershire, the winners of the 1987 Sunday League, were helped immeasurably in their cause by its opening pair of Tim Curtis and Ian Botham, who struck a record four century partnerships in their last four matches.

104	Curtis 86 & Botham 57	v Glamorgan at Swansea
119	Curtis 68 & Botham 56	v Yorkshire at Worcester
159	Curtis 47* & Botham 80	v Surrey at Hereford
172	Curtis 69* & Botham 61	v Northamptonshire at Worcester

•

During the 1986 Sunday League, Gordon Greenidge, playing for Hampshire, became the first batsman to register 10 centuries—he also became the first to appear in 100 successive innings in the competition without being dismissed without scoring.

Gordon Greenidge

Adrian Kuiper

South African batsman Adrian Kuiper hit a blistering century (117) off just 49 balls against England in an unofficial one-day match at Bloemfontein in 1989–90. His innings included eight sixes and eight fours.

•

West Indies batsman Phil Simmons turned out to be a surprise package with the ball during the 1992–93 World Series Cup, taking seven wickets for just 14 runs in consecutive appearances at the SCG. In one match, against Pakistan, he captured 4 for 3 off 10 overs with eight maidens, the most economical bowling performance on record in one-day internationals. His seamers demolished Pakistan, reducing them to 1 for 2, 2 for 4, 3 for 9, 4 for 9 and 5 for 14, a record low score for the fall of the fifth wicket in one-day international cricket. Quite remarkably, though, Pakistan then broke that record in its next World Series match, again against West Indies at Brisbane, by losing its fifth wicket with the score on just 12. Pakistan was dismissed for 71 in 23.4 overs, at the time the shortest completed innings on record in one-day international competition. It was just a few weeks later that Pakistan broke that record as well. Playing against the West Indies in a triangular series in South Africa, the World Cup holders set a new record low, being bowled out for 43 in 19.5 overs. The previous lowest run total was 45, set by Canada against England in a 1979 World Cup match at Manchester. On a treacherous Cape Town pitch, they lost their fourth, fifth and sixth wickets with the score on 14 and saw their ninth depart on 26. Six of the Pakistan batsmen made ducks, including Ramiz Raja, who was out to the first ball of the match. When the West Indies came in to bat, one of their openers, Desmond Haynes, also went to the first ball of the innings, and at one stage found themselves in a similar position to that of Pakistan's, stumbling to three wickets down for 11.

•

When Pakistan made 3 for 315, and Sri Lanka replied with 8 for 288 at Adelaide in 1989–90, it was the first time 600 runs had been scored in a single 50-overs-a-side one-day international. Prior to this game, Sri Lanka had been involved in another three matches which also realised over 600 runs.

626–14	(120 overs)	Pakistan & Sri Lanka at Swansea in 1983
619–19	(118 overs)	England & Sri Lanka at Taunton in 1983
604–9	(120 overs)	Australia & Sri Lanka at The Oval in 1975

•

Sri Lanka was involved in another run-feast during the 1992 World Cup. Chasing Zimbabwe's 312 at New Plymouth, they made 314 with four balls to spare. This was the first time in one-day international cricket that any country had scored 300 batting second to win a match.

•

When Sri Lanka went down by 114 runs at Sharjah in 1990, it completed, for the first time, a run of 10 successive one-day international victories for Australia. Five different countries contributed to the success, with New Zealand the victims four times.

New Zealand seam bowler Martin Snedden opened the bowling and the batting in three World Cup matches in 1987 and each time contributed to a 50-run first wicket partnership —59 v Zimbabwe at Hyderabad, 67 v India at Bangalore and 72 v Australia at Chandigarh.

•

In successive seasons the West Indies established new records in the World Series Cup for the fastest team 50 and the slowest. Batting against Pakistan at Melbourne in 1983–84, the West Indies were reduced at one stage to 4 for 10 and took 25.3 overs to reach 50, and 39.5 overs for 100, which was also a new record. They avenged that effort next season by humiliating Sri Lanka at Adelaide—openers Gordon Greenidge (110*) and Desmond Haynes (51) made 50 in just 6.3 overs and forged a partnership of 133 in 22.

•

During the World Series Cup match against the West Indies at Brisbane in 1984–85, Australia suffered four run outs—three of which were effected by Clive Lloyd.

•

With a stand of 204 against Sri Lanka in the final of the 1992–93 Sharjah Trophy, the Pakistani pair of Saeed Anwar (110) and Ramiz Raja (109*) became the first openers to record two double-century first-wicket partnerships in one-day internationals. In their earlier stand—of 202, also against Sri Lanka, at Adelaide in 1989-90—Ramiz scored 107 not out and Saeed 126.

•

Score	*Opposition and total*	*Venue*	*Series*	*Victory margin*
3–163	Pakistan (162)	Melbourne 1989–90	World Series Cup	7 wickets
6–255	Pakistan (186)	Sydney 1989–90	World Series Cup	69 runs
9–187	India (169)	Christchurch 1989–90	Rothman's Cup	18 runs
8–244	New Zealand (94)	Christchurch 1989–90	Rothman's Cup	150 runs
3–212	India (8–211)	Hamilton 1989–90	Rothman's Cup	7 wickets
6–239	New Zealand (2–167)	Auckland 1989–90	Rothman's Cup	Faster scoring rate
2–164	New Zealand (162)	Auckland 1989–90	Rothman's Cup	8 wickets
5–258	New Zealand (7–195)	Sharjah 1990	Australasia Cup	63 runs
3–140	Bangladesh (8–134)	Sharjah 1990	Australasia Cup	7 wickets
3–332	Sri Lanka (218)	Sharjah 1990	Australasia Cup	114 runs

Australia's best sequence of wins prior to 1990 was nine in a row, against New Zealand, Sri Lanka and England, at home in 1987–88.

•

New Zealand batsman Bev Congdon and Indian all-rounder Ravi Shastri share the misfortune of recording one of the worst bowling stints in one-day international cricket. Both bowlers conceded 11 runs per over with identical figures:

Bev Congdon	7–0–77–1	New Zealand v Australia	Christchurch	1973–74
Ravi Shastri	7–0–77–1	India v West Indies	Jamshedpur	1983–84

•

Australia lost its first three matches to the West Indies in the 1983–84 World Series Cup by margins which were nearly identical—27 runs, 28 runs and 26 runs.

•

When Graham Gooch hit 129 not out at Port-of-Spain in 1985–86, he became only the second batsman to reach three figures since one-day internationals came to the Caribbean in 1976–77. Desmond Haynes was the only other batsman to score a century, recording six of them between 1977–78 and 1984–85:

148	v Australia	St John's	1977–78
133*	v Australia	Berbice	1983–84
102*	v Australia	Castries	1983–84
104*	v Australia	Kingston	1983–84
146*	v New Zealand	Berbice	1984–85
116	v New Zealand	Bridgetown	1984–85

The next highest score in the West Indies before Gooch's century was also achieved by Haynes—97 v India at Port-of-Spain in 1982–83.

•

Waqar Younis

In 1990 Pakistan's Waqar Younis dominated the headlines with a string of outstanding bowling performances in one-day internationals. Within the space of eight matches he collected over 30 wickets, including 17 at 7.41 in the Australasia Cup in Sharjah—4-42 v India, 6-26 v Sri Lanka, 5-20 v New Zealand and 2-38 v Australia.

Hauls of five wickets in two successive matches and his aggregate of 17 gained him the Man of the Series award. A few months later he went one better, becoming the first bowler to take five wickets in three successive one-day internationals:

5-11 v New Zealand at Peshawar 1990-91
5-16 v New Zealand at Sialkot 1990-91
5-52 v West Indies at Lahore 1990-91

•

Two batsmen promoted to the relatively unfamiliar role of opener hit rich form in the early part of 1993—the West Indies' Brian Lara scored a phenomenal 523 runs at 174.33 in six successive matches in two series over a period of six weeks—128 v Pakistan at Durban, 111* v South Africa at Bloemfontein, 26* v Pakistan at Cape Town, 49 v Pakistan at Johannesburg, 114 v Pakistan at Kingston and 95* v Pakistan at Port-of-Spain. Mark Waugh, opening for the first time in his career, was Australia's leading batsman in the five-match series against New Zealand, hitting three half-centuries and a maiden one-day international hundred—60, 57, 0, 108 and 83.

•

Due to the weather, the second Prudential Trophy match between England and India at The Oval in 1974 was extended to include play the following day. This was the first one-day international to become a 'two-day international'.

•

When Warwickshire made 5 for 392 against Oxfordshire in the 1984 NatWest Bank Trophy, two of the opposition bowlers conceded over 100 runs—Derek Gallop 12-0-106-2 and Simon Porter 12-0-105-1. Warwickshire's total was a record for the competition and was a personal triumph for Alvin Kallicharran who, with 206, became the first batsman to score a double century in a one-day match in England. Named Man of the Match, Kallicharran was also the chief wicket-taker, snaring 6 for 32 in Oxfordshire's total of 8 for 165.

•

In September 1985 the Essex opening pair of Graham Gooch and Brian Hardie put on two double-century first wicket stands, on successive days and against Nottinghamshire on each occasion:

202	G.A. Gooch (91) & B.R. Hardie (110)	Lord's
239	G.A. Gooch (171) & B.R. Hardie (60)	Manchester

Their stand of 202 came in the final of the NatWest Bank Trophy, while the following day's effort was a record for the first wicket in the Sunday League.

•

Two batsmen scored in excess of 400 runs in the World Series Cup of 1987-88—Dean Jones made 461 runs at an average of 57.62, while New Zealand's Andrew Jones hit 416 runs at 52.00. Both of them scored five fifties.

Andrew Jones

Imran Khan

Despite a record Pakistani bowling performance of 6 for 14 by Imran Khan at Sharjah in 1985, his side still lost the match by 38 runs. After confining India to a total of only 125, Pakistan collapsed to be all out for 87.

•

When the West Indies played India at Jamshedpur in 1983-84, seven of its batsmen could not manage a score higher than 5—Desmond Haynes 1, Clive Lloyd 3, Eldine Baptiste 1, Malcolm Marshall 5, Andy Roberts 1*, Roger Harper 0 and Michael Holding 0*. Even so, they compiled their then highest score in one-day internationals—8 for 333—thanks to centuries from Gordon Greenidge (115) and Viv Richards (149).

•

In a low-scoring affair at Arnos Vale in 1980-81, nine West Indians and eight of England's batsmen failed to reach double-figures—Faoud Bacchus 1, Alvin Kallicharran 2, Clive Lloyd 2, Larry Gomes 8, David Murray 1, Andy Roberts 2, Joel Garner 4, Michael Holding 1, Colin Croft 2*, Geoff Boycott 2, Peter Willey 0, Roland Butcher 1, Mike Gatting 3, David Bairstow 5, John Emburey 5, Graham Stevenson 6* and Chris Old 1.

•

Allan Lamb was run out in three consecutive innings during the 1986-87 World Series Cup, a misfortune experienced by Dean Jones in the 1989-90 series and by Mark Waugh in 1992-93.

•

In the 1974 John Player League, Yorkshire bowled out Middlesex at Leeds for a record low score of 23 in 19.4 overs. No batsman reached double figures, five of them made ducks.

•

During the one-day series against South Africa in 1986-87, Australia recorded one of the most inexplicable batting collapses ever seen in international cricket. In the first match at Port Elizabeth, Australia was cruising at 2 for 298 in reply to the South African total of 6 for 316 off 50 overs. Needing only 19 runs for victory off 3.2 overs, they lost their last eight wickets for 12 runs in 19 deliveries and lost the match by six runs.

•

Kris Srikkanth was the first Indian to twice take five wickets in a one-day international, securing both hauls in the same series, against New Zealand in 1988-89—5-27 at Visakhapatnam and 5-32 at Indore. In the first game, when opening the batting, he scored 70 and became only the second player, after Viv Richards, to record a half-century and five wickets in the same match.

•

A high-scoring match at Hyberabad in 1991-92 saw Pakistan reach a total of 241 off 40 overs. In reply, Sri Lanka could only manage 182, having got off to a flying start with 70 runs off the first 10 overs.

•

Glenn Bishop hit 31 sixes in a score of 246 in a limited-overs match for South Australia against a Malaysian Cricket Association XI in Kuala Lumpur in 1991. His team amassed 8 for 528 off 50 overs and then won the match by 426 runs, dismissing the Malaysian XI for 102.

Glenn Bishop

When Kepler Wessels made his international debut for South Africa against India at Calcutta in 1991, he became the first player to have represented two countries in one-day international cricket, following 54 matches for Australia in the 1980s. His innings of 50 in South Africa's total of 8 for 177 backed up his half-century (79) on his Australian debut, against New Zealand at Melbourne in 1982–83. Wessels was named the South African player of the series, top-scoring in each of the three matches with consecutive half-centuries—50, 71 and 90.

•

Pakistan stalwarts Imran Khan and Javed Miandad are the only two players to have appeared in the first five World Cups. During the 1992 tournament, Javed became the highest run-scorer in the Cup with 1,029, while Imran became the first all-rounder to achieve the double of 600 runs and 30 wickets.

•

The Australia–England one-day international at Sharjah in 1985, was the first match between the two countries played on neutral ground.

•

Brian Langford, an off-spinner who played for Somerset, gave nothing away in a John Player League match in 1969, returning figures of 8–8–0–0 against Essex at Yeovil.

•

Although Sunil Gavaskar scored 34 centuries in Test cricket, he made only one in 107 one-day internationals. His hundred off 85 balls came in his penultimate match, against New Zealand at Nagpur in the 1987 World Cup, and included three sixes and 10 fours. This was in stark contrast to an innings he played in India's inaugural World Cup match, against England at Lord's in 1975, when he batted throughout the entire 60 overs scoring a mere 36 not out.

•

Pakistan's Aaqib Javed made history in 1991, when he took a world record haul of 7 for 37 against India in the final of the Sharjah Cup. His figures bettered Winston Davis' 7 for 51 against Australia in the 1983 World Cup, and included an all-lbw hat-trick, the first of its kind in one-day internationals. His hat-trick was also the first not to include middle or lower-order batsmen, his victims being Ravi Shastri (15), Mohammad Azharuddin (0) and Sachin Tendulkar (0).

•

After winning its first-ever one-day international, against Australia in 1983, Zimbabwe then lost its next 18 matches, all of them in the World Cup—five in 1983, six in 1987 and seven in 1992.

•

When the West Indies and Pakistan met in the World Series Cup at Brisbane in 1988–89, the match produced a world-record 90 extras. Pakistan's total of 7 for 258 was boosted by 59 extras, which included 37 wides.

•

Although not recognised as an official one-day international, the South Africa–West Indies match at Durban in 1982–83 contained a remarkable spell of bowling by Franklyn Stephenson returning figures of 6 for 9 off 6.5 overs. In the previous match, at Johannesburg, Rupert Hanley took a hat-trick on his South African debut.

Franklyn Stephenson

•

Dean Jones hit exactly 300 runs at an average of 100.00 in the three-nation Rothman's Cup tournament in New Zealand in 1990.

•

During the first six months of 1983, New Zealand bowler Martin Snedden appeared in nine one-day internationals against England—in four of them, he conceded over 50 runs, including a world record return of 2 for 105 at The Oval.

•

Although Australia won its first one-day international against Sri Lanka, by 52 runs at The Oval in 1975, it lost its first series, with two defeats and two matches abandoned in 1982–83.

•

During the calendar year of 1990, Pakistan won 10 consecutive one-day internationals—four, against various countries, in the Australasia Cup, three against New Zealand and three against the West Indies.

•

Of the first five hat-tricks in one-day internationals, two were achieved by Pakistan's Wasim Akram at Sharjah in 1989–90. The first came against the West Indies in the Sharjah Champion's Trophy, the second against Australia in the final of the Australasia Cup—a match in which he also contributed 49 with the bat.

•

During an Australia Day carnival at Chinchilla in Queensland in 1991–92, the local Colts cricket team scored a mammoth 600 runs, for the loss of four wickets, off 55 overs against Jandowae. Sean Slinger, a schoolteacher, and farmer Ken Young both hit double centuries in a second wicket partnership of 359. Another Queensland cricket team, the Gold Coast Dolphins, hit the big time the following season, when its teenage opening pair, Andrew Symons (220*) and Matthew Mott (208*) put on an unbeaten world record stand of 446 in a 50-overs match against Souths.

•

Greg Matthews is responsible for two of Australia's worst bowling performances in one-day internationals. In 1986–87 he conceded over 10 runs per over in a match in New Delhi, and nearly nine runs per over against the West Indies at Sydney in 1988–89:

5-0-54-0 v India 1986-87	(10.80 runs per over)
7-0-62-0 v West Indies 1988-89	(8.86 runs per over)

•

For four consecutive seasons Dean Jones was the leading batsman in the World Series Cup, each time scoring 400 runs at an average of over 50. His record run in the competition ended in 1991–92, when he could muster only 196 runs in nine matches. The world's leading one-day batsman even suffered the extreme misfortune of being dropped for one of the matches against India.

Season	*M*	*I*	*NO*	*Runs*	*HS*	*100s*	*50s*	*Avge*
1987-88	10	10	2	461	92	0	5	57.62
1988-89	10	10	2	404	93*	0	3	50.50
1989-90	10	9	3	461	85*	0	5	76.83
1990-91	10	10	1	513	145	1	3	57.00

•

Gary Gilmour marked Australia's berth in the finals of the 1975 World Cup by obtaining two five-wicket hauls in consecutive matches—6-14 v England at Leeds at 5-48 v the West Indies at Lord's. Although he played only twice, Gilmour took the most wickets (11) and topped the bowling averages (5.64). Another Australian bowler, Graeme Porter headed the averages in the next World Cup, in 1979. Porter took three wickets at 11.00 in his only two appearances in one-day internationals.

•

On his way to the milestone of 2,000 runs in one-day internationals, Kepler Wessels scored five fifties in succession, the first of which came seven years before the fifth:

57	Australia v England	Birmingham 1985
50	South Africa v India	Calcutta 1991
71	South Africa v India	Gwalior 1991
90	South Africa v India	Delhi 1991
81*	South Africa v Australia	Sydney 1991-92

•

During a seven-month period in 1987 Javed Miandad hit nine consecutive half-centuries in one-day internationals:

78	v India at Nagpur
78*	v India at Jamshedpur
74*	v Australia at Sharjah
60	v England at Sharjah
52*	v India at Sharjah
113	v England at The Oval
71*	v England at Nottingham
68	v England at Birmingham
103	v Sri Lanka at Hyderabad

•

During the 1982–83 World Series Cup, David Gower hit three centuries in four matches against New Zealand—122 at Melbourne, 158 at Brisbane and 109 at Adelaide. His aggregate for the series against the Kiwis was 424 runs in five matches at an average of 106.00.

•

David Gower

Wasim Akram

Although Wasim Akram was the most effective bowler in the 1992 World Cup with 18 wickets, he was also the most wayward, recording the most wides (48) and the most no-balls (22).

•

South Africa's Peter Kirsten suffered a double blow during a one-day international against India at Port Elizabeth in 1992–93, firstly being run out by Kapil Dev when he backed up too far, and then being fined half his match fee for using offensive language.

•

At Sharjah in 1986, Courtney Walsh recorded the amazing analysis of 4.3–3–1–5 against Sri Lanka.

•

As many as three batsmen made 400 runs in the 1987 World Cup—two of them were Australia's opening pair of David Boon (447 at 55.88) and Geoff Marsh (428 at 61.14). The other batsman to reach the target was Graham Gooch (471 at 58.88).

8 The Don

Don Bradman was responsible for almost a quarter (24.35%) of Australia's total runs in Test matches during his 52-match career.

•

It took Bradman only 126 innings to reach the milestone of 10,000 runs in first-class cricket. By way of comparison, W.G. Grace needed 188, Vijay Merchant 171, Bill Ponsford 161 and Barry Richards 200.

•

The highest aggregate by Bradman in a single first-class match was 455—3 & 452* for New South Wales v Queensland at Sydney in 1929-30.

•

Bradman was never dismissed in the nineties in Test cricket. Every time he reached 90, he went on to score a century, his highest double-figure innings in a Test match being 89 at Lord's in 1948.

•

During the 1934 Test series against England, Bradman scored consecutive double centuries—304 and 244—and reached the coveted series mark of 500 runs in the two innings. With 77 in his next outing, he made a staggering 625 runs at an average of 208.33. Only a few of the world's best batsmen have ever made 500 runs in three Test innings—Bradman did it four times:

500 RUNS IN THREE TEST INNINGS	
254, 1, 334	589 runs v England 1930
304, 244, 77	625 runs v England 1934
270, 26, 212	508 runs v England 1936-37
187, 234, 79	500 runs v England 1946-47

•

Until Bradman came along, the feat of a batsman scoring more runs in a single innings than the entire opposition in either innings was fairly rare in Test cricket. Prior to his Test debut, nine batsmen had done so—Bradman went on to achieve the feat five times between 1931 and 1947:

223 v West Indies (193 & 148)	Brisbane 1930-31
152 v West Indies (99 & 107)	Melbourne 1930-31
226 v South Africa (170 & 117)	Brisbane 1931-32
187 v England (141 & 172)	Brisbane 1946-47
185 v India (58 & 98)	Brisbane 1947-48

•

In 1931-32, Bradman achieved a double-century average in the Test series against South Africa—201.50—and a century average (116.91) in all first-class matches for the season—the first time such a double had been recorded by any batsman in first-class cricket.

•

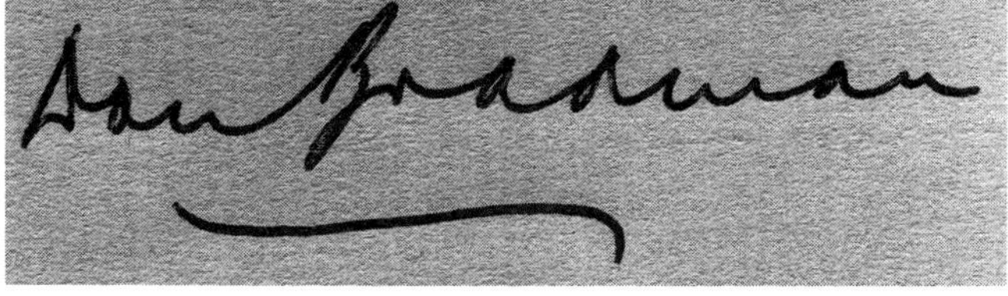

Bradman scored over 1,000 runs in a season in Australia on nine successive occasions, and 12 times in all—both are records.

1,000 RUNS IN AN AUSTRALIAN SEASON BY DON BRADMAN

Season	*I*	*NO*	*Runs*	*HS*	*100s*	*Avge*
1928–29	24	6	1,690	340*	7	93.88
1929–30	16	2	1,586	452*	5	113.28
1930–31	18	0	1,422	258	5	79.00
1931–32	13	1	1,403	299*	7	116.91
1932–33	21	2	1,171	238	3	61.63
1933–34	11	2	1,192	253	5	132.44
1935–36	9	0	1,173	369	4	130.33
1936–37	19	1	1,552	270	6	86.22
1937–38	18	2	1,437	246	7	89.81
1939–40	15	3	1,475	267	5	122.91
1946–47	14	1	1,032	234	4	79.38
1947–48	12	2	1,296	201	8	129.60

•

Although he was out for a duck in his last Test innings in 1948, the Don did manage to score a century in his last three first-class innings on English soil:

150 v Gentlemen of England at Lord's
143 v South of England at Hastings
153 v H.D.G. Leveson Gower's XI at Scarborough

•

When Bradman scored 138 at Adelaide in 1939–40 it was his fifth hundred in successive innings against Queensland, a record sequence in Australian first-class cricket against a single state.

•

After starting with a duck in his initial first-class appearance against Queensland, Bradman went on to score 13 centuries in just 18 matches. Eleven of the hundreds came in the space of 14 innings, and included three successive double centuries—452*, 0, 200, 253, 233, 31, 123, 246, 39*, 107, 113, 225, 186 and 138.

•

In 1936–37, Bradman hit two double centuries in successive innings for the fourth time in his career, beating the previous record of three by Walter Hammond:

DOUBLE CENTURIES IN SUCCESSIVE INNINGS

226 & 219 for New South Wales in 1931–32
304 & 244 for Australia in 1934
233 & 357 for South Australia in 1935–36
369 & 212 for South Australia in 1936–37

•

In Sheffield Shield cricket, Bradman's record was supreme, recording a century average for both New South Wales and South Australia:

	M	*I*	*NO*	*Runs*	*HS*	*100s*	*Avge*
NSW	31	52	9	4,633	452*	17	107.74
SA	31	44	6	4,293	357	19	112.97
All Shield	62	96	15	8,926	452*	36	110.10

•

Bradman had a batting average of over 50 against all his opponents in Test cricket. His highest average was 201.50 against South Africa, his lowest 74.50 against the West Indies. In domestic first-class cricket he had an average exceeding 50 against all states, while in England his record extended to 14 of the 17 counties and six other first-class teams he opposed on his four overseas tours.

D.G. BRADMAN—MAJOR TEAMS AGAINST WHICH HIS AVERAGE EXCEEDED 50

Opponents	*M*	*I*	*NO*	*Runs*	*HS*	*100s*	*50s*	*Avge*
England	37	63	7	5,028	334	19	12	89.78
West Indies	5	6	0	447	223	2	0	74.50
South Africa	5	5	1	806	299*	4	0	201.50
India	5	6	2	715	201	4	1	178.75
South Australia	11	20	0	1,269	258	4	6	63.45
Victoria	27	41	6	3,648	357	14	9	104.22
Queensland	17	25	4	2,957	452*	13	4	140.81
Tasmania	5	5	0	751	369	3	1	150.20
Western Australia	6	7	1	731	209*	5	0	121.83
New South Wales	10	16	5	1,205	251*	5	3	109.54
Worcestershire	4	4	0	807	258	4	0	201.75
Leicestershire	3	3	1	331	185*	1	2	165.50
Yorkshire	5	7	0	460	140	1	4	65.71
Lancashire	5	10	4	446	133*	2	0	74.33
Derbyshire	3	4	1	183	71	0	2	61.00
Surrey	7	8	2	839	252*	4	2	139.83
Hampshire	3	3	1	336	191	2	0	168.00
Middlesex	4	6	1	254	160	1	0	50.80
Somerset	3	3	0	336	201	2	0	112.00
Kent	3	4	1	355	205*	1	2	118.33
Essex	2	2	0	206	187	1	0	103.00
Warwickshire	2	3	1	179	135	1	0	89.50
Nottinghamshire	2	3	0	286	144	1	2	95.33
Sussex	1	1	0	109	109	1	0	109.00

•

Bradman's average in Test cricket was 99.94. In first-class cricket it was 95.14. For first-class matches in Australia his average was 94.45, in England it was 96.44.

•

In 18 seasons of first-class cricket in Australia, only twice did Bradman fail to record an average of over 50; on eight occasions his average exceeded 100:

		M	*I*	*NO*	*Runs*	*HS*	*100s*	*Avge*
1929–30	NSW	11	16	2	1,586	452*	5	113.28
1931–32	NSW	10	13	1	1,403	299*	7	116.91
1933–34	NSW	7	11	2	1,192	253	5	132.44
1935–36	SA	8	9	0	1,173	369	4	130.33
1938–39	SA	7	7	1	919	225	6	153.16
1939–40	SA	9	15	3	1,475	267	5	122.91
1945–46	SA	2	3	1	232	112	1	116.00
1947–48	SA	9	12	2	1,296	201	8	129.60

•

In 1929–30, Bradman achieved an average of over 100 at all levels of cricket:

	I	*NO*	*Runs*	*HS*	*Avge*
Sheffield Shield	10	2	894	452*	111.75
Other first-class	6	0	692	225	115.33
All first-class	16	2	1,586	452*	113.28
First grade	7	2	549	187	109.80
Second-class	28	8	2,073	228*	103.65

•

•

N.S.W. XI v ENGLAND A

Bradman Oval, Bowral NSW
January 31 1993

Illustration : Frank Reynolds

Hours of Play

10.30am - 2 pm, First Innings
2 pm - 2.30 pm, Lunch
230 pm - 6.00 pm, Second Innings

$1.00

The New South Wales town of Bowral houses the Bradman Museum and the Bradman Oval. The ground has staged several important matches since its redevelopment, including a 1992 World Cup warm-up match between a Bradman XI and South Africa, and a New South Wales XI v England A in 1993.

•

Although he failed to impress on his Test debut, Bradman scored a century on his first-grade debut, his first-class debut, in his first international match, in his first first-class match overseas, in his first Test overseas, and in his first Sheffield Shield match for South Australia. He also scored a century in his first Test against the West Indies and India.

In a career which spanned three decades Bradman crammed his best performances with both bat and ball into a single 12-month period. He made his highest score and produced his best bowling performances in both first-class and Test cricket during the calendar year of 1930:

Highest Score			
First-Class	452*	N.S.W. v Queensland	Sydney 1929-30
Test	334	Australia v England	Leeds 1930
Best Bowling			
First-Class	3-35	Australians v Cambridge University	Fenner's 1930
Test	1-8	Australia v West Indies	Adelaide 1930-31

•

During his record-breaking knock of 270 against England at the MCG in 1936-37, Bradman became the first batsman to score 1,000 Test runs on one ground. He got there in just 11 innings and hit five hundreds along the way. He was also the first to register 1,500 runs on one ground—1,671 in 17 innings with nine centuries at Melbourne.

Bradman only played Test cricket on 10 grounds around the world, scoring 500 or more runs on eight of them, including 963 at an average of 192.60 at Headingley. He averaged over 100 runs per innings at five venues, and scored a double century at the five grounds he played on in Australia.

AROUND THE GROUNDS

	Total runs	*Avge*
MCG—Melbourne		
79, 112, 123, 37*, 152, 2, 167, 0, 103*, 13, 270, 169, 79, 49, 132, 127*, 57 retired hurt	1,671	128.54
Adelaide Oval—Adelaide		
40, 58, 4, 299*, 8, 66, 26, 212, 0, 56*, 201	970	107.77
Headingley—Leeds		
334, 304, 103, 16, 33, 173*	963	192.60
Woolloongabba—Brisbane		
226, 76, 24, 38, 0, 187, 185	736	105.14
SCG—Sydney		
25, 43, 0, 112, 48, 71, 0, 82, 234, 12, 63, 13	703	58.58
The Oval—London		
232, 244, 77, 0	553	138.25
Lord's—London		
254, 1, 36, 13, 18, 102*, 38, 89	551	78.71
Trent Bridge—Nottingham		
8, 131, 29, 25, 51, 144*, 138, 0	526	75.14
The Exhibition Ground—Brisbane		
18, 1, 223	242	80.66
Old Trafford—Manchester		
14, 30, 7, 30*	81	27.00
Total Runs	6,996 @	99.94

9 Captains and Captaincy

When Graham Dowling made 239 against India at Christchurch in 1968, not only was it the highest Test innings to date by a New Zealander, but it was also the first time a double century had been achieved by a player in his first Test as captain. The previous highest was 191 by Australia's Clem Hill, against South Africa at Sydney in 1910–11.

•

In 1989–90 Mark Taylor celebrated his elevation to captaincy with two centuries—127 & 100—in the Sheffield Shield final against Queensland. This was only the second occasion that twin centuries had been scored in a Shield final, and the first by a captain.

Mark Taylor

•

In 1990 Graham Gooch and Mohammad Azharuddin provided the first example in Test cricket of rival captains scoring centuries in the same Test on more than one occasion. They also managed to achieve the feat in successive matches:

G.A. Gooch (333 & 123)	M. Azharuddin (121)	England v India	Lord's 1990
G.A. Gooch (116)	M. Azharuddin (179)	England v India	Manchester 1990

Of all the captains to lead their country in more than 30 Tests only a few can claim any real sustained success. New Zealand's John Reid, for example, led the Kiwis in 34 Tests and finished with a win-loss ratio of 3:18. Mike Brearly, though, won 18 matches and lost only 4 in 31 Tests, a success rate of over 58%.

•

When India beat England at The Oval in 1971 it brought to an end England's record run of 26 Tests without defeat. It was also the first loss experienced by England's captain Ray Illingworth since he took over the reins from Colin Cowdrey in 1969. No country was able to defeat England under the guidance of Illingworth in his first 19 Tests as captain. This is a record for the most successive matches by any player starting his Test captaincy career. Mike Brearley is next on the list—under his leadership, England was not beaten in his first 15 Tests as captain, and was never beaten in 19 Tests at home.

•

When you win the toss—bat. If you are in doubt, think about it, then bat. If you have very big doubts, consult a colleague—then bat.

—W.G. Grace

•

Of the 25 Tests England played under the captaincy of Mike Smith, 17 were drawn.

•

Stuart Surridge, who played for Surrey between 1949 and 1960, captained the county in five seasons (1952–56) and won the Championship each time.

•

W.G. Grace captained Gloucestershire for 28 consecutive seasons between 1871 and 1898, an English record shared by Yorkshire's Lord Hawke (1883–1910).

•

Tony Lewis captained England on his Test debut, against India at Delhi in 1972–73.

•

During the 1988 Test series against the West Indies, England for the first time, used four captains. Previously only Australia, the West Indies and India had used as many captains in one series.

Australia v England 1884-85		*West Indies v England 1929-30*	
Billy Murdoch	First Test	Teddy Hoad	First Test
Tom Horan	Second & Fifth Tests	Nelson Betancourt	Second Test
Hugh Massie	Third Test	Maurice Fernandes	Third Test
Jack Blackham	Fourth Test	Karl Nunes	Fourth Test
India v West Indies 1958-59		*England v West Indies 1988*	
Polly Umrigar	First Test	Mike Gatting	First Test
Ghulam Ahmed	Second & Third Tests	John Emburey	Second & Third Tests
Vinoo Mankad	Fourth Test	Chris Cowdrey	Fourth Test
Hemu Adhikari	Fifth Test	Graham Gooch	Fifth Test

•

When England lost the Lord's Test of 1989 to Australia, it was their eighth successive defeat under the captaincy of David Gower, a new Test record.

•

'Gerry' Alexander was the last white player to captain the West Indies in a Test match—v England in 1959-60.

•

Laurie Potter, who lived in Perth but was born in Kent, has the unique distinction of captaining both the Young Australia and Young England 'Test' sides.

•

During the 1982-83 Ashes series, the captain who won the toss in each of the first four Tests put the opposition in to bat—this was the first time this had happened in any Test series, and the decisions yielded one win, two losses and a draw. The captains were Greg Chappell and Bob Willis.

•

In the England-Australia Test at Edgbaston in 1981 half of the players who took part were either past, present or future Test captains—Geoff Boycott, Mike Brearley, David Gower, Graham Gooch, Mike Gatting, Ian Botham, John Emburey, Bob Willis, Allan Border, Kim Hughes and Graham Yallop. Five months later, when England played India at Calcutta, 14 captains were present—Gooch, Boycott, Gower, Botham, Gatting, Emburey, Willis, Keith Fletcher, Sunil Gavaskar, Kris Srikkanth, Dilip Vengsarkar, Kapil Dev, Ravi Shastri and Gundappa Viswanath.

•

In 1990 Allan Lamb became the first English player this century to score a hundred in his first Test as captain when he made 119 against the West Indies at Bridgetown. Archie MacLaren was the last captain to perform the feat for England, with 109 against Australia at Sydney in 1897-98.

•

Dilip Vengsarkar broke a rather unusual captaincy record in 1987 when he led India against the West Indies at Delhi. It was Vengsarkar's 95th Test, but his first as captain. The previous record for the number of Tests played before gaining the captaincy was 73 by Tom Graveney, who skippered England for the only time in his career against Australia at Leeds in 1968. Desmond Haynes, playing in his 87th Test, captained the West Indies for the first time in 1990, against England at Port-of-Spain.

•

When Andrew Hilditch took over the captaincy of New South Wales in 1977-78, he did so in only his second first-class match.

Andrew Hilditch

•

New South Wales skipper Geoff Lawson made Sheffield Shield history in 1991-92 when he declared his side's first innings at 0 for 0 in the match against Tasmania at Sydney without a ball being bowled. His bold attempt to win the rain-affected match backfired, with the visitors gaining victory by 48 runs.

•

With Ian Healy on Test duty and Carl Rackemann sidelined through injury, Queensland's selectors recalled the retired Dirk Wellham to captain the Maroons in 1992-93. In doing so, Wellham became the first Australian cricketer to lead three states in the Sheffield Shield, having previously captained New South Wales and Tasmania.

•

When Allan Border captained Australia at Melbourne in 1990-91 it was the 20th time he'd done so against England, an achievement which broke Don Bradman's record. In the fifth Test at Perth Border then overtook England's Archie MacLaren, who held the overall captaincy record of 22 Tests. After the Perth match, Border had led Australia in 13 consecutive Tests against England without defeat, another record by a Australian captain.

•

Jamie Siddons hit centuries in his first two innings as captain of South Australia, in his first two matches for the state—149 v Queensland at Brisbane and 141 v Tasmania at Adelaide in 1991-92.

Jamie Siddons

•

Two of the highest scores by Test captains were recorded within the space of a few months in the early 1990s. At Lord's, Graham Gooch scored 333 against India, only the second triple century by a Test captain, beating the previous best of 311 by Bob Simpson at Manchester in 1964. Martin Crowe then came tantalisingly close to a triple hundred, scoring 299 against Sri Lanka at Wellington in 1990-91, his innings the third-highest by a captain in Test cricket.

By taking 11 wickets for 96 against the West Indies at Sydney in 1988-89, Allan Border became the first Australian captain to achieve a 10-wicket haul in a Test match.

•

Playing against a team with Ian Chappell as captain turns a cricket match into gang warfare.

—Mike Brearley, 1980

•

On three successive tours of England the West Indies, under the captaincy of Clive Lloyd, lost only two first-class matches:

	P	*W*	*L*	*D*
1976	26	18	2	6
1980	16	8	0	8
1984	14	8	0	6
Total	56	34	2	20

His record of no losses in 1980 and 1984, emulated the feats of Intikhab Alam in 1974, and Don Bradman in 1948, who also returned home from England with no defeats in first-class matches.

•

Percy Sherwell, South Africa's number 11 against England in 1905-06, opened the batting in the return series in 1907 and scored a century at Lord's. He was also the wicket-keeper and captain, an all-round feat not seen again in Test cricket until 1958-59, when the West Indian skipper 'Gerry' Alexander kept wicket and opened the innings in two matches against Pakistan.

•

In his first Test as captain, and in his country's first Test, Zimbabwe's David Houghton scored 121 against India at Harare in 1992-93. This was the first time a captain had scored even a half-century in his country's inaugural Test.

CAPTAIN'S SCORES IN EACH COUNTRY'S FIRST TEST

Dave Gregory	1 & 3	Australia v England at Melbourne 1876-77
James Lillywhite	10 & 4	England v Australia at Melbourne 1876-77
Owen Dunell	26* & 11	South Africa v England at Port Elizabeth 1888-89
Karl Nunes	37 & 10	West Indies v England at Lord's 1928
Tom Lowry	0 & 40	New Zealand v England at Christchurch 1929-30
C.K. Nayudu	40 & 10	India v England at Lord's 1932
Abdul Kardar	4 & 43	Pakistan v India at Delhi 1952-53
Bandula Warnapura	2 & 38	Sri Lanka v England at Colombo 1981-82
David Houghton	121 & 41*	Zimbabwe v India at Harare 1992-93

10 The Theatre, Film, Television and Radio

Ian Botham swapped his bat for a sword in 1991, when he made his theatrical debut in a production of *Jack and the Beanstalk*. Another to tread the boards was former England bowler Richard Ellison, who in 1985 appeared in a Canterbury Opera Society version of *Fiddler on the Roof*.

> **I have often thought what a pity it is, what a better life I would have had, what a better man I would have been, how much healthier an existence I would have led, if I had been a cricketer instead of an actor.**
>
> **—Laurence Olivier**

•

The 1953 British film *The Final Test*, which starred Robert Morley and Jack Warner, also featured England Test cricketers Len Hutton, Denis Compton, Jim Laker, Cyril Washbrook, Godfrey Evans and Alec Bedser. A light comedy, the storyline revolves around a cricketer, played by Warner, who makes a duck in his final Test match at The Oval.

•

> **I do love cricket, it's so very English.**
>
> **—Sarah Bernhardt**

> **Cricket is basically baseball on valium.**
>
> **—Robin Williams**

•

C. Aubrey Smith, who captained England against South Africa in 1888–89, later found fame and fortune as an actor in Hollywood. During the 1930s and '40s, Smith appeared in dozens of films, including *Morning Glory, The Prisoner of Zenda, The Adventures of Mark Twain, Little Lord Fauntleroy* and *Rebecca.*

•

It's been said that one of Walt Disney's best-known cartoon characters, Donald Duck, was named after Don Bradman scored a duck during a match on the Australian tour of North America in 1932. Disney, a keen cricket fan, was a member of the Hollywood Cricket Club.

•

Ian Botham as The King in *Jack and the Beanstalk*

C. Aubrey Smith

C. Aubrey Smith was one of the leading lights behind the legendary Hollywood Cricket Club, formed in the early 1930s. Some of its famous players included Boris Karloff, David Niven, Leslie Howard and Frank Lawton.

•

England bowler Derek Pringle made a brief appearance in the award-winning 1981 film *Chariots of Fire.*

•

Greg Chappell, Dennis Lillee and Rod Marsh were amongst the financial backers of Paul Hogan's box-office hit *Crocodile Dundee.*

> **Cricket needs brightening up a bit. My solution is to let the players drink at the beginning of the game, not after. It always works in our picnic matches.**
>
> **—Paul Hogan**

•

> **Cricket is like sex films. They relieve frustration and tension.**
>
> **—Linda Lovelace, star of *Deep Throat***
>
> **Is there any sex in it?**
>
> **—Peter Sellers, as the psychiatrist learning about cricket in the 1965 film *What's New Pussycat?***

•

After his retirement from cricket, West Indies batsman Learie Constantine became a governor of the BBC.

•

Alan McGilvray, Australia's most celebrated cricket commentator, gained the captaincy of the New South Wales Sheffield Shield team in 1933–34, in only his third match.

•

Follow the Tests

through the

A.B.C. Sporting Service

WITH

TEAM OF EXPERT COMMENTATORS

Alan McGilvray

Full Description of Play each Day

Evening Summaries

★

Charles Fortune

Arthur Gilligan

Descriptions M.C.C. and Sheffield Shield Matches

Johnnie Moyes

WATCH "A.B.C. WEEKLY" FOR BROADCASTING DETAILS

2FC REGIONALS 2BL

The first time a radio station provided live cricket reports took place during the 1924–25 season, when Clem Hill and Hyam Marks gave updates on 2BL on the Sydney Test match between Australia and England. Ball-by-ball commentary came a few years later, in 1926–27, with Lionel Watt, a former grade cricketer, going to air live on Sydney's 2FC with a continuous broadcast of a first-class match at the SCG. In England, radio broadcasts began in 1927 when Frank Gillingham and 'Plum' Warner gave commentary and scores on the New Zealand–Essex match at Leyton.

•

The first TV broadcasts of cricket took place in England in 1938, when the BBC covered play in the second Test against Australia at Lord's. In Australia, the first telecast was carried by GTV-9 and ATN-7 in 1959, with viewers in Melbourne and Sydney receiving the last two hours of play on each day of the Australia–England Test series. The first Test to be televised in its entirety was the fifth Test between Australia and the West Indies in 1960–61, which was shown on the ABC in Sydney. Australia-wide coverage of Test cricket began in 1970–71 when the national broadcaster covered every day's play of the Ashes series in all states.

•

How McDougall Topped the Score, made in 1924, is the only full-length Australian feature film with cricket as its theme. It cost £800 to produce, was seen only in Adelaide, and starred Leslie Gordon and Dorothy May.

•

British actor John Le Mesurier, famous for his appearance on the TV show *Dad's Army*, used to play cricket for the Gentlemen of Suffolk team in the 1930s.

•

When Viv Richards married his childhood girlfriend, Miriam, in 1981, the ceremony was broadcast live on national radio in Antigua.

•

A number of Australian cricketers, including Dean Jones, Mark Waugh and Terry Alderman, have made celebrity appearances on quiz and game shows like *Sale of the Century*, *Family Feud* and *The Main Event*. Greg Matthews was a regular contributor to the Channel 9 program *Live at 5*, while Simon O'Donnell became a reporter on Ray Martin's *Midday* show. In 1991 Merv Hughes went one step further by guest starring in the Channel 9 drama *Flying Doctors*—he was brought in to coach the 'Broken Hill Brumbies' for a local grudge match against the 'Coopers Crossing Crusaders'.

Merv Hughes on the *Flying Doctors* set with Maurie Fields

The Channel 9 commentary team—Greg Chappell, Ian Chappell, Richie Benaud, Bill Lawry and Tony Greig

•

Australian actress Kate Fitzpatrick was employed as a commentator by Channel 9 in 1983–84.

•

Peter Gibbs, who played for Oxford and Derbyshire during the 1960s and '70s, gained international recognition as a playwright, taking out two prestigious drama competitions in 1983. After winning the Prix Futura contest in Berlin for BBC Radio with his comedy *Supersaver*, he then won the *Radio Times* television award for his play *Benefit of Doubt*, a drama about a cricket umpire appearing in his first match.

•

Channel 9's television ad *C'Mon Aussie C'Mon* for the World Series Cricket was voted Commercial of the Year in 1979 by FACTS, the Federation of Australian Television Stations.

•

Radio and television commentator Henry Blofeld played 17 matches in first-class cricket in a career that spanned three seasons. His highest score was 138 for Cambridge University against the MCC at Lord's in 1959.

•

The batsman's Holding, the bowler's Willey.

—BBC commentator Brian Johnston

Patrick Cargill, who starred in the television comedy *Father Dear Father* and appeared in films such as *Inspector Clouseau* and *Help!* is an uncle of the England medium-pace bowler Robin Jackman, who played in four Tests in the early 1980s

Sarah Potter, who played Test cricket for England, is the daughter of Dennis Potter, the award-winning television playwright (*Pennies from Heaven* and *The Singing Detective*)

Laurence Olivier's father played cricket at Oxford, and for Hampshire and the MCC

Nick Wisdom, who appeared in two matches for Sussex in 1974, is the son of the English actor-comedian Norman Wisdom

A cousin of *The Goodies*' Tim Brooke-Taylor—David Brooke-Taylor—played 15 times for Derbyshire in the late 1940s. David's father, G.P. Brooke-Taylor, an uncle of Tim's, also played first-class cricket

Russell Crowe, who appeared in the Australian film *Romper Stomper*, is a cousin of Jeff and Martin Crowe

Tim Brooke-Taylor

•

Throughout the 1932–33 'Bodyline' Test series, radio listeners in Britain received most of their match reports not through the BBC, but via a commercial radio network in France. With the BBC carrying only brief scores in its news bulletins, the Paris station Poste Parisien hired the former Australian Test cricketer Alan Fairfax who, perched in the Eiffel Tower, gave detailed 'synthetic' two hour commentaries of the Tests off cables.

•

Before turning to cricket commentary, John Arlott worked as a poetry producer for the BBC. During his time with the Overseas Services section, he worked alongside Dylan Thomas, as well as E.M. Foster and George Orwell.

Michael Charlton, a newsreader who became one of the BBC's top cricket commentators, was the first face seen on ABC television when it opened in 1956. He was also the first compere of the current affairs show *Four Corners.*

11 The Wicket-Keepers

England's Edmund Tylecote, who scored 66 at Sydney in 1882–83, was the first wicket-keeper to record a half-century in Test cricket. In the next Test, also at Sydney, Australia's Jack Blackham became the first keeper to score two fifties (57 & 58*) in a match, a performance not equalled until Dilawar Hussain's 59 and 57 for India v England at Calcutta in 1934. Harry Wood scored the first century by a wicket-keeper in a Test when he made 134 not out against South Africa at Cape Town in 1892. The first double hundred (209) came off the bat of Pakistan's Imtiaz Ahmed against New Zealand at Lahore in 1955–56.

•

In 1986–87 Transvaal wicket-keeper Ray Jennings took 10 catches in a match twice during the season, a unique performance in first-class cricket. The feat was achieved a third time in the summer, by Steve Rixon for Australia v South Africa at Johannesburg, repeating his performance at the same venue in 1985–86.

•

Peter Richardson, the England opener, was caught at the wicket by either Gil Langley or Len Maddocks in each of his eight innings in the 1956 Test series against Australia.

•

Colin Bremner, who had a brief first-class career of four matches for the Services and Dominions teams, marked his debut in 1945 by twice stumping Walter Hammond.

•

During Australia's match against Somerset in 1985, Ray Phillips, deputising for Wayne Phillips, made two stumpings in the first innings and held five catches for the match. This was only the second time in all first-class cricket that a sub had achieved a pair of stumpings in a single innings.

•

With Dennis Lillee, Rod Marsh holds the world record for most wicket-keeper/bowler dismissals in a Test career—95 in 69 Tests at a rate of 1.38 per match. The first batsman to be dismissed 'c Marsh b Lillee' was England's John Hampshire at Sydney in 1970–71; the last was Abdul Qadir, also at Sydney, in 1983–84. Their most profitable association in a particular Test series was against England in 1972, when they combined to dismiss 10 batsmen.

CAUGHT MARSH BOWLED LILLEE

	Series	*Tests*	*Dismissals*
1970–71	England	2	1
1972	England	5	10
1972–73	Pakistan	3	4
1972–73	West Indies	1	–
1974–75	England	6	5
1975	England	4	4
1975–76	West Indies	5	9
1976–77	Pakistan	3	6
1976–77	New Zealand	2	5
1976–77	England	1	4
1979–80	West Indies	3	4
1979–80	England	3	7
1979–80	Pakistan	3	1
1980	England	1	1
1980–81	New Zealand	3	3
1980–81	India	3	7
1981	England	6	6
1981–82	Pakistan	3	5
1981–82	West Indies	3	3
1981–82	New Zealand	3	3
1982–83	England	1	1
1983–84	Pakistan	5	6
Totals		69	95

•

During the six-match Test series against Australia in 1979–80, India's wicket-keeper Syed Kirmani had a good time behind the stumps but also impressed with the bat, scoring 285 runs at an average of 57.00. Twice during the series he scored a 50 when batting as a nightwatchman—57 at Madras and 101* at Bombay.

•

Bob Taylor, of Derbyshire, twice dismissed seven batsmen in an innings in 1975—first against Lancashire in a John Player League match and then in the County Championship match against Yorkshire at Chesterfield. In a first-class career which saw him make a world-record 1,649 dismissals, Taylor achieved seven dismissals in an innings three times and 10 in a match twice.

•

Taslim Arif, a Pakistani wicket-keeper, had a memorable match against Australia at Faisalabad in 1980 when he opened the batting and scored 210 not out—a new record for a wicket-keeper in a Test match. His unbroken partnership of 223 with Javed Miandad was a Pakistan record for the third wicket. He finished the three-match series with an aggregate of 307 runs at 102.33, six dismissals and one wicket.

•

Alan Knott batting in the fourth Test against Australia at Sydney in 1974–75

•

During the fifth Test at Adelaide in 1974–75, England's Alan Knott became the second wicket-keeper, after Godfrey Evans, to reach the milestone of 200 dismissals in Test cricket. Later in the same match he became the second keeper, after Les Ames, to score a century in England–Australia Tests.

•

In 1989–90 Darren Berry broke a world record of 24 years standing in his debut first-class season. He did not concede a bye in the course of 2,446 runs scored against South Australia, beating the previous best of 2,132 by Northamptonshire's Keith Andrew in 1965.

•

In 1935–36 Don Tallon achieved five dismissals in an innings for the first time in his career. Representing Queensland against the touring Englishmen at Brisbane, Tallon made six dismissals in the MCC's only innings, five of which were stumpings.

•

South Australian wicket-keeper Charlie Walker made eight dismissals on his first-class debut, against New South Wales at Sydney in 1928–29, with five stumpings all off the bowling of Clarrie Grimmett.

•

Only seven wicket-keepers have achieved 100 dismissals in a season. Les Ames did it three times, in 1928, 1929 and 1932. The last man to perform the feat was Worcestershire's Roy Booth, who dismissed exactly 100 batsmen in 1964.

100 DISMISSALS IN A SEASON

Total	*Ct*	*St*			
128	79	49	Les Ames	Kent	1929
122	70	52	Les Ames	Kent	1928
110	63	47	Hugo Yarnold	Worcestershire	1949
107	77	30	George Duckworth	Lancashire	1928
107	96	11	Jimmy Binks	Yorkshire	1960
104	40	64	Les Ames	Kent	1932
104	82	22	John Murray	Middlesex	1957
102	69	33	Fred Huish	Kent	1913
102	95	7	John Murray	Middlesex	1960
101	62	39	Fred Huish	Kent	1911
101	85	16	Roy Booth	Worcestershire	1960
100	91	9	Roy Booth	Worcestershire	1964

•

When Australia made 551 at The Oval in 1884, it was England's wicket-keeper, Alfred Lyttelton, who came away from the Test with the most wickets. For the fifth time in Test cricket all 11 players bowled in Australia's innings, Lyttelton grabbing 4 for 19 in 12 overs. W.G. Grace, deputising for Lyttelton, took a leg-side catch to dismiss Billy Midwinter—the first time a player had made a dismissal to the first ball received as a wicket-keeper in Test cricket.

New South Wales wicket-keeper Billy Murdoch, who in 1881–82 scored 321 against Victoria in Sydney. It was the first century for the state and the first triple-century in a first-class match in Australia.

•

During the first Test against Australia at Johannesburg in 1966–67, both wicket-keepers—Denis Lindsay and Brian Taber—took five catches in the first innings, Lindsay's six equalling the then world record. Taber, on his Test debut, made eight dismissals in the match, as did Lindsay, and their combined total of 16 established a new Test record. Lindsay also scored a century (182) to become the first wicket-keeper to score 100 runs and claim five dismissals in an innings of a Test match.

Others to achieve the wicket-keepers' 'double' include New Zealand's Ian Smith, and Sri Lanka's Amal Silva who scored 111 and held five catches in the second innings against India at Colombo in 1985–86. Silva's nine catches in the match followed a similar number in the previous Test, a unique performance. He made a total of 22 dismissals in the three-Test series, another world record.

•

English wicket-keeper Lisa Nye claimed a Test record eight dismissals in an innings on the first day of the third Women's Test against New Zealand at New Plymouth in 1991–92.

Jack Blackham

Jack Blackham kept wicket for Australia in its first 17 Test matches.

•

Alan Smith, who kept wicket in four Tests against Australia in 1962–63, took a hat-trick when bowling for Warwickshire against Essex in Clacton in 1965. This was only the second recorded instance in first-class cricket, after Bengal's Probir Sen in 1954–55, of a hat-trick taken by the appointed match wicket-keeper.

•

Rod Marsh is the only wicket-keeper to achieve five dismissals in a Test innings against five different countries. He took five catches in an innings three times against England, three times against New Zealand and Pakistan, twice against the West Indies and once against India.

•

On his first-class debut in 1990–91, Tasmanian wicket-keeper Joe Holyman took seven catches in the first innings of the match against Western Australia in Hobart. This was a new record for Tasmania, and a world record for any keeper in his first first-class match.

•

In 1989 two county wicket-keepers—Alec Stewart and Warren Hegg—took 11 catches in a first-class match to give them a share of the world record. Previously, only three others had performed the feat—Surrey's Arnold Long in 1964, Rod Marsh in 1975-76 and Yorkshire's David Bairstow in 1982. South Australia's Tim Nielsen joined the list in 1990-91 with 11 catches against Western Australia in Perth.

•

When England wicket-keeper Bruce French was forced to leave the field due to injury in the 1986 Lord's Test against New Zealand, three other players stood behind the stumps—Bill Athey, Bob Taylor and Bobby Parks.

•

An Indian wicket-keeper by the name of V. Rajindernath only played in one Test match, and although he failed to take a catch he etched his appearance in the record books by making four stumpings. His one Test was against Pakistan at Bombay in 1952-53, a series which saw India use a different keeper for each of the first four Tests—Probir Sen at Delhi, 'Nana' Joshi at Lucknow, Rajindernath at Bombay and Ebrahim Maka at Madras.

•

An unusual dismissal took place during Victoria's Sheffield Shield clash with Western Australia at the Junction Oval in Melbourne in 1992-93—Darren Berry was stumped by Mike Veletta off Tim Zoehrer. All three were wicket-keepers.

•

The New South Wales wicket-keeper Steve Rixon and Carl Rackemann proved to be a formidable combination during the unofficial Australian tour of South Africa in 1985-86. In one first-class match alone, at Johannesburg, Rixon took 10 catches with nine off the bowling of Rackemann.

•

When Bob Taylor caught New Zealand's John Bracewell in the fourth Test at Nottingham in 1983, Chris Smith became the 100th different bowler off whom Taylor had made a dismissal in first-class cricket.

•

Bob Taylor will long remember the 1981 season. He was recalled to the England Test side, established a world record for catches and scored his maiden first-class century 21 years after making his debut. His score of exactly 100, against Yorkshire at Sheffield, came in his 744th first-class innings.

•

In 1984 Wayne Phillips became the first Australian wicket-keeper to score a century *and* not to concede a bye in a total of over 500 in Test cricket. Both feats came in the same match—against the West Indies (509) at Bridgetown. When he made 120 he became only the second Australian keeper, after Rod Marsh, to score a Test hundred, and matched the deeds of James Kelly, in 1897-98, and Bert Oldfield, in 1928-29, behind the stumps.

•

Queensland's Ray Phillips secured a similar double in a Sheffield Shield match at Geelong in 1981-82—he did not concede a bye during Victoria's first innings total of 7 declared for 536 and in Queensland's first innings scored an unbeaten 111. In the return match the following season, at St Kilda, Phillips repeated the feat while Victoria scored 510.

•

In 1982, Geoff Humpage became the first wicket-keeper to score a double-century in a match in England after the Second World War. His score of 254 for Warwickshire v Lancashire at Southport was part of a record fourth-wicket stand of 470 with Alvin Kallicharran (230*). In 1986-87 South Australian keeper Wayne Phillips (213*) and David Hookes (306*) came close to matching the feat of Humpage and Kallicharran by recording an unbroken fourth wicket partnership of 462 against Tasmania at Adelaide. For Phillips this was his third double-century in first-class cricket, but his first as a wicket-keeper.

•

Of the record-breaking 28 catches taken by Rod Marsh in the 1982-83 Test series against England, 16 came off the bowling of Geoff Lawson. This in itself was a record for a Test series, the previous most successful pair being Wally Grout and Alan Davidson with 15 against the West Indies in 1960-61.

Rod Marsh

Jack Russell

Alec Stewart

Jack Russell had the unusual experience of making his first-class debut and his Test debut against Sri Lanka. In his initial first-class appearance for Gloucestershire in 1981 he dismissed eight of the tourists in the match at Bristol, a record-equalling performance for a debutant wicket-keeper. His Test debut, at Lord's in 1988, saw him score 94, then his highest innings in first-class cricket and the third instance of a night-watchman reaching 90 in a Test match for England. When he made 128 not out against Australia at Manchester the following season he became the fourth Englishman to record his maiden first-class century in a Test match.

•

Despite a lack of success with the gloves in the Auckland Test match of 1970–71, England's Alan Knott came close to achieving the rare feat of a century in each innings. His double of 101 and 96 was followed by a century in his next Test innings—116 against Pakistan at Birmingham in 1971.

•

During the first Test in 1990–91 New Zealand scored a record 4 for 671 against Sri Lanka in Wellington. Sri Lanka did not concede a single bye in the innings, their wicket-keeper being Hashan Tillekeratne. His performance was a Test record beating Godfrey Evans, who conceded no byes in Australia's 8 declared for 659 at Sydney in 1946–47. It was also one off the all-time first-class record set by Somerset's Archdale Wickham against Hampshire (7d–672) at Taunton in 1899.

•

During the 1991 England–Sri Lanka Test match at Lord's, five international wicket-keepers were on the field at the same time. While Jack Russell and Alec Stewart were batting, Hashan Tillekeratne was behind the stumps, and former keepers Brendon Kuruppu and Asanka Gurusinha were fielding.

•

In 1976–77 Rod Marsh became the first Australian wicket-keeper, and the second after Northamptonshire's Laurence Johnson, to achieve 10 dismissals in a first-class match more than once. Marsh's accomplishment of 10 catches, for Western Australia v South Australia at Perth, was coupled with a century (104)—a unique double in first-class cricket. Marsh also had the distinction of captaining his team and winning the match by an innings.

Fourteen years later, Steve Marsh—no relation—established a similar double, also unique at first-class level. Playing for Kent against Middlesex at Lord's in 1991, Marsh took a world record-equalling eight catches in the first innings of the match and then scored 108 not out.

A CENTURY AND SEVEN DISMISSALS IN AN INNINGS IN THE SAME FIRST-CLASS MATCH

Score	*Dismissals*			
108*	8 (8c)	Steve Marsh	Kent v Middlesex	Lord's 1991
163*	7 (6c & 1st)	Robert East	Orange Free State v Western Province B	Cape Town 1984–85

•

Brendon Kuruppu

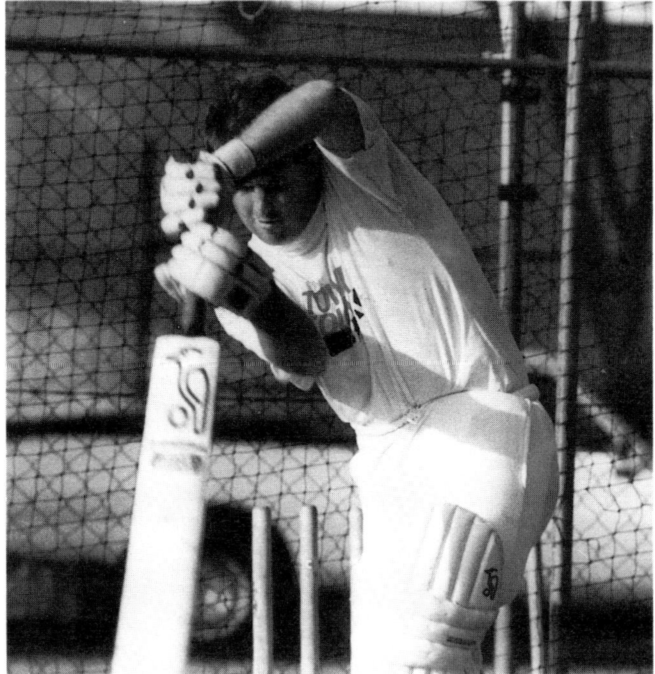

Tim Zoehrer

In 1987 Sri Lanka's Brendon Kuruppu hit 201 not out on his Test debut against New Zealand at Colombo. The 25-year-old opening batsman became the first wicket-keeper to score a century on debut, it was also the first double century by a Sri Lankan in a Test match. After spending 776 minutes at the crease, he then kept wicket throughout New Zealand's innings, the first time a player on his Test debut had been on the field all five days. With the gloves he also excelled, not conceding a single bye in New Zealand's total of 406.

•

Australia's John Maclean and England's Bob Taylor both took five catches in an innings in the first Test at Brisbane in 1978–79. Taylor's effort was a first for England against Australia, while Maclean took his five on his Test debut.

•

On five occasions during his career, Rod Marsh achieved the wicket-keeper's double of 500 runs and 50 dismissals. His most productive season was 1974–75, in which he scored 865 runs and made 64 dismissals.

Season	*M*	*I*	*NO*	*Runs*	*HS*	*Avge*	*Ct*	*St*	*Total*
1974–75	14	26	3	865	168	37.61	58	6	64
1975–76	15	23	0	631	76	27.44	63	4	67
1976–77	11	18	4	600	110*	42.86	53	0	53
1980–81	14	23	2	625	91	29.76	59	2	61
1982–83	13	20	0	538	110	26.90	61	0	61

Australia's two wicket-keepers on the 1989 tour of England opened the batting in the match against Essex at Chelmsford. Ian Healy scored 45 and Tim Zoehrer, in the match as a batsman, made 93 in an opening stand of 89.

•

Hampshire's Bobby Parks was the only wicket-keeper to achieve 600 first-class dismissals during the 1980s and not play Test cricket.

•

South African Percy Sherwell made a record 37 dismissals in Australia in 1910–11—his tally included more stumpings (20) than catches (17), a unique achievement in Australian first-class cricket.

•

On his first-class debut for Natal in 1956–57, Roland Pearce made eight dismissals in the match against Western Province at Durban, and scored 95 in his dual role as an opening batsman.

•

Rohan Kanhai, who ended his career as one of the world's best number-3 bats, began his Test career, against England in 1957, as West Indies wicket-keeper. He marked his last appearance in Test cricket in 1973–74 behind the stumps as well, when he filled in for the injured Deryck Murray during the fifth Test against England at Port-of-Spain.

12 Imports and Exports

In 1962–63 Garry Sobers, playing for South Australia, became the first man to achieve the Australian double of 1,000 runs and 50 wickets in a season. On his return to Adelaide the following season he attained the double again, and remains the only player to reach the target once.

•

In 1907 two Australians, Albert Trott and Frank Tarrant, took four wickets in four balls in first-class matches for Middlesex. However, Trott went one better by taking a hat-trick in the same innings of the match against Somerset at Lord's—a unique performance in first-class cricket.

•

Australia's Chris Matthews marked his debut for Lancashire in 1988 by dismissing Worcestershire's Tim Curtis with his first ball in the Sunday League—he was only the third such bowler to achieve the feat in the competition's history.

•

Sydney Callaway, a medium-fast bowler who played in three Tests for Australia, took a record 15 wickets for 60 when representing the New Zealand provincial side Canterbury in 1904. In doing so, he became the only bowler to capture 15 wickets in a match in New Zealand twice:

15–175	New South Wales v New Zealand	Christchurch 1895–96
15–60	Canterbury v Hawke's Bay	Napier 1903–04

•

One of the most famous all-round performances in the County Championship came from Graham McKenzie in 1971. In the match against Glamorgan at Leicester, he top-scored with 53 not out, batting at number 10, before a decisive spell of bowling which saw the visitors all out for 24 and 66. McKenzie's bowling figures were 11.4–6–8–7 and 14–3–29–4.

•

A former Tasmanian batsman, Peter Bowler, was the first player to score a century on his first-class debuts for two English counties. His 155 not out for Derbyshire v Cambridge University in 1988 followed his 100 not out on debut for Leicestershire v Hampshire in 1986. In between, Bowler played in a couple of matches for Tasmania in 1986–87, scoring 7 and 1 against England at Hobart and 7 against New South Wales at Newcastle.

•

Jason Gallian, who captained Australia's Youth Test team against England in 1990, claimed a wicket with his first ball on his first-class debut, for Lancashire v Oxford University at The Parks in 1990.

•

Keith Miller and Mike Haysman both scored centuries on their debuts in English county cricket, having already achieved the feat on their first-class debuts in Australia.

K.R. Miller	
181	Victoria v Tasmania at Melbourne 1937–38
102*	Nottinghamshire v Cambridge University at Nottingham 1959
M.D. Haysman	
126	South Australia v Queensland at Adelaide 1982–83
102*	Leicestershire v Cambridge University at Cambridge 1984

•

Damien Martyn celebrated his first-class debut with county side Leicestershire in 1991 by scoring an unbeaten 60 against the touring West Indians. He top-scored in Leicestershire's second-innings total of 4 declared for 136. His innings included eight fours and a six and was scored off 81 balls. Later in the season, as captain of the Australian Under-19s, Martyn hit 179 in the first 'Test' against England at Leicester, and 181 not out in the second match at Chelmsford.

Damien Martyn

The highest partnership for Lancashire's ninth wicket in first-class cricket was set by two Australians in 1907—142 by Les Poidevin and Alex Kermode v Sussex at Eastbourne.

•

In 1985-86 two of Test cricket's leading openers, Gordon Greenidge and India's Chetan Chauhan, were the opening batsmen for the Adelaide first-grade cricket club. Greenidge hit two successive centuries in the local competition, including 210 on his debut.

•

Graeme Hick scored 1 on his first-class debut for Queensland in 1990-91. He fared little better in his next match with scores of 5 and 11 not out, but finished the season on a high note with centuries in three successive Shield matches.

•

Brian Davison, who also played for Rhodesia and Leicestershire, scored five centuries in successive matches for Tasmania in the early 1980s.

•

Coaxed out of retirement in 1987-88 at the age of 41, Bob Holland took 31 wickets for Wellington in the Shell Trophy.

•

Wes Hall's 43 wickets for Queensland in the 1961-62 Sheffield Shield was a state record for 22 seasons, until Jeff Thomson took 47 wickets in 1983-84.

•

David Gower played club cricket for Claremont-Cottesloe in Perth in 1977-78.

•

England's 18th first-class county, Durham, marked its entry in the Sunday League competition in 1992 with a nine-run win over Lancashire, thanks mainly to a debut hundred by Dean Jones. He hit 114 off just 85 balls in Durham's total of 4 for 246.

•

In 1973-74 Pakistan's Majid Khan took a record number (16) of catches in the field when representing Queensland. His record was broken in 1987-88 by another import, Ian Botham, who held 18 catches.

•

Former Australian Test batsmen Kepler Wessels and Kim Hughes both hit match-winning centuries in the opening round of South Africa's Nissan Shield in 1990-91. For Eastern Province, Wessels made 122 in an opening stand of 246 with Philip Amm. Rod McCurdy, with bowling figures of 3 for 12, and John Maguire 3 for 7, then combined to dismiss Natal County Districts for 46—the lowest-ever total in the one-day competition. Kim Hughes made 119 for Natal against Border, while another Australian, Mike Haysman, scored 66 not out for Northern Transvaal against Western Transvaal.

•

Albert Trott twice scored 1,000 runs and took 100 wickets in a season when playing for Middlesex

Albert Trott twice performed the double of 1,000 runs and 200 wickets for Middlesex, and did so in successive seasons:

1899	1,175 runs and 239 wickets
1900	1,337 runs and 211 wickets

Frank Tarrant, who also played for Middlesex, produced some extraordinary all-round feats, obtaining the 1,000 run/100-wicket double in eight successive seasons (1907-14), including 2,000 runs and 100 wickets in 1911. George Tribe, another Victorian, achieved the double seven times for Northamptonshire during the 1950s.

•

Australia's Tom Moody has the distinction of being the first batsman to score a century in his first three matches in English first-class cricket. After an innings of 147 on his debut for Warwickshire in 1990, he then made hundreds against the touring New Zealanders and Derbyshire, scored 96 in his next match and hit centuries in his next four.

147	v Cambridge University	Cambridge
44 & 106	v New Zealanders	Birmingham
168	v Derbyshire	Derby
30 & 96	v Lancashire	Coventry
40 & 103*	v Glamorgan	Swansea
48 & 101*	v Hampshire	Birmingham
110	v Sussex	Eastbourne
26 & 117	v Leicestershire	Birmingham

Tom Moody

His sensational form saw him collect several other records, including the milestone of 1,000 runs for Warwickshire in just 12 innings, and then the fastest century of all time. Although scored in contrived circumstances, Moody's 100, against Glamorgan at Swansea, was reached in 26 minutes off 36 balls, and included seven sixes and 11 fours.

TOM MOODY'S HISTORY-MAKING CENTURY

103 v Glamorgan at Swansea 1990*

0,1,1,6,4,4,6,6,4,4,0,4,1,4,4,1 (50)
2,6,2,0,0,6,0,0,4,1,1,4,4,0,4,1,6,2,1,6 (100)

When not engaged on the first-class circuit, Moody proved just as valuable playing the one-day competitions, scoring half-centuries in his first two matches in both the NatWest Bank Trophy and the Sunday League.

Forced to move from Warwickshire for the following season, Moody continued his winning ways with Worcestershire. In his first match at New Road, Moody scored 160 in a Sunday League match against Kent, a record innings by a Worcestershire batsman in the competition. He hit 16 fours and six sixes, reaching 50 in 51 balls. His second 50 came off 35 balls, his third off just 19. Six weeks later, Moody notched his 500th run for the season in only six matches; his sequence of scores included three centuries in four innings—160, 128*, 50, 100, 45 and 62. He ended the season as he began it—with a century—and a record 917 runs.

TOM MOODY'S RECORDS IN THE 1991 SUNDAY LEAGUE

- Scored 500 runs in record time, beating David Gower's performance for Leicestershire in 1982.
- Reached 1,000 runs in the competition in 24 innings, a record previously held by Hampshire's Barry Richards.
- Scored 1,000 runs opening the batting with Tim Curtis, becoming the first pair to record the feat, eclipsing the 949 runs scored by the Yorkshire openers Geoff Boycott and John Hampshire in 1975.
- Scored a record total of 917 runs for the season, beating Jimmy Cook's 902 for Somerset in 1990.
- Scored a record four centuries in a Sunday League season—160, 128*, 100 and 128*.

His performance in first-class matches were equally impressive, and mirrored his extraordinary form with Warwickshire the previous summer. In his first half-a-dozen-or-so matches in the County Championship, Moody hit at least one fifty, with four hundreds. He later scored his maiden double century in county cricket, a career-best 210 against his old club Warwickshire at Worcester.

A FIFTY IN HIS FIRST SEVEN MATCHES IN THE 1991 COUNTY CHAMPIONSHIP

82*	v Gloucestershire	Worcester
135	v Lancashire	Worcester
118	v Glamorgan	Worcester
71	v Northamptonshire	Northampton
181*	v Essex	Ilford
73	v Sussex	Hove
107 & 96	v Nottinghamshire	Worcester

1,000 FIRST-CLASS RUNS IN DEBUT SEASON FOR TWO COUNTIES

M	*I*	*NO*	*Runs*	*HS*	*100s*	*50s*	*Avge*
Warwickshire 1990							
9	15	2	1,163	168	7	1	89.46
Worcestershire 1991							
22	34	4	1,887	210	6	9	62.90

•

Imran Khan took his 1,000th wicket in first-class cricket while playing for New South Wales, against Western Australia at Perth in 1984–85.

•

During the 1950s, two Australian spinners, Bruce Dooland and George Tribe, set English county bowling records, which still stand, for most first-class wickets in a season:

Bruce Dooland (Nottinghamshire) 181 wickets at 14.96 in 1954
George Tribe (Northamptonshire) 175 wickets at 18.70 in 1955

•

Victorian all-rounder Tony Dodemaide was one of only three players to achieve the double of 1,000 runs and 50 wickets in English first-class cricket in 1990. In 24 matches for Sussex, he hit 1,001 runs at 33.36 and took 61 wickets at 40.27.

•

As well as scoring over 1,500 runs for Essex in 1989, Mark Waugh was also the leading fieldsman for the county with 31 catches.

•

In 1982–83 Joel Garner became the first bowler to achieve 50 Sheffield Shield wickets in a season for South Australia. In eight matches he took 55 wickets, with a best return of 7 for 78 against Tasmania at Launceston. In all first-class matches for the state, Garner was the eighth South Australian bowler to reach 50 wickets in a season, and the second West Indian after Garry Sobers.

In 1975–76 Tony Greig took 75 wickets at 12.36 for the Waverley club in Sydney, the best haul in grade cricket since the Second World War. The following season Geoff Boycott became the first batsman to top 1,000 runs in a year for Waverley, with an aggregate of 1,160 at an average of 165.71.

•

	Season	*M*	*O*	*M*	*R*	*W*	*BB*	*5wi*	*10wm*	*Avge*
Joel Garner	1982–83	8	403.2	131	976	55	7–78	4	2	17.74
Garry Sobers	1962–63	10	384.3	49	1,355	51	7–110	4	–	26.56
Garry Sobers	1963–64	9	411.4	50	1,441	51	6–71	2	–	28.25

Peter Sleep

Martin McCague

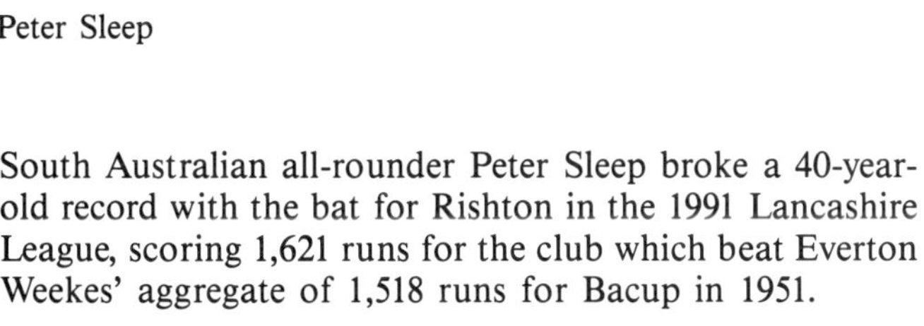

South Australian all-rounder Peter Sleep broke a 40-year-old record with the bat for Rishton in the 1991 Lancashire League, scoring 1,621 runs for the club which beat Everton Weekes' aggregate of 1,518 runs for Bacup in 1951.

•

In Dennis Lillee's first stint of county cricket, in 1988, he made his highest score for the season and produced his best bowling figures on his Championship debut—22 & 22 and 6 for 68, a match-winning double for Northamptonshire v Gloucestershire at Northampton. Lillee took seven wickets for the match, all without assistance from the field.

•

When Kent met Leicestershire at Grace Road in 1991, the best bowling performances for each side came from their Australian state imports—for the visitors, Martin McCague took a career-best 6 for 88, while John Maguire returned a Championship-best 7 for 57 in Kent's first innings total of 130.

•

Greg Chappell was the first batsman to score a century in the Sunday League one-day tournament—128* for Somerset v Surrey at Brislington in 1969.

•

In 1981 the Esso oil company and the Australian Cricket Board initiated a scholarship program which enabled up-and-coming state players to gain further experience playing second XI cricket in England. Of the 24 players who won scholarships nearly half went on to play Test cricket for Australia:

1981	Greg Geise (NSW), Carl Rackemann (Q), Wayne Phillips (SA), Stuart Saunders (T)
1982	Greg Ritchie (Q), Steve Smith (NSW), Malcolm Dolman (SA), Ken MacLeay (WA)
1983	Merv Hughes (V), Mike Haysman (SA), Robbie Kerr (Q), Greg Matthews (NSW)
1984	Ian Carmichael (SA), Brett Mulder (WA), Peter Faulkner (T), Brett Henschell (Q)
1985	Steve Waugh (NSW), Andrew Courtice (Q), Tony Dodemaide (V), Glenn Bishop (SA)
1986	Mark Waugh (NSW), Glenn Trimble (Q), Keith Bradshaw (T), Denis Hickey (V)

Between 1976–77 and 1983–84 a similar scheme offered young English players scholarships with cricket clubs in Australia. Twenty-seven cricketers won awards—among them were Mike Gatting, Ian Botham, John Emburey and Neil Foster.

•

The first overseas Test player to appear in the English County Championship was Australia's J.J. Ferris, for Gloucestershire against Surrey at The Oval in 1892.

•

On his first-class debut for Tasmania in 1981–82, the West Indian all-rounder Franklyn Stephenson took 10 for 46 against Victoria at Melbourne, the best figures by a bowler in his first match in Australia for 50 years.

•

In the 1989 Lancashire League the most successful bowlers were the Victorian pair of Simon O'Donnell and Paul Reiffel. O'Donnell finished the season with 102 wickets at 12.42 for his club Haslingden, while Reiffel captured 97 at 12.61 for East Lancashire.

•

Apart from one season of county cricket with Essex in 1986, Allan Border played once for Gloucestershire in 1977, scoring 15 not out against Oxford University. He spent most of the season playing second XI cricket, scoring 355 runs in 12 matches and topping the bowling averages with 15 wickets at 14.80.

•

Australian bowlers figured prominently in the 1989–90 domestic season in South Africa. John Maguire was the leading wicket-taker, claiming 60 victims at an average of 15.05. Rod McCurdy was next on the list with 45 wickets at 23.40.

•

In 1971 the New South Wales batsman Bruce Francis marked his first season of English County Championship cricket by scoring 1,563 runs in 24 matches for Essex—a record number of runs for the county by a batsman in his debut season in the Championship.

•

Graham McKenzie

The first bowler to take a hat-trick and 50 wickets in the Benson & Hedges Cup was Western Australia's Graham McKenzie, who achieved the feats while playing for Leicestershire.

•

John McMahon, a leading left-arm spinner from Adelaide, who played for both Surrey and Somerset, had the unusual experience of recording his best first-class bowling figures with both counties. In 1948 he took 8 for 46 for Surrey v Northamptonshire at The Oval, then 8 for 46 for Somerset v Kent at Yeovil in 1955.

•

Gladstone Small marked his first-class debut with South Australia in 1985–86 by taking five wickets in an innings. His haul in the Shield match against Western Australia in Adelaide included the top three in the batting order—Graeme Wood, Mike Veletta and Geoff Marsh.

•

Bill Alley, who appeared in 12 matches for New South Wales and 350 for Somerset, made over 3,000 first-class runs for the county in 1961, and took over 100 wickets and scored close to 2,000 runs in 1962.

•

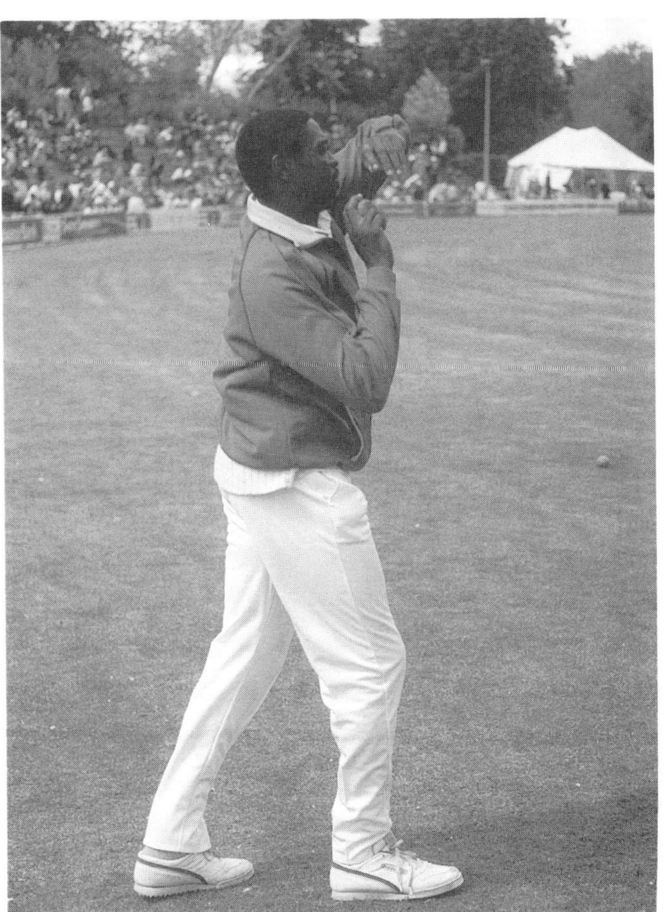
Patrick Patterson

Former New Zealand captain Jeff Crowe began his first-class career not in New Zealand but in Australia. Crowe's initial matches at first-class level were with South Australia from 1977–78. In his first match with the Croweaters he made 0 and 1 against the touring Indians in Adelaide.

•

Jason Gallian, the Australian Youth captain in 1989–90, hit twin centuries in three consecutive matches, and seven hundreds in eight innings for the Lancashire seconds in 1992.

•

During his one season with Tasmania in 1984–85, West Indies fast bowler Patrick Patterson was dropped for disciplinary reasons from the Sheffield Shield side for the match against New South Wales at Newcastle. It appeared he was unable to see eye-to-eye with captain Roger Woolley, and was sidelined after sending down a succession of bouncers to Woolley during net practice.

•

Ian McLachlan, who became nationally known in his roles as president of the Farmers Federation and as a federal coalition shadow minister, played first-class cricket for South Australia and Cambridge University. He played 35 matches in England in the 1950s and toured the West Indies with E.W. Swanton's XI in 1960–61.

•

13 Cricket and Other Sports

Bobby Moore, captain of England's 1966 World Cup-winning soccer team, was an opening batsman who was once offered the chance to play for Essex. Moore's West Ham United team-mate, Geoff Hurst, who played in one first-class match for Essex, was instrumental in England's 4–2 victory over West Germany in the 1966 final, kicking three goals.

A triumphant England soccer captain Bobby Moore with the 1966 World Cup trophy. Before turning to football, Moore was a talented cricketer who captained the Essex, London and South of England schoolboy teams

•

The first two men's singles champions at Wimbledon were both first-class cricketers—Surrey's Spencer Gore won the title in 1877 while Patrick Hadow, of Middlesex, was the winner the following year.

•

Jack Massie, a fast bowler with New South Wales and a son of Test batsman Hugh Massie, also represented his state at rugby, rowing and athletics. In 1914 he was the New South Wales heavyweight boxing champion.

•

W.G. Grace won the 400-yard hurdles event at the National Olympic Association meeting in London in 1866. He was also a keen bowler and a founding member of the English Bowls Association. His brother, E.M. Grace, broke the world triple-jump record in 1866.

•

Apart from being a squash and tennis professional, Norman Cowans won an athletics championship for javelin throwing and sprinting.

•

Mark Taylor played first-grade Aussie Rules football in Sydney, and represented Combined Universities at rugby league.

•

Keith Stackpole, the father of the former Australian vice-captain, played Sheffield Shield cricket for Victoria and VFL football. He represented Collingwood in the 1930s and was a member of Fitzroy's premiership side in 1944.

•

Victor Trumper was a rugby union full-back for South Sydney—he was also a member of the Paddington baseball team.

•

Jack Scott, a fast bowler who played for New South Wales and South Australia and later became a Test match umpire, also played rugby league for Newtown, scoring the club's first-ever try in 1908.

•

England Test batsman Chris Balderstone once played in a first-class cricket match and a first-grade soccer match on the same day (15 September 1975)—Leicestershire v Derbyshire at Chesterfield (1130–1830) and Doncaster Rovers v Brentford at Doncaster (1930–2110).

•

'Dave' Nourse, who played in 45 Tests for South Africa, also represented Natal at soccer and rugby union, and was a competing member of the Natal Rowing Club.

•

Two of cricket's knights who shared a love for the game of golf. Don Bradman (left) once took out his club championship in South Australia, while Garry Sobers (right) was, at one time, rated one of Barbados' top players

•

Former Australian Test player Tony Mann was selected for a West Australian soccer squad to take on Manchester City.

•

Tennis champion John Newcombe is a nephew of former Australian Test batsman Warren Bardsley.

•

David Acfield, of Cambridge and Essex, won a gold medal for sabre fencing at the 1970 Commonwealth Games.

•

Ray Lindwall was a full-back for St George in the Sydney rugby league competition, appearing in their losing grand final sides in 1942 and 1946.

•

New South Wales batsman Reg Bettington won the Australian Amateur Golf Championship in 1932.

•

C.B. Fry played association football, and also held the world record for the long jump.

•

Viv Richards is the only man to have played World Cup soccer—a preliminary match—and World Cup cricket. He and his brother, Mervyn, both played soccer for Antigua.

•

Former Tasmania captain Brian Davison appeared in 12 hockey internationals for Zimbabwe.

•

The New Zealand Test player Phil Horne represented his country at badminton at the 1986 Commonwealth Games.

•

Les Poidevin, who played for New South Wales and Lancashire, played Davis Cup tennis for Australia in 1906.

•

England went into the third Test against New Zealand at Leeds in 1958 with two international football players as their opening batsmen—Mike Smith, who had represented England at rugby union against Wales, and Arthur Milton, a soccer player who was capped by England in 1951–52.

•

Alison Inverarity, daughter of former Test cricketer John, won a gold medal in the high-jump section at the 1991 World Student Games.

•

Former Australian captain Vic Richardson also played baseball for Australia and golf, tennis and Aussie Rules football for South Australia.

•

Steve Waugh, with rounds of 84, 82 and 81, took out the amateur section of the 1991 Vanuatu Invitation golf tournament.

•

Brian Booth, who appeared in 29 Tests for Australia during the 1960s, had previously represented his country at hockey in Melbourne at the 1956 Olympic Games.

•

Don Bradman won the South Australian Squash Championship in 1939.

•

Simon O'Donnell, Keith Miller, Sam Loxton, Jimmy Matthews and Fred Burton all played Test cricket for Australia and VFL football for St Kilda.

•

As a teenager, Bruce Reid was a talented basketball player who gained selection for Western Australia's Under-16 squad in 1978.

•

South African captain Percy Sherwell was the national lawn tennis champion in 1904.

•

Leonard Crawley, of Worcestershire and Essex, won the English Amateur Golf Championship in 1931. He also won a gold medal for ice-skating and was a lawn tennis doubles champion.

•

Rachael Heyhoe Flint, a former England's women's captain, was also a hockey international and a county squash player.

•

Brian McKechnie, the New Zealander who faced the infamous Trevor Chappell underarm delivery, made 10 Test appearances for the All Blacks.

•

Alan Walker, of New South Wales and Nottinghamshire, played for Australia on the 1947–48 rugby league tour of Britain.

•

Hampshire captain Mark Nicholas caddied for professional golfer Chris Moody in the 1992 Johnnie Walker Classic in Bangkok. He also partnered Australian golfer Rodger Davis in the 1992 Asian Pro-Am Tournament.

•

Mark Ella, the former rugby union international, was manager of the Australian Aboriginal cricket team that toured England in 1988.

•

Jack Wilson, who played for Yorkshire, won the Grand National horse race on Double Chance in 1925.

•

Uvaisul Karnain, who took 5 for 26 on his one day international debut in 1983–84, is a former Sri Lankan hockey player.

•

England's Andy Ducat captained Aston Villa to victory in the FA Cup final of 1920.

•

Britain's first amateur squash champion was Hampshire's Tommy Jameson, who won the title in 1922–23.

•

Cota Ramaswami played in two Davis Cup ties for India in 1922, and made his Test debut aged 40, against England, in 1936.

•

Geoff Miller, who appeared in 34 Test matches, played table tennis for Derbyshire.

•

South African Test batsman Eric Dalton was the republic's amateur golf champion in 1950.

•

West Indies Test umpire Steve Bucknor, who officiated in the 1992 World Cup final in Melbourne, had previously stood in a World Cup soccer match.

Steve Bucknor

Bill Alley, the New South Wales and Somerset batsman, won 28 consecutive professional boxing matches in Australia.

•

'Tip' Foster is the only man to have captained England at both cricket and soccer. He also represented Oxford at football, rackets and golf.

•

Henry Palairet, who turned out for the MCC in first-class cricket, was Britain's top archer in 1876.

•

Graham Gooch got a hole-in-one on a golf course in Calcutta on England's 1981–82 tour of India.

•

Ben Barnett, who kept for Australia in four Tests in 1938, was a delegate to the International Lawn Tennis Federation.

•

Two of Australia's leading international umpires during the 1980s, Dick French and Ray Isherwood, had strong connections with other sports. French represented New South Wales at table tennis, while Isherwood was a goal umpire for the Victorian Football Association.

•

Allan Lamb's brother-in-law, Tony Bucknall, won 10 Test caps for England at rugby union.

•

Terry Alderman's father, Bill, was a top-grade footballer who played for Western Australia.

•

Tony Harris represented South Africa on eight occasions—three times in cricket, five in rugby. He was also the Griqualand West junior tennis champion five times.

•

West Indian cricketer, Maurice Foster, is a former Jamaican table tennis champion.

•

Apart from playing both cricket and rugby union for New Zealand, Eric Tindall also umpired Test matches and refereed rugby internationals. His sons, Peter and Dennis, also played rugby for Wellington.

•

Former Victorian wicket-keeper Michael Dimattina played for the Melbourne Tigers in the National Basketball League.

•

A.N. 'Monkey' Hornby was the first man to captain England at both cricket and rugby union. Andrew Stoddart also achieved the double, and went on to captain England to victories in both sports.

•

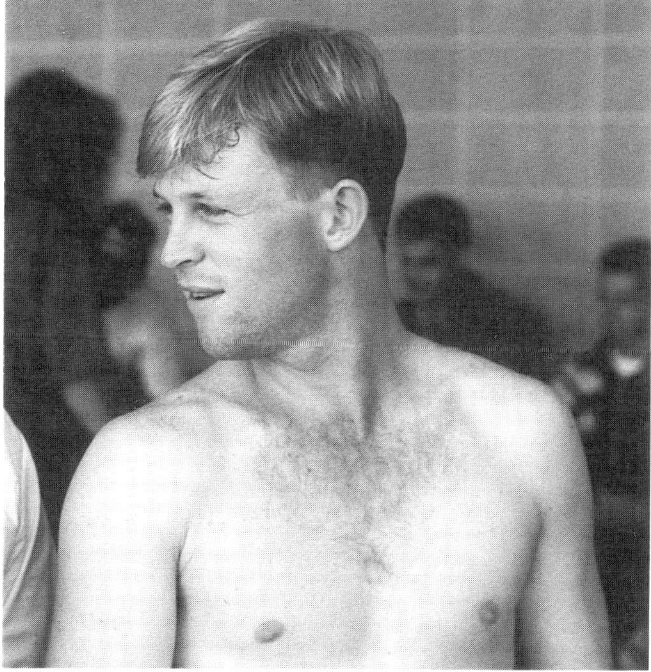

'Jonty' Rhodes

South African batsman 'Jonty' Rhodes, who hit a century on his first-class debut for Natal in 1988–89, also played international hockey.

•

Merv Hughes played Australian Rules football for Werribee in the VFA competition.

•

Soccer's Gary Lineker, a playing member of the MCC, hit a century in a benefit match for David Gower in 1987. He represented the MCC in a match against Germany at Lord's in 1992.

•

Bronko Djura, who kept wicket for Australia in an Under-19 tour of England in 1983, had previously toured New Zealand with a schoolboy rugby league team—a unique double at junior level.

•

In 1973 Kepler Wessels was the number-one ranked junior tennis player in South Africa and was offered a tennis scholarship at Houston University in Texas.

•

England Test player Johnny Douglas won a gold medal for boxing at the 1908 Olympic Games, an event refereed by his father. Douglas also represented England at amateur association football.

•

Tony Pawson, who played in 43 first-class matches for Kent, was World Fly Fishing Champion in 1984.

•

Rugby league player Adam O'Neill, whose father Norman (Australia) and brother Mark (NSW & WA) both played first-class cricket

Adam O'Neill, son of former Australian Test batsman, Norman O'Neill, played rugby league for South Sydney. A sister of Adam's married former Australian rugby league player, Les Davidson.

•

Ian Healy played alongside Peter Jackson and Michael Hagan in an under-12 Queensland Primary Schools rugby league team.

•

Peter Cazalet, who played for Oxford and Kent, also excelled at tennis and squash. After a short career as a jockey he turned to training horses for the Queen Mother.

•

Neil Harvey's great-nephew, Robert Harvey, carved a successful career playing Aussie Rules football for St Kilda in the AFL.

•

David Boon was a first-grade Australian Rules footballer who played in the Northern Tasmanian Football League. His mother, Leslie, is a former international hockey player.

•

Brendon Bracewell, the New Zealand fast bowler, is a past captain of the West Australian rugby team.

•

Herbie Collins, who captained Australia in the early 1920s, was a member of the Easts football club which won the Sydney rugby league competition in 1911.

•

Alistair McCorquodale, of Middlesex, was an international sprinter who appeared in the finals of the 100 metres at the 1948 Olympic Games.

•

West Indian Test player Rolph Grant was a former heavyweight boxing champion.

•

Graham McKenzie's uncle, Doug McKenzie, captained Western Australia at both cricket and hockey.

•

Martin Faull, who made his first-class debut for South Australia in 1990–91, is the elder brother of Australian tennis player Jo-Anne Faull.

•

Australia's Bill Ponsford was an accomplished baseball player who was invited to join the Brooklyn Dodgers.

•

Ian Botham played football for Scunthorpe United and was a junior champion at badminton doubles for Somerset. Always one to accept a new challenge, Botham made his motor-racing debut in 1991 at England's Donington Park circuit driving a Ford Sierra Cosworth.

Ian Botham, the footballer

New Zealand Test bowler Ian Cromb distinguished himself at golf, winning both the Canterbury and South Island championships.

•

Peter Borwick, who played for Northamptonshire in 1932, won a bronze medal for England in an equestrian event at the 1948 Olympics.

•

Alan Wharton, who played in a Test for England in 1949, also played rugby league for Salford and for Broughton Park.

•

Australian fast bowler Laurie Nash kicked over 200 goals for the South Melbourne VFL football club.

•

Louis Devereaux played cricket for Middlesex, Worcestershire and Glamorgan and table tennis for England.

•

Charles Hooman, who helped Kent win the County Championship in 1910, played golf for England against Scotland in the same year.

•

Bill Greswell, an all-rounder who played for Middlesex and Ceylon, played hockey for Somerset and the West of England, and captained various hockey and football teams in Sri Lanka.

•

Verdun Scott represented New Zealand at both Test cricket and rugby league.

•

Alan Brown played first-class cricket for Warwickshire and was a top-class snooker player who made the English amateur championship final in 1946.

•

Terry Gale, runner-up to Greg Norman in the 1981 Australian Masters golf tournament, was 12th man for Western Australia in the Sheffield Shield match against South Australia at Perth in 1966–67.

•

Rugby league half-back Allan Langer once played cricket for Queensland at under-16 level as an opening batsman.

•

Two of England's squad for the 1991 World Cup rugby union final at Twickenham had scored centuries in first-class cricket—Rob Andrew, England's five-eighth, had a top score of 101 not out for Cambridge v Leicestershire at Fenner's in 1984, while their utility back Simon Halliday scored 113 not out for Oxford v Kent at The Parks in 1982. For Australia, its two wingers for the final, Rob Egerton and David Campese, had both played cricket together for an ACT under-14 side in Canberra in the mid-1970s.

•

The England bowler Bernard Bosanquet, best remembered for developing the 'googly', represented Oxford University at hammer-throwing and billiards.

•

John Thompson, who captained Warwickshire in 1947, was Britain's squash champion in 1959.

•

Austin Matthews, who played against New Zealand at The Oval in 1937, also played rugby for Northamptonshire and table tennis for Wales.

•

Eric Freeman, the Australian and South Australian fast bowler, was a top-grade Australian Rules footballer.

•

England's Gilbert Jessop was a scratch golfer who played in the 1914 Amateur Championship.

•

Surrey batsman Cyril Wilkinson captained England at hockey, and represented Great Britain in the 1920 Olympic Games.

•

Lennox Giddy, who played for Eastern Province, was an outstanding tennis player who won the South African singles championship five years in a row from 1894 to 1898.

•

Jamie Siddons, who made his Australian debut in a one-day international in 1988, is a former Sydney Swans player.

•

Roger Hartigan, who played only twice for Australia but scored a century on his Test debut in 1907, represented Queensland at lacrosse and New South Wales at baseball.

•

Harry Makepeace, who appeared in four Test matches for England, also appeared four times at international level playing soccer. He was a member of the Everton side that won the 1906 FA Cup.

•

Ted McDonald, the Australian fast bowler of the 1920s, not only played cricket, but also rugby and soccer for Victoria.

•

In 1982 Rod Marsh's brother, Graham, became the first golfer to win the Australian PGA and the Australian Masters in the same year.

•

Graham Winter, a former South Australian first-class cricketer, was Australia's psychologist for the 1992 Barcelona Olympic Games.

•

When Alfred Lyttelton made his Test debut against Australia in 1880 he became the first double international at cricket and soccer, having played football for England in 1877. The first female to achieve the double was Clare Taylor, who in 1990 followed her England cricket appearances with a berth in the European Soccer Championships in Germany.

•

Chris Old's brother, Alan, played first-class cricket for Warwickshire and rugby union for England.

•

'Gerry' Alexander, the West Indies wicket-keeper who hit at least one fifty in each of the five Tests against Australia in 1960-61, played amateur association football for England.

•

Graeme Hughes—cricket and rugby league for New South Wales

Television sports commentator Graeme Hughes was the last man to represent New South Wales at both cricket and rugby league.

•

David Houghton, who scored Zimbabwe's first century in a Test and a one-day international, is a former international hockey player. He also represented Zimbabwe at tennis and squash.

•

Rugby league great Reg Gasnier played first-grade cricket in Sydney.

•

Eddie McLeod, who played in New Zealand's second Test match, against England at Wellington in 1929-30, also played in New Zealand's first hockey Test.

•

Chris Cairns played rugby for the New Zealand Under-17s in 1987.

•

The game of Australian Rules football was developed by Victorian all-rounder Tom Wills. Rugby league was introduced into Australia by Victor Trumper and J.J. Giltinan in 1907. Alfred Brice, who played first-class cricket for New Zealand, represented Wellington at rugby union and brought the game of rugby league to the province in 1908.

•

Craig McDermott, who played squash, tennis and rugby at club level, was his school's athletics champion for three successive years.

•

Phil Emery—a first-class cricketer and first-grade rugby footballer

New South Wales wicket-keeper Phil Emery is a former rugby union player, who represented both Gordon and Sydney University. His father, Neville, a Mosman and Sydney University first-grade cricketer, was an Australian rugby five-eighth who played on the Wallabies tour of the British Isles in 1947-48.

•

England captain Norman Yardley won the North of England Squash Championship six times.

•

In 1983 Tex Dexter won the Oxford and Cambridge President's Putter golf tournament, after being runner-up in 1969, 1972 and 1977. In the same year, and at his first attempt, he made it through to the third round of the English amateur championship at Wentworth.

•

Glenn Turner represented Worcestershire at both cricket and hockey. His elder brother, Brian, played hockey for New Zealand in the 1960s, while their younger brother, Greg, is a professional golfer.

•

Colin Cowdrey was a champion rackets player.

•

Robin Smith is an under-19 South African record-holder in shot-put and hurdles.

•

Peter Bedford, an all-rounder who scored over 1,500 first-class runs for Victoria, won Australian Rules' most prestigious award, the VFL Brownlow medal in 1970.

•

Michael Mortensen, the brother of Derbyshire fast bowler Ole Mortensen, played Davis Cup tennis for Denmark and doubles tennis at Wimbledon. Michael, who used to play club cricket, was involved in the longest tie-break—26-24—in the history of international tennis during the first round of the men's doubles at Wimbledon in 1985. Playing with Sweden's Jan Gunnarsson, they defeated Australia's John Frawley and Paraguay's Victor Pecci 6-3, 6-4, 3-6, 7-6.

•

When a schoolboy, Steve Waugh was captain of the New South Wales primary schools soccer team, while Mark Waugh was a one-time captain of the state's junior tennis team. Both Steve and Mark played soccer professionally for the Sydney club Croatia.

I have not seen a better goal this year than the one scored by East Hills High School's Stephen Waugh in the Commonwealth Bank Cup at Mt Druitt Town Soccer Centre last Wednesday evening. It was a goal of which the legendary Franz Beckenbauer would have been proud.

—Former Socceroo Johnny Warren, 1983

Both of the Waughs' parents were tennis champions. Their father Rodger, once beat Tony Roche in a state Under-14 final; he also won a national Under-19 doubles final. Their mother, Bev, was a New South Wales Under-14 champion and a national Under-19 mixed doubles winner. Later in life, Bev turned her attention to squash, and in 1990 appeared in the World Open in Sydney.

•

Mark Levy, who played rugby league for Balmain, Parramatta and Penrith, was a first-grade cricketer before turning to full-time football. He once took part in a state trial match and played alongside a young Allan Border.

•

During their Australian tour in 1991-92, West Indies captain Richie Richardson skippered an 18-foot skiff *Prudential* to victory in the fourth Cricketers Cup sailing event on Sydney Harbour.

•

Australia's Sammy Woods, who played county cricket for Somerset and Test cricket for England and Australia, won 13 rugby caps for England in the 1890s.

•

Australian Test batsman Peter Burge is a former chairman of the Queensland Harness Racing Board.

•

England all-rounder Walter Robins played soccer for Nottingham Forest.

•

Cambridge University batsman Max Woosnam captained England at tennis in the Davis Cup in 1921, and at association football against Wales in 1922. He won the doubles event with R. Lycett at Wimbledon in 1921 and a gold medal with O.G.N. Turnbull in the men's doubles at the 1920 Olympic Games.

•

Denis Compton won an FA Cup winners' medal for Arsenal in 1949-50. His elder brother, Leslie, also played cricket for Middlesex, and soccer for Arsenal and England.

Denis Compton

Ralph Legall, a West Indies wicket-keeper who appeared in four Tests against India in 1952–53, is a Canadian Over-60s tennis champion.

•

Paul Reiffel's father and a grandfather both played VFL football. His dad, Ron Reiffel, played for Richmond, while his grandfather, Lou, played for Melbourne and South Melbourne.

•

The Nawab of Pataudi, who appeared in three Tests for England and in three for India, also represented India at hockey.

•

George Ede, who appeared in 15 first-class matches for Hampshire during the 1860s, was a successful jockey who was killed during the running of the 1870 Grand National.

•

Apart from his 51 Test matches for England, 'Patsy' Hendren played football for Coventry, Queens Park Rangers, Manchester City and Brentford.

•

South Africa's Peter Kirsten was a leading rugby five-eighth who, at the age of 19, played for the Barbarians against the touring British Lions.

•

Leslie Balfour, who played for Scotland and the MCC, won the Scottish Tennis Championship in 1905—he also represented Scotland at rugby and excelled at billiards.

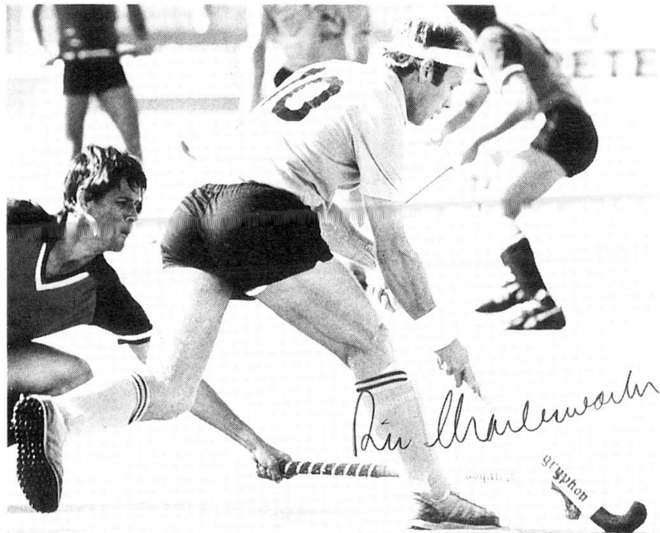

Former Western Australian cricket captain Ric Charlesworth, who led Australia's hockey team on 130 occasions between 1977 and 1984

Ric Charlesworth, who scored over 2,000 first-class runs for Western Australia during the 1970s, represented Australia in over 200 hockey internationals between 1972 and 1988. He played in five Olympic Games, winning a silver medal at Montreal in 1976.

•

J.W. Barnato, a noted long-distance racing car driver, played first-class cricket for Somerset between 1928 and 1930.

•

Graham Gooch ran in the 1993 London Marathon.

14 Duck Soup

Some of the greatest batsmen of all time began their first-class careers with a duck. They include W.G. Grace, Clem Hill, Walter Hammond, C.B. Fry, Frank Woolley, Len Hutton, Ted Dexter, Everton Weekes and Victor Trumper.

•

Victorian bowler Tom Antill played only one first-class match, against Tasmania at Launceston in 1850–51, and recorded Australia's first-ever duck. John Watson, another one-timer at first-class level, made the first pair in Australian cricket, a misfortune he suffered opening Tasmania's batting at Melbourne in 1851–52.

•

In 1985 Australia's Bob Holland scored a record five consecutive ducks in Test matches:

0 & 0 v England at Edgbaston
0 & 0 v New Zealand at Brisbane
0 v New Zealand at Sydney

•

In 1989 Desmond Haynes marked his first season of county cricket with three consecutive ducks after gaining his Middlesex cap.

•

India's match-winning spinner B.S. Chandrasekhar can probably lay claim to the unfortunate tag of being one of cricket's worst batsmen. In a first-class career which spanned three decades, he scored a mere 600 runs at 4.61. In Test cricket he registered more wickets (242) than runs (167), and was dismissed for a duck 23 times, and a pair four times, both Test records.

•

During the Australia–New Zealand Test at Perth in 1980–81, the Kiwis' left-handed opener Bruce Edgar and Australia's left-handed opener Graeme Wood were both dismissed for a pair.

•

Terry Alderman was unable to score a single run in his first eight matches in first-class cricket. He was required to bat only four times, scoring 0*, 0*, 0* and 0.

•

There were 12 ducks in the first-ever match between Victoria and New South Wales, at Melbourne in 1855–56. The home side recorded four noughts, while New South Wales scored eight. In their return match, at Sydney in 1856–57, the home team made four ducks while Victoria made nine.

•

Despite three consecutive ducks in June 1949, Len Hutton managed 1,294 runs for the month—a record in first-class cricket.

•

In 1905–06, South Australian bowler Alby Wright began his first-class career with three consecutive pairs, his six ducks constituting a world record.

•

Jack Davies, a spinner who later became President of the MCC, was the first bowler to dismiss Don Bradman for a duck in England. The dismissal, which happened in Australia's match against Cambridge University in 1934, was such a sensation it was front-page news.

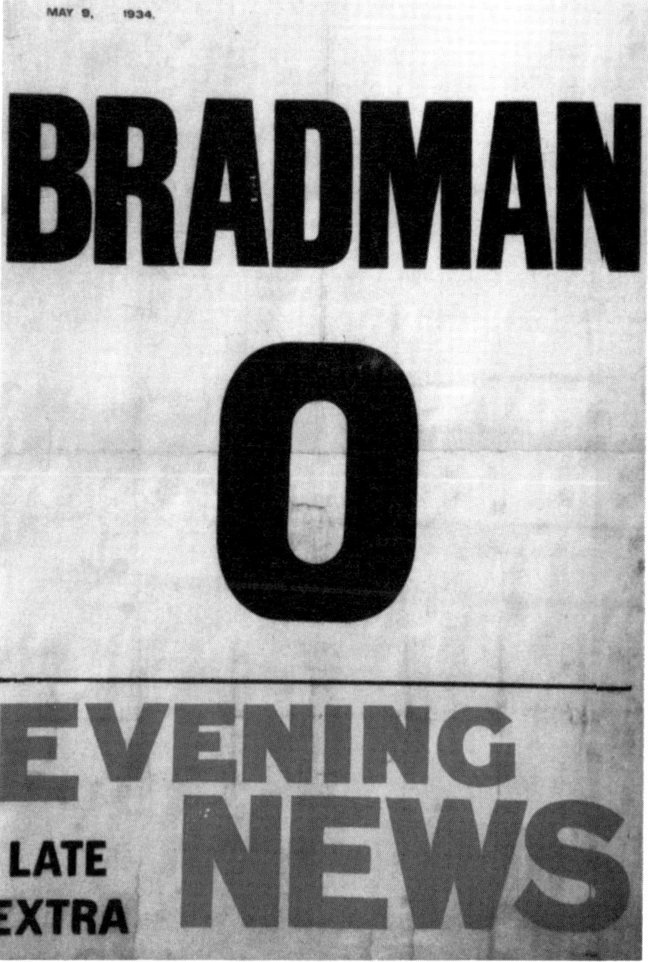

Mark Waugh made three ducks in the 1988–89 Sheffield Shield—all scored in the first innings of the first three matches of the season:

0 & 18 v Queensland at Brisbane
0 & 46 v Victoria at Sydney
0 & 100* v Tasmania at Devonport

•

In 1958–59 the West Indies were dismissed for 76 by Pakistan at Dacca. Their last six batsmen failed to score a single run between them.

•

New Zealand bowler Danny Morrison made four noughts in his first five Test innings.

•

Three Pakistan batsmen—Majid Khan, Wasim Bari and Sikander Bakht—were each dismissed for a pair in the same Test, versus Australia at Perth in 1978–79.

•

South African batsman Colin Wesley suffered the terrible fate of being dismissed first ball in both innings of a Test match—against England at Nottingham in 1960. In doing so he became the 100th batsman to record a pair in Test cricket.

•

With the bat, England fast bowler Brian Statham had a frustrating time against Australia in the 1950s, failing to score a run in six successive Test innings—0 and 0 in 1954–55; 0* & 0*, 0 and 0 in 1956.

•

When Australia was bundled out for 81 and 70 in the third Test at Manchester in 1888, no fewer than eight different batsmen were dismissed for a duck.

•

Steve Perryman failed to score a run in his first eight first-class innings for Worcestershire in 1982.

•

Len Hutton, who made over 6,000 Test runs, was dismissed for a duck on his Test debut. Other leading batsmen to have suffered this fate include Victor Trumper, Joe Darling, Maurice Leyland, Glenn Turner, Graham Gooch and Richie Richardson.

•

Kim Hughes ended his Test career with a pair, against the West Indies at Melbourne in 1984–85, having scored 0 and 2 in his previous two innings.

•

Fred Trueman was the first bowler to dismiss 50 batsmen for a duck in Test matches.

•

The record for most matches in a first-class career without scoring a single run is 13, by John Howarth (Nottinghamshire 1966/67).

•

One of the most unproductive spells of batting in the history of first-class cricket belongs to George Deyes of Yorkshire, who in 1907 in successive innings made 0, 0 & 0*, 1, 1* & 0, 0, 0 & 0, 1*, 0, 0, 0 & 0.

•

Majid Khan was out for a duck in his last Test match for Pakistan at Lahore in 1982–83. His father, Jahangir Khan, made a duck in his first Test, for India at Lord's in 1932.

•

'Patsy' Hendren, of Middlesex, was out for a duck in his first and last innings in first-class cricket.

•

Alan Hurst, who suffered 10 ducks in his 12-match Test career, recorded three pairs in the space of seven Tests, against England and Pakistan in 1978–79. He went on to complete the season with nine ducks in all first-class matches, a new Australian record.

•

B.S. Chandrasekhar began the 1977–78 tour of Australia without a single run in his first eight first-class innings. In the Test matches he batted eight times, recording two pairs and four runs at an average of 0.66. He made seven ducks in total on the tour, his first-class batting average was 1.20.

•

Two of the batsmen who hit centuries in the first innings of the Adelaide Test match in 1986–87 made ducks in the second innings—David Boon (103 & 0) and Mike Gatting (100 & 0). Gatting nearly did the same in reverse in the fifth Test at Sydney, scoring 0 & 96.

•

Bob Crisp was dismissed for a duck four times in five balls during the South African–Australia Test series in 1935–36.

•

Mohammad Ghazali, a Pakistani batsman, was out for a duck twice within two hours during the third Test against England at Manchester in 1954—this is believed to be the quickest pair in Test history.

•

One of India's leading batsmen, Mohinder Amarnath, made five ducks in the 1983–84 Test series against the West Indies. He went to the crease six times and finished the series with a single run at an average of 0.16.

•

Dennis Lillee had the better of Dennis Amiss in 1974–75, dismissing the England opener for a duck in three successive innings, with a pair in the fifth Test at Adelaide.

•

Half-a-dozen batsmen out for a duck in a single innings has been fairly common in the history of first-class cricket. But all six being dismissed by a single bowler is a feat that's fairly rare—Edward Barratt dismissed seven Australians for nought at The Oval in 1878, and Tim Wall accounted for six New South Wales batsmen in his haul of 10 for 36 for South Australia at the SCG in 1932–33. In postwar cricket, Tony Merrick got six out for a duck for Warwickshire v Derbyshire in 1988. The West Indian-born fast bowler took six wickets, including a hat-trick, in 10 balls without conceding a run.

DERBYSHIRE v WARWICKSHIRE
Derby 1988

J.G. Wright	b Gifford	48
P.D. Bowler	lbw b Small	3
B.J.M. Maher	b Small	39
J.E. Morris	not out	54
B. Roberts	c Din b Gifford	9
S.C. Goldsmith	lbw b Merrick	0
K.J. Barnett	c Humpage b Merrick	0
P.G. Newman	lbw b Merrick	0
O.H. Mortensen	c Moles b Merrick	0
S.J. Base	b Merrick	0
D.E. Malcolm	b Merrick	0
Extras	(lb 10 nb 3)	13
		166

•

South Africa's Jimmy Cook was the first Test debutant to be dismissed by the first ball of a match. His dismissal, by Kapil Dev at Durban in 1992–93, was the 17th instance overall of a batsman out first ball of a Test.

•

Pat Pocock, who was resurrected to face the West Indies in 1984 after an eight-year absence, marked his comeback at Manchester with a pair. He followed it up with another two ducks in the next Test at The Oval.

•

Paul Garlick failed to disturb the scorers in nine successive innings for Cambridge University in 1984—0, 0, 0 & 0, 0, 0* & 0, 0 & 0.

•

The Indian opening batsman Pankaj Roy was dismissed for a duck in five of his seven innings in the 1952 Test series against England, on each occasion to the bowling of Fred Trueman.

•

On his first-class debut in 1939–40, Queensland bowler John Stackpoole had the distinction of dismissing Don Bradman for a first-ball duck.

•

Mark Waugh made it into double-figures only once during the 1992 Test series against Sri Lanka, earning ducks in his last four innings.

•

David Boon

When Pakistan's Wasim Akram dismissed David Boon first ball at Melbourne in 1989–90, it was his second successive golden duck and his third nought in three Tests.

•

Simon O'Donnell, fresh from a magnificent century against the MCC at Lord's in 1985, was out first ball on his Test debut three weeks later at Leeds.

•

Twelve different batsmen made ducks in the County Championship match against Northamptonshire at Leicester in 1990, including six in Leicestershire's second innings total of 165. One of the dozen ducks was Northants bowler Mark Robinson, who failed to score for the 12th time in successive innings in first-class matches. This beat by two the previous world record held by Jim Griffiths of Northamptonshire and Peter Visser, who represented the New Zealand provincial side Central Districts.

M.A. ROBINSON (NORTHAMPTONSHIRE)
12 scoreless innings 1990

0, 0* & 0, 0* 0*, 0* & 0, 0 & 0, 0*, 0*, 0

Prior to his 'feats' of 1990, Robinson had only ever recorded runs on 16 occasions in 46 first-class innings. From his debut in 1987 to the end of the '89 season, Robinson failed to score in 30 innings and was out for a duck 14 times. His first 70 appearances at the crease in first-class matches yielded only one double-figure score and saw him out first ball six times. In 1992 he reached a noteworthy landmark, passing a career total of 100 first-class runs in his 84th match (v Yorkshire at Headingley).

•

Andy Afford, a slow left-armer bowler with Nottinghamshire, gave Mark Robinson a run for his money in 1990, when he failed to score a run 12 times in 15 successive first-class innings—0*, 0, 0* & 0, 0*, 0, 0* & 1, 0 & 0, 1 & 0, 0, 1* and 0. For the season, Afford batted 22 times and failed to score on 14 occasions with nine ducks.

•

Former England Test all-rounder David Capel made six ducks in seven successive first-class innings for Northamptonshire in 1991.

•

Allan Border marked his 100th Test match, at Melbourne in 1988–89, with his first duck in 89 innings since Brisbane 1982–83.

•

Yorkshire batsman Phillip Robinson, who scored over 1,000 runs in 1988, collected two history-making ducks in a Championship match against Kent at Canterbury—he was run out in the first innings without facing a ball and dismissed lbw first ball in the second.

•

David Gower was out for a pair when England met Western Australia on their tour in 1986–87. Wilf Slack, Allan Lamb and Mike Gatting all made ducks. When England took on New South Wales at Newcastle a fortnight later, five of them, including both openers—Chris Broad and Bill Athey—failed to score in its second-innings total of 82.

•

One of the most celebrated hat-tricks in Test cricket took place at Leeds in 1899, when Jack Hearne dismissed Clem Hill, Syd Gregory and Monty Noble for ducks.

•

Kim Hughes, who was dismissed for a pair in his last Test match, suffered a 'king pair' in the third unofficial Test against South Africa at Johannesburg in 1985–86.

•

The nearly always dependable West Indies opening pair of Gordon Greenidge and Desmond Haynes were both dismissed for a duck in the same innings by India's Balwindersingh Sandhu in the second Test at Port-of-Spain in 1982–83.

•

There were seven ducks in the World Series Cup match between Australia and England at Sydney in 1979–80.

•

Former Queensland bowler Ross Duncan was out for a duck seven times for Victoria in 1971–72.

Chris Tavaré

England opener, Chris Tavaré bagged a pair in the tour match against Western Australia in 1982–83. Both times he was out to the 'c Marsh b Lillee' combination.

•

Seymour Clark of Somerset went to the crease nine times in first-class cricket and never scored a run—0 & 0, 0 & 0, 0* & 0*, 0 & 0 and 0.

•

Craig McDermott dismissed 11 batsmen for a duck in the first three matches of the Sheffield Shield season in 1990–91. Most of his victims were top-order batsmen—Andrew Hilditch, David Hookes, Dean Jones, Jamie Siddons, and Warren Ayres who collected a pair. In McDermott's first Test of the season he got another two specialist batsmen out for a duck—Michael Atherton and Allan Lamb, in the first innings at Adelaide.

•

Francis Kendall, selected three times for Northamptonshire in 1930, made five consecutive ducks in the six innings of his first-class career.

•

Eight Oxford University batsmen failed to score in their first innings total of 24 against Leicestershire at The Parks in 1985.

Jim Higgs

Kim Barnett

On Australia's 1975 tour of England, Jim Higgs played in eight matches and was bowled by the only ball he received (v Leicestershire at Leicester).

•

When Allan Border made two noughts in the fifth Test against the West Indies at Perth in 1992–93, it gave him his first pair in his 325-match first-class career, which began in 1976–77.

•

Thirty-seven ducks were recorded in the 1978–79 Ashes series.

•

Aaqib Javed, the Pakistan fast bowler, was out for a duck in his first five first-class innings on the 1989–90 Australian tour:

0 & 0	v Western Australia at Perth
0	v Queensland at Brisbane
0 & 0	v Australia at Melbourne

•

John Candler, who played in seven matches (10 innings) for Cambridge University in 1894 and '95, failed to score in nine successive first-class innings.

England batsman Kim Barnett was out for a duck on his Test debut, against Sri Lanka at Lord's in 1988. The player who dismissed him, Matibage Samarasekera, was also making his Test debut, and he too was out for nought.

•

The first father and son to play Test cricket—Ned and Syd Gregory—were both dismissed for a duck on their Test debuts. Jack Gregory, a cousin of Syd, also made a duck in his first Test.

•

Tasmanian wicket-keeper Richard Soule, the scorer of a first-class century, was bowled first ball in both innings of his first-class debut, against the touring Pakistanis in 1983–84.

•

The record for the most wretched of all first-class careers must surely go to the Northamptonshire bowler Harry Wilson, who was run out for a duck in both innings of his only first-class match, against the touring New Zealanders at Peterborough in 1931.

•

Six Pakistan batsmen—Shafiq Ahmed, Sadiq Mohammad, Majid Khan, Ijaz Faqih, Iqbal Qasim and Nazir Junior—were dismissed for a duck in the first innings of the third Test against the West Indies at Karachi in 1980.

Both Leonard Butterfield and Gordon Rowe made an inauspicious start to Test cricket when they were dismissed for pairs in their only Test appearance, against Australia at Wellington in 1945–46. Bill O'Reilly, in the last of his 27 Tests, was the bowler who remarkably got both batsmen each time:

C.G. Rowe	b O'Reilly 0 & b O'Reilly 0
L.A. Butterfield	lbw O'Reilly 0 & lbw O'Reilly 0

•

Sunil Gavaskar, who scored 34 Test centuries for India, was out to the first ball of a Test match on three occasions.

Test	*Bowler*
v England Birmingham 1974	Geoff Arnold
v West Indies Calcutta 1983–84	Malcolm Marshall
v Pakistan Jaipur 1986–87	Imran Khan

•

England bowler Richard Ellison faced 52 balls in 50 minutes before being out for a duck in the first Test against India at Bombay in 1984–85.

•

In a Benson & Hedges Cup match against Nottinghamshire in 1987, five Leicestershire batsmen were out for a duck, four to Winston Benjamin when the score was on 46. A few days later in the same competition five Essex batsmen were dismissed for a duck, including the top four in the batting order, against Hampshire at Chelmsford.

•

Everton Weekes was out for a pair in his final Test match against England, at The Oval in 1957.

•

When Greg Matthews took David Gower's wicket at Melbourne in 1990–91, it brought to an end an extraordinary run of 119 innings without a duck—a record sequence in Test cricket. The last time Gower failed to score was way back in 1982 when Pakistan's Mudassar Nazar got him out for nought in the second Test at Lord's.

•

In 1958–59 England experienced one of its worst starts to a Test match when Ray Lindwall struck two vital blows in the fifth Test at Melbourne. Trevor Bailey, appearing in his final Test, was dismissed for a pair by Lindwall, and with his opening partner Peter Richardson gave England starts of 0 and 0.

The South African opener 'Jackie' McGlew made a pair in the second Test at Lord's in 1955, falling twice in three balls to Brian Statham.

•

Apart from collecting a pair on his Test debut in 1975, Graham Gooch suffered the ignominy of back-to-back pairs on his home ground at Chelmsford in 1987. The first two ducks came in a County Championship match against Warwickshire, the next two a week later in a game against the touring Pakistanis.

•

John Trim, a West Indian fast bowler, ended his brief four-match Test career by being run out for a duck in both innings at Melbourne in 1951–52.

•

An unusual record came Sri Lanka's way in its very first Test match, against England at Colombo in 1982. Four of England's batsmen—Chris Tavaré, John Emburey, Derek Underwood and Bob Willis—were dismissed for a duck in the first innings—a record number for a country playing its inaugural Test. Geoff Cook's dismissal for nought in the second innings brought to five the number out for a duck, another Test record. The previous match record was three ducks inflicted on Australia in England's first Test at Melbourne in 1877.

•

Richard Hadlee had Graeme Wood out for a pair and a duck in consecutive innings during the 1980–81 Test series in Australia.

•

In Test matches against England, Victor Trumper was dismissed for a duck seven times, including three in a row in 1907–08.

•

Garry Sobers made a duck in his only one-day international, against England at Leeds in 1973.

•

There were eight ducks in Hampshire's total of 15 against Warwickshire at Birmingham in 1922.

•

When Victoria made its world record score of 1,107 at Melbourne in 1926–27, Frank Morton was run out for a duck.

•

OTHER INSTANCES OF 0 AND 0 OPENING PARTNERSHIPS IN TEST CRICKET

Sir Timothy O'Brien & George Lohmann (1st inns)	E v SA Port Elizabeth 1895–96
Charles Wright & Harry Butt (2nd inns)	
Tom Hayward & Wilfred Rhodes (1st inns)	E v A Melbourne 1903–04
Len Braund & 'Tip' Foster (2nd inns)	
Vic Richardson & Bill Woodfull	A v E Sydney 1932–33
Jack Moroney & Arthur Morris	A v E Brisbane 1950–51
'Jackie' McGlew & Trevor Goddard	SA v E Lord's 1955
Rick McCosker & Alan Turner	A v WI Perth 1975–76
Majid Khan & Mudassar Nazar	P v A Perth 1978–79
Mudassar Nazar & Mohsin Khan	P v E Birmingham 1982

Don Bradman's last innings in Test cricket—a duck at The Oval in 1948

Test cricket's most famous duck was probably that of Don Bradman at The Oval in 1948. Playing in his last Test, Bradman was out second ball for a duck to the bowling of Eric Hollies. A boundary would have taken him past 7,000 Test runs, and his average to 100.00.

•

Immediately prior to his first-class debut for Queensland in 1989–90, a match in which he scored a century, Geoff Foley had made four successive ducks in club cricket.

•

Geoff Boycott made a duck in his final Test match innings against Australia, in the sixth Test at The Oval in 1981.

•

Brendon Bracewell, who appeared in six Tests for New Zealand, scored only twice in his first nine innings—0 & 0, 0 & 0*, 4 & 0, 0* & 5 and 0 (1978–80).

•

John Bracewell, like his brother Brendon, was out for a duck on his Test debut, at Brisbane in 1980–81.

•

There were 11 ducks in the Sheffield Shield match between Victoria (4) and New South Wales (7) at Melbourne in 1988–89. Victorian spinner Mark Osborne, who had three batsmen out for a duck in a row, himself suffered a pair, as did Wayne Holdsworth who was making his first-class debut for New South Wales.

In the previous Shield match between the two sides at Sydney, Simon O'Donnell—who made a pair—dismissed Steve and Mark Waugh and Steve Smith all without scoring in one over.

•

Six Pakistanis made ducks in the third Texaco Trophy match against England at Birmingham in 1987. Mudassar Nazar, in his 100th one-day international, was out to the first ball of the match.

•

Keith Stackpole, who was out to the first ball of the third Test at Auckland in 1973–74, finished the match, and his Test career, with a pair.

•

Former Test batsman John Morris made 12 ducks during the 1992 English season—seven in first-class matches, with three in a row, and five in one-day matches.

Derek Randall

England Test player Reg Sinfield began his first-class career with Gloucestershire in 1921 scoring seven ducks in his first 11 innings. He eventually went on to pass 1,000 runs in a season on 10 occasions.

•

When Surrey bowled out the MCC for 16 at Lord's in 1872, the first seven wickets fell before the first run was scored.

•

Vincent Hogg batted for 87 minutes before being out for a duck for Rhodesia B v Natal B at Pietermaritzburg in 1979–80.

•

New South Wales opening batsman Sammy Jones marked the beginning of the Sheffield Shield competition with a duck to the third ball of the match at Adelaide in 1892–93.

•

When South Africa made its debut in one-day international cricket, at Calcutta in 1991, opening batsman Andrew Hudson was out for a duck in the opening over. Hudson also made a duck in his first Test, at Bridgetown in 1992, having made a century in the first innings of the match, the first South African batsman to reach three figures on his Test debut.

During a County Championship match at Nottingham in 1989, Derek Randall completed one of the oddest pairs on record in first-class cricket. Out for a duck in the first innings on a pitch considered sub-standard, the match was transferred to another, upon which he was also out for a duck. Being dismissed for a duck on two different pitches in the same match is an occurrence believed to be unique in first-class cricket.

•

Mark O'Neill, who hit three centuries in successive innings for New South Wales in 1985–86, made four consecutive ducks to finish the 1990–91 season, achieving pairs against Tasmania and Victoria, in the Sheffield Shield final.

•

When Pakistan's Sarfraz Nawaz took his record 9 wickets for 86 at Melbourne in 1978–79, five of his victims made a duck.

•

Ravi Shastri got three New Zealand batsmen out for a duck in four balls on his Test debut, at Wellington in 1980–81.

•

Ian Botham made a pair in his last Test as England captain, against Australia at Lord's in 1981.

•

The Pakistani opening batsman Rizwan-uz-Zaman was out for a duck on his Test debut, at Perth in 1981–82, to Terry Alderman who earned his first Test wicket on home soil with his first delivery.

Andrew Hudson

Denis Compton made four ducks in six first-class innings in 1946.

•

Sussex brothers Alan and Colin Wells were both dismissed for a first-ball duck in the first innings of the County Championship match against Surrey at Guildford in 1990. On the same day, at Northampton, another pair of brothers made ducks, when Curtly Ambrose dismissed the Kent pair of Chris and Graham Cowdrey.

•

Sri Lanka's Arjuna Ranatunga suffered three successive ducks in the 1991–92 Test series against Pakistan.

•

Frank Hayes, who began his Test career with a century on his debut at Lord's in 1973, made a duck in six of his next eight appearances—29 & 0, 8 & 0, 12 & 8, 10 & 0, 6, 24 & 0, 0 & 18, and 7 & 0. His poor form was due in part to the fact he played all of his nine Tests against the West Indies.

•

On his Test debut at Manchester in 1912, South African wicket-keeper Tommy Ward picked up a 'king pair'. On both occasions he was the third victim of a hat-trick to Australia's Jimmy Matthews.

•

Clyde Walcott was out for a duck only once in his 44-match Test career for the West Indies. Clive Lloyd played in 58 successive Test innings before his first duck, at Port-of-Spain in 1973–74, and suffered only four in 175 innings.

•

Although Bob Simpson scored over 1,500 first-class runs in 1963–64, he also scored six ducks.

In the opening match of the 1992–93 Mercantile Mutual Cup, the last six batsmen in Victoria's all-out total of 132 failed to score in the match against Western Australia.

•

Hans Ebeling, a Victorian fast bowler, dismissed seven Queensland batsmen for a duck in the Sheffield Shield match at Melbourne in 1928–29. He got five of them out for nought in the first innings on his way to a match-winning haul of 7 for 33.

•

Seven batsmen failed to score in South Australia's total of 96 against Queensland at Brisbane in 1976–77.

•

In successive first-class matches in 1940–41, Don Bradman suffered two first-ball ducks.

•

John Cockett, who was good enough to score a century for Cambridge in his brief eight-match career, made a pair in his final two first-class appearances.

•

In 1989 Gloucestershire fast bowler Kevin Jarvis had a lean trot with the bat, recording six consecutive scoreless innings, and only one successful knock in a run of nine—0, 0*, 0, 0, 0, 0, 32, 0 and 0.

•

During a Shell Trophy match in New Zealand in 1988–89, there was the unusual sight of three first-ball ducks affecting opening batsmen. Going in first for Northern Districts at Morrinsville, Lindsay Croker was dismissed by the first ball of the match. Graham Burnett was out first ball in Wellington's first innings; Croker then completed a 'king pair', out first ball in Northern Districts' second innings.

15 What's in a Name?

Although Smith is the most common surname in Test cricket, with over 20 having played to date, only two have done so for Australia:

Dave Smith	2 matches v England in 1912
Steve Smith	3 matches v West Indies in 1983–84

•

During a Sheffield Shield match at Perth in 1984–85, three of the players' surnames began with the letter Z—Bob Zadow and Andrew Zesers for South Australia and Western Australia's Tim Zoehrer. The trio met again on two other occasions in the Sheffield Shield, once the following season and once in 1986–87.

•

Keith (Ross) Miller was named after two famous Australian aviators—Keith Smith and Ross Smith.

•

The two middle names of West Indian fast bowler Colin Croft are Everton Hunte, after Everton Weekes and Conrad Hunte.

•

The First Test at Christchurch in the 1991–92 season featured two players on each side with the same surname—Ian Smith and Chris Pringle for New Zealand and Robin Smith and Derek Pringle for England.

•

In three consecutive Tests against Pakistan in 1987, England's first three in the batting order were all known by their second christian name, rather than their first—Brian Christopher (Chris) Broad, Robert (Tim) Robinson and Charles William (Bill) Athey.

•

E.B. Dwyer, a Sydney-born bowler who represented Sussex, can lay claim to the unusual record of being the first-class cricketer with the most christian names—John Elicius Benedict Bernard Placid Carrington Dwyer.

•

Unable to cope with the burden of his father's name, John Bradman changed his surname to Bradsen.

•

I.L. Bula, a Fijian batsman, holds a record which nobody will ever claim, that of the longest name in first-class cricket. His full name is ILEKENA LASARUSA TALEBULA-MAINEIILIKENAMAINAVALENIVEIVAKABULA-IMAINAKULALAKEBA—a grand total of 59 letters for the surname alone.

•

England batsman Neil Fairbrother has the middle name of Harvey. He was named after Australian batsman Neil Harvey, his mother's favourite cricketer.

•

In 1919 two county cricketers played in a first-class match under an assumed name—Guy Bignell played for Hampshire using the name 'G. Newcombe', while Somerset's Arthur Rippon played under the name of 'S.C. Trimnell' in a match against Gloucestershire.

•

One of the longest and perhaps most complicated dismissals in all first-class cricket surfaced during a Ranji Trophy match between Andhra and Kerala in 1990–91:

V. Chamundeswaranath c Balasubramaniam b Anantapadamanabhan

The letters in their surnames totalled 50, average 16.66.

•

When Warwickshire met Hampshire in the 1991 NatWest one-day semi-final at Edgbaston, both teams fielded two Smiths—Chris Smith and Robin Smith (Hants) and Paul Smith and Neil Smith (Warks).

•

The middle name of Chris Kuggeleijn, who played Test cricket for New Zealand in the late 1980s, is Mary.

16 LBW

The first recorded instance of an lbw decision occurred in 1795 in a match between Surrey and an England XIII—the batsman to fall was John Tufton.

•

In a Ranji Trophy match between Patiala and Delhi in 1953–54, 19 of the 33 dismissals were lbw decisions—this is a record number in any first-class match.

•

In 1979 Mike Procter, bowling for Gloucestershire, repeated his earlier feat in 1972 of taking an all-lbw hat-trick:

v Essex at Westcliff in 1972
v Yorkshire at Cheltenham in 1979

•

Eight Oxford University batsmen were dismissed lbw in the second innings of the match against Warwickshire in 1980, an English first-class record, equalled by Sussex in 1992 against Essex at Hove.

•

Indian opener Kris Srikkanth had a terrible time against Wasim Akram in the 1989 Test series with Pakistan. Srikkanth fell lbw to Wasim in four of his seven innings. In the other three he was bowled by Wasim for 13 and 0, and caught by Wasim off the bowling of Imran Khan for 3.

•

When Sri Lanka's Ravi Ratnayeke dismissed Javed Miandad lbw for 40 at Sialkot in 1985–86, it was the first time the Pakistani batsman had fallen this way in 35 Tests at home.

•

Seven of Richard Hadlee's 11 wickets against the West Indies at Dunedin in 1979–80 were leg before wicket. For the first time in Test history, there were 12 lbws in a single Test.

•

Of the 100 Test wickets taken by Terry Alderman against England, 36, more than a third of them were lbw decisions. Nineteen of his 41 wickets in the 1989 series were leg before.

•

During a run of 10 consecutive Test innings against Australia (1989–1990/91), Graham Gooch was out lbw six times.

•

During the 1981 Benson & Hedges Cup, David Gower of Leicestershire was the subject of a most unusual hat-trick. For the third time in succession at Northampton, Tim Lamb had Gower dismissed lbw for a duck. The other two dismissals came in a County Championship match in 1980.

•

When Malcolm Marshall dismissed Australia's Roger Woolley lbw at St John's in 1983–84, it was his 100th Test wicket. He also got his 200th wicket—Paul Downton at Port-of-Spain in 1985–86—and his 300th—David Boon at Melbourne in 1988–89—with lbw decisions.

•

No Australian batsman was given out lbw in the six-Test series against England in 1970–71.

•

Abdul Qadir took seven wickets lbw in the first Test against England at Lahore in 1987.

Abdul Qadir

Of the 27 wickets which fell in the Yorkshire–Middlesex match at Sheffield in 1982, 13 were lbw. Two of the openers were dismissed leg before in both innings—Geoff Boycott for Yorkshire and Wilf Slack for Middlesex.

•

In the three-Test series in Sri Lanka in 1985–86, three of Pakistan's top-order batsmen—Mohsin Khan, Javed Miandad and Ramiz Raja—were dismissed lbw three times in four innings. A fourth Pakistani, Qasim Omar, was adjudged lbw twice in a row during the series.

•

Mike Gatting was given out lbw five times in his first six innings against Australia in the 1981 Ashes series.

•

Don Bradman was only ever dismissed lbw 27 times in his 338 first-class innings. Strangely, two of those dismissals came in his first match for South Australia, against the MCC at Adelaide in 1935–36.

•

When Sussex made 278 against Gloucestershire at Eastbourne in 1928, its first six in the batting order were out lbw.

•

England's Graham Gooch fell leg before to Michael Holding for 51 in both innings of the fifth Test at St John's in 1985–86.

•

There were 17 lbw victims in the first Test between the West Indies and Pakistan at Port-of-Spain in 1992–93. This was a Test record, beating the 14 at Faisalabad, when Sri Lanka played Pakistan in 1991–92.

Curtly Ambrose

In Pakistan's second innings at Melbourne in 1989–90, no fewer than six batsmen were dismissed lbw—a number which equalled the Test record. Terry Alderman got five of the leg-before decisions, the first time this had been achieved by one bowler in a single Test match innings. Curtly Ambrose, just two months later, became the second bowler to achieve the feat when he got five leg befores in the second innings against England at Bridgetown.

•

Garry Sobers was dismissed lbw three times in a row by Pakistan's Fazal Mahmood in the 1958–59 series.

17 Cricket Stamps

The first postage stamp featuring cricket was issued in 1962 by an unlikely place, the Portugese colony of Cape Verde Islands.

•

Garry Sobers was the first cricketer to be the subject of a stamp, when Barbados released a 35¢ issue in 1966.

•

Australia's first cricketer to be depicted on a stamp was Victor Trumper, in 1981. Other Australian cricketing issues include a set of six stamps which celebrated the 1977 Centenary Test, a $1 stamp for the Bicentenary in 1988 and two commemorating the centenary of the Sheffield Shield in 1992. The 45¢ and $1.20 Shield stamps, featuring illustrations by artist Mark Sofilas, brought to 12 the number of cricket stamps released by Australia.

•

It wasn't until 1973 that England released its first cricket stamps—a set of three, featuring W.G. Grace, commemorating 100 years of county cricket.

•

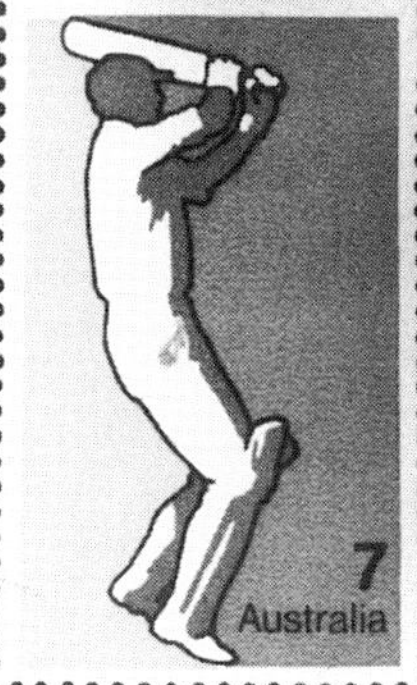

World Record
Most Wickets In
Test Cricket
New Zealand Record
Most First Class Wickets

BANGALORE INDIA
FIRST TEST

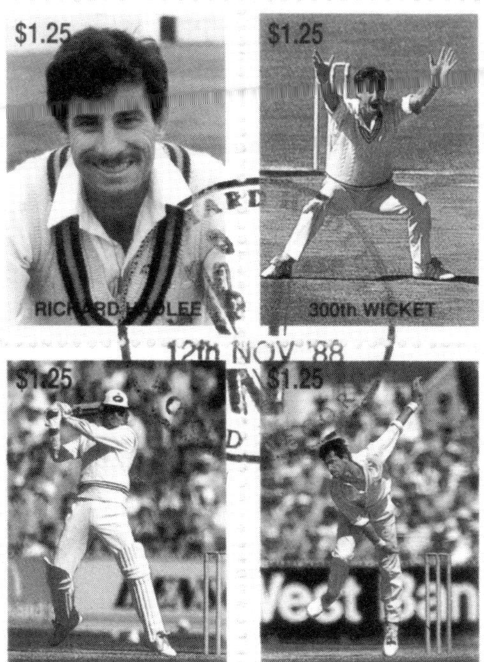

18 Births and Deaths

Two cricketing legends W.G. Grace and Dennis Lillee share the same birthday—18 July. W.G.'s mother, Martha—the first woman to appear in *Wisden*'s 'Births and Deaths' section—was also born on 18 July.

•

Australian captain Bill Woodfull twice won the Ashes in England on his birthday—22 August—in 1930 and 1934.

•

Syd Gregory, who played 58 times for Australia, was born on the site of the present Sydney Cricket Ground.

•

Australian Test players James Kelly and Hugh Trumble both played Test cricket together around the turn of the century. Kelly was born on 10 May 1867; Trumble two days later. Both died at the age of 71 on 14 August 1938.

•

The first cricketer to die from injuries received in a first-class match was George Summers in 1870. Playing for Nottinghamshire against the MCC at Lord's, a ball from John Platts struck Summers and he died of the injury four days later.

•

Leslie Hylton, a West Indies fast bowler, was excuted in 1950 for the murder of his wife.

•

Australian Test cricketers Sid Barnes, Jack Iverson, William Bruce, Albert Trott and Jim Burke committed suicide.

•

Two members of Australia's first-ever Test team, Dave Gregory and Tom Garrett, were born in the New South Wales coastal city of Wollongong. Four were born in England, one in Ireland, one in India, two in Melbourne and two in Sydney.

AUSTRALIAN TEST PLAYERS BORN IN ENGLAND

Name	*Birthplace*	*Tests*	*Debut*
Charles Bannerman	Woolwich, Kent	3	1877
Hanson Carter	Halifax, Yorkshire	28	1907–08
William Cooper	Maidstone, Kent	2	1881–82
Tony Dell	Lymington, Hampshire	2	1970–71
James Hodges	England	2	1877
Tom Kendall	Bedford, Bedfordshire	2	1877
Percy McDonnell	London	19	1880
Billy Midwinter	St. Braviels, Gloucestershire	8[a]	1877
Harry Musgrove	Surbiton, Surrey	1	1884–85

[a]Midwinter also played 4 Tests for England

•

Clarrie Grimmett was born on Christmas Day in 1891 at Dunedin in New Zealand.

•

In 1991 England's Test selectors set a new record when they chose the team to take on the West Indies in the second Test at Lord's. Seven of the XI were born outside England—Graeme Hick (Zimbabwe), Allan Lamb (South Africa), Robin Smith (South Africa), Derek Pringle (Kenya), Phillip DeFreitas (Dominica), Steve Watkin (Wales) and Devon Malcolm (Jamaica).

Before 1991, one of the most cosmopolitan England teams was the XI which played New Zealand in the second and third Tests in 1931. Its captain—Douglas Jardine—was born in India, Freddie Brown was born in Peru, 'Gubby' Allen Australia and K.S. Duleepsinhji India.

•

In 1987–88 at Faisalabad, every England player in the second Test against Pakistan was English-born. Not since the inaugural Test against Sri Lanka at Colombo in 1981–82 had England selected a home-grown XI. For the next 60 successive Tests through until 1987–88, at least one of England's Test team was born overseas.

•

The two captains for the 1905 Australia-England Test series—F.S. Jackson and Joe Darling—were both born on 21 November 1870.

•

Jeffrey Stollmeyer, who captained the West Indies in 14 Tests during the 1950s, was shot dead by an intruder at his home in Trinidad in 1989.

•

Two of Australia's finest wicket-keepers were born on 17 February—Don Tallon in 1916 and Barry Jarman in 1936.

•

Francis MacKinnon, who played for England in 1878–79, is Test cricket's longest-lived player. Born in 1848, he died in 1947 aged 98 years and 324 days. Australia's most durable Test cricketer was Ken Burn, who passed away in 1956 at the age of 93 years 307 days.

•

In 1892 Hong Kong's national cricket team was lost at sea. On its return from a cricket match in Shanghai their boat,

The Bokhara, struck a typhoon in the China Sea and sank, with the loss of 125 lives, including the 13 touring cricketers.

•

In 1991 two first-class cricketers passed away just one year short of their 100th birthday—Willis Walker, who played for Nottinghamshire from 1913 to 1937, and Stan Rimington, who scored 91 in his only first-class innings, for Victoria in 1921–22.

•

Five of England's most famous Test cricketers were born on 24 November—Herbert Sutcliffe (1894), Roly Jenkins (1918), Ken Barrington (1930), Fred Titmus (1932) and Ian Botham (1955).

•

During a match at Nagpur in India in 1987–88, the wicket-keeper, dissatisfied with one of his appeals being turned down, hit the umpire Uday Pimple about the head with a stump. The 20-year-old official later died in hospital.

•

In 1978 no fewer than six overseas batsmen scored 500 runs in the County Championship for Sussex—Pakistan's Imran Khan and Javed Miandad, Sri Lanka's Gehan Mendis, the Rhodesian-born Paul Parker, John Barclay from West Germany and Paul Phillipson, who was born in India. The best-placed 'local' batsman was the wicket-keeping captain, Arnold Long, who made 405 runs.

Gehan Mendis

19 Music, Music, Music and Other Cricket Records

Francis Parr, who captained Lancashire in 1953, was a professional jazz trombonist. He played with George Melly in the Mick Mulligan Band and managed Acker Bilk, of 'Stranger on the Shore' fame, from 1963 to 1974.

•

England bowler Maurice Allom was a well-regarded saxophonist who played at the Savoy Hotel in London during the 1920s. He was also a member of the Quinquaginta Club Ramblers, a university group which recorded a number of songs on the Brunswick label.

•

Former England captain Tony Lewis was a violinist with the Welsh Youth Orchestra.

•

Bev Congdon, a New Zealand batsman of the 1960s and '70s, used to play trumpet in a jazz band.

•

David Measham, who was conductor of the West Australian Symphony Orchestra for 16 years, used to play club cricket in England and was once offered a position on the ground staff at Nottingham.

•

David English, who turned out for Middlesex and the MCC, is a former record company president who once managed the Bee Gees. He also founded a charity cricket team in 1986 with guitarist Eric Clapton.

•

In 1930 one of cricket's most famous songs was released when Art Leonard recorded the Jack O'Hagan composition 'Our Don Bradman'. The flipside was 'Our Eleven', a number written by Jack Lumsdaine in recognition of the 1930 Australian touring team. It was on that tour that Bradman himself recorded some music, a 78 rpm disc that featured two piano solos—'Old-Fashioned Locket' and 'Our Bungalow of Dreams'. Bradman also composed the music for another Jack Lumsdaine song, 'Everyday Is a Rainbow Day for Me'.

•

In 1971 the England Test side, fresh from securing the Ashes in Australia in 1970–71, celebrated the win by recording 'The Ashes Song'. It turned out to be a flop, unlike 'Here Come the Aussies' by the '72 Australians, which made it into the Australian Top 20.

•

Elton John, a frequent spectator at Test matches, dressed up in cricket gear for the cover of his *Greatest Hits Volume II* album.

•

Geoff Hurst, the former Essex first-class cricketer, was a member of the England World Cup soccer squad, which went to the top of the British charts in 1970 with the song 'Back Home'.

•

Some cricketing records which deserve a mention include: 'How to Improve Your Cricket' by Jack Hobbs (1920s); 'Leg Theory' by Harold Larwood (1933); 'Victory Calypso' by Lord Beginner (1950); 'King Cricket'/'The Constantine Calypso' by Cy Grant (1966); 'When An Old Cricketer Leaves the Crease' by Roy Harper (1975); 'The Umpire Strikes Back' by Fred Trueman (1980); and 'The Cricket EP' by Percy Pavilion (1983).

Don Bradman at the recording of his composition 'Everyday is a Rainbow Day for Me' at Columbia's Sydney studios

The Ashes-winning MCC side of 1970–71 in the studio recording 'The Ashes Song', a performance that proved to be far less successful than their cricket

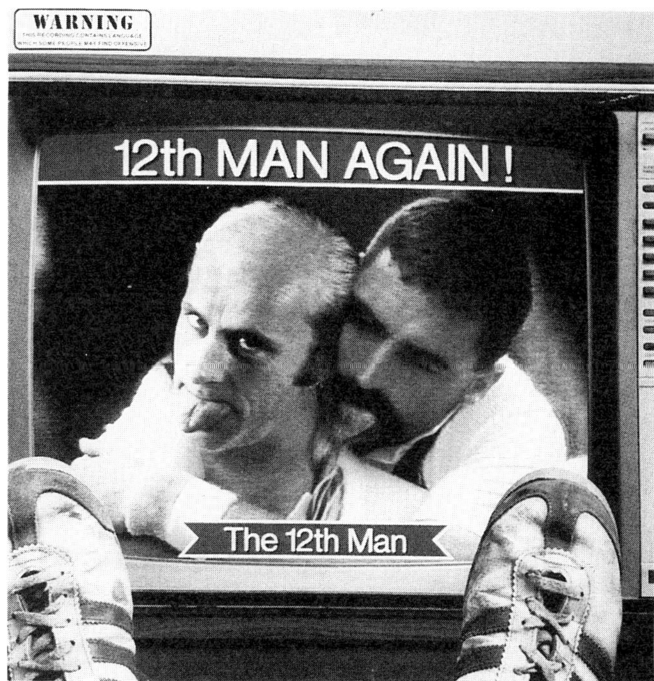

A hat-trick of hits for the Twelfth Man, Billy Birmingham

The Australian pop group Sherbet had a number-one hit in 1976 with their single 'Howzat'. It was the first record of a cricketing nature to hit the top of the Australian charts; it was also a number one in England. Other cricket singles to go to number one in Australia include 'C'Mon Aussie C'Mon' by the Mojo Singers in 1979, and 'It's Just Not Cricket' in 1984, '12th Man Again!' in 1990 and 'Marvellous' in 1992—three comedy tracks by Billy Birmingham that lampooned the Channel 9 television commentary team. 'Marvellous', his first musical offering, featured the backing vocals of Jimmy Barnes and John Farnham, and the guitar of Johnny Diesel. An album, *Still The 12th Man*, the fourth in his cricket series, was issued in 1992—it too went to number one.

•

If I have my time again (God help us all), I won't be coming back as a rock'n'roller, video buff or TV presenter. . . I'll be a cricketer and loving it.

—Molly Meldrum

David Gower's batting average of 19.00 against the 1984 West Indians fuelled a Top 20 hit in Britain in 1985, when Rory Bremner, as The Commentators, recorded 'N-N-Nineteen Not Out'. As with the Twelfth Man, Bremner's record was built around impersonations of commentator Richie Benaud and was based on the 1985 hit 'Nineteen' by Paul Hardcastle.

•

In 1992 the ABC dedicated an entire album to the words and music of Australian cricket. The CD, *Classic Cricket Hits*, contained 16 tracks, among them 'The Game is Not the Same Without McGilvray' by Mike Brady, 'Who's for Cricket?' by Ward Leopold, Paul Kelly's 'Bradman' tribute, 'I Made 100 in the Backyard of Mum's' by Greg Champion, 'It's Got Me Stumped' by Tony Miles, and Don Bradman's instructional piece 'How it's Done'.

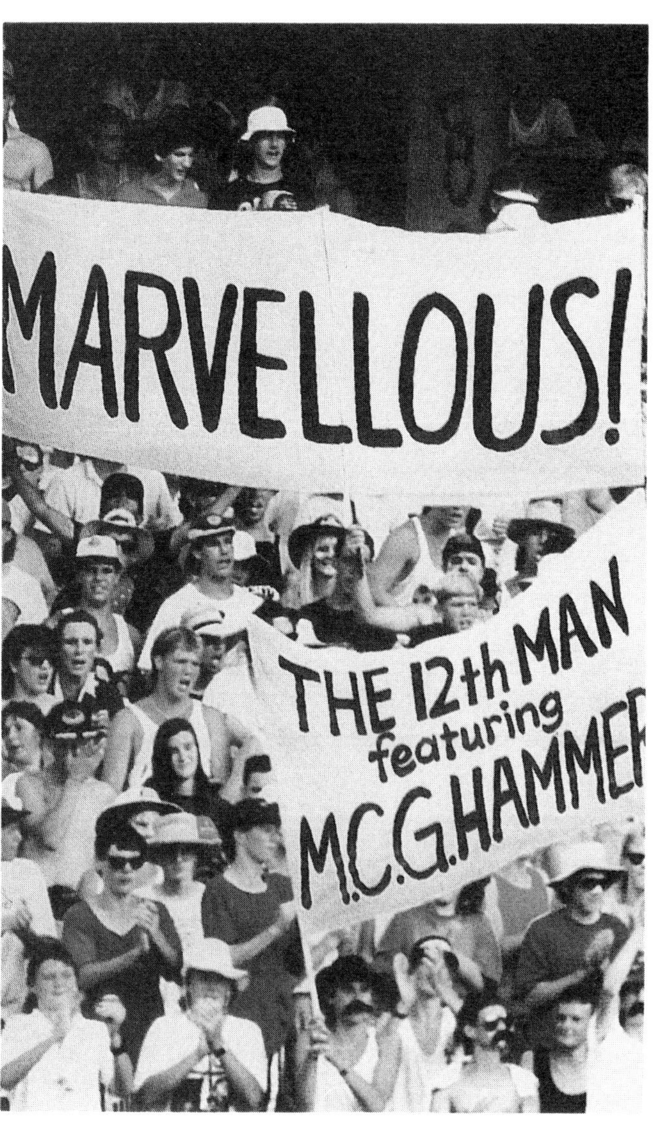

20 Averages

On the 1989 Ashes tour Steve Waugh had a Test batting average of 393.00 after the first three Tests. His world-record sequence of scores was 177*, 152*, 21* and 43. He finished the six-Test series with 506 runs at 126.50, becoming only the second Australian batsman after Don Bradman to gain a century average in a Test series against England.

•

An American, John Barton King, was the surprise bowler to top England's first-class averages in the summer of 1908. He took 81 wickets at 11.01 for the touring Gentlemen of Philadelphia team.

•

Walter Hammond holds the Test record for the highest batting average in a single Test series—563.00 v New Zealand in 1932-33. He made it to the crease only twice in the series, scoring back-to-back double-centuries—227 and 336*.

•

Dirk Wellham had the distinction of topping both the batting and bowling averages on his first overseas tour for Australia, against England in 1981—497 runs at 55.22 and 1 wicket at 11.00.

•

When the West Indies played New Zealand in 1979-80 a bowler topped the batting averages and a batsman topped the bowling—Andy Roberts with 78 runs at 78.00 beat Desmond Haynes' total of 339 runs at 56.50 and Alvin Kallicharran's three wickets at 5.33 pipped Joel Garner's 14 wickets at 16.78.

•

Geoff Boycott's average of 56.83 is the highest of any batsman with over 30,000 runs in first-class cricket. Walter Hammond comes second with 56.10.

•

In 1985 Viv Richards became the first batsman in over 100 years to top England's first-class averages with no not outs. Only two others had achieved this feat—W.G. Grace in 1874 and 'Monkey' Hornby in 1881.

In 1985-86 against Sri Lanka, Javed Miandad had a batting average of 153.00 in the three-match Test series. This was the fifth time he'd averaged over 100 in a series, and moved him one place in front of Don Bradman, Garry Sobers, Geoff Boycott and Zaheer Abbas who had all achieved the feat four times. Javed averaged over 100 again in 1988-89.

	T	*I*	*NO*	*Runs*	*HS*	*Avge*
v New Zealand 1976-77	3	5	1	504	206	126.00
v England 1977-78	3	5	3	262	88*	131.00
v India 1978-79	3	5	3	357	154*	178.50
v India 1982-83	6	6	1	594	280*	118.80
v Sri Lanka 1985-86	3	3	1	306	203*	153.00
v New Zealand 1988-89	2	2	0	389	271	194.50

•

In his brief Test match career for Australia, Albert Trott had a batting average of 102.50. In three Tests he scored 205 runs with three not outs in five innings. For England his average with the bat was less flattering—23 runs at 5.75 in two Tests.

•

Four batsmen finished the first-class season in India in 1990-91 with an average in excess of 100:

	M	*I*	*NO*	*Runs*	*HI*	*100s*	*Avge*
M.D. Gunjal (Maharashtra)	5	7	3	533	204	2	133.25
Ajay Sharma (Delhi)	6	6	1	614	216	3	122.80
C.S. Pandit (Bombay)	8	14	7	784	100*	2	112.00
R.J. Shastri (Bombay)	6	6	0	623	217	3	103.83

•

When Bob Willis took 12 wickets at 25.50 against New Zealand in 1983-84, it was the fifth time he'd topped England's bowling averages in successive Test series:

15 wickets at 22.00 v India 1982
10 wickets at 22.20 v Pakistan 1982
18 wickets at 27.00 v Australia 1982-83
20 wickets at 13.65 v New Zealand 1983
12 wickets at 25.50 v New Zealand 1983-84

•

	County	*Season*	*M*	*I*	*NO*	*Runs*	*HS*	*Avge*
W.G. Grace	Gloucestershire	1874	21	32	0	1,664	179	52.00
A.N. Hornby	Lancashire	1881	25	38	0	1,534	188	40.36
I.V.A. Richards	Somerset	1985	19	24	0	1,836	322	76.50

In his four seasons of County Championship cricket with Northamptonshire, fast bowler Mark Robinson found himself at the bottom of the batting averages each time. In 1987 and 1990 he was also the worst-placed batsman in the national averages.

Year	*M*	*I*	*NO*	*Runs*	*HS*	*Avge*
1987	7	6	2	4	2	1.00
1988	13	16	7	32	19*	3.55
1989	16	21	10	16	9	1.45
1990	17	16	10	3	1*	0.50

•

Larry Gomes topped both the batting and bowling averages for the West Indies in the five-Test series against Australia in 1984-85. With the bat he made 451 runs at 64.42 and his two wickets were taken at a cost of 15.00.

•

Five batsmen came away from the 1988-89 Test series between New Zealand and Pakistan with an average of over 100.00—Javed Miandad (194.50), Imran Khan (140.00), Shoaib Mohammad (137.50), Ian Smith (127.00) and Salim Malik (118.00).

•

The 'Three W's'—Frank Worrell, Clyde Walcott and Everton Weekes—all had a batting average of over 50 in first-class cricket.

	First-class career		*Test career*	
	Runs	*Avge*	*Runs*	*Avge*
C.L. Walcott	11,820	56.55	3,798	56.68
E.D. Weekes	12,010	52.90	4,455	58.61
F.M.M. Worrell	15,025	54.24	3,860	49.48

•

The lowest bowling average by a bowler taking at least 1,000 wickets in a career is 12.12 by Alfred Shaw, who took 2,027 wickets for Nottinghamshire and Sussex between 1864 and 1897. Three times during that period he took 100 wickets in a season at an average under 10:

County	*Season*	*O*	*M*	*R*	*W*	*Avge*
Nottinghamshire	1880	2,133	1,257	1,589	186	8.54
Nottinghamshire	1875	1,755.1	1,023	1,495	160	9.34
Nottinghamshire	1879	1,501	870	1,232	128	9.62

•

Allan Border averaged 50 in 10 successive Test series during the 1980s:

Allan Border

A.R. BORDER: CONSECUTIVE TEST SERIES WITH A 50 AVERAGE

Season	*Opposition*	*M*	*I*	*NO*	*Runs*	*HS*	*100s*	*Avge*
1985	England	6	11	2	597	196	2	66.33
1985-86	New Zealand	3	6	1	279	152*	1	55.80
1985-86	India	3	5	0	298	163	1	59.60
1985-86	New Zealand	3	5	1	290	140	2	72.50
1986-87	India	3	4	1	245	106	1	81.66
1986-87	England	5	10	1	473	125	2	52.56
1987-88	New Zealand	3	4	0	288	205	1	72.00
1987-88	England	1	2	1	50	48*	0	50.00
1987-88	Sri Lanka	1	1	0	88	88	0	88.00
1988-89	Pakistan	3	5	1	230	113*	1	57.50
	Totals	31	53	8	2,838	205	11	63.06

Sunil Gavaskar, who had a Test career batting average of 51.12, averaged over 50 in almost half of his 33 Test series. His best series was his first—774 runs at 154.80 against the West Indies in 1970–71. He also achieved a century average in the 1985–86 series against Australia—352 runs at 117.33.

•

Two highly unlikely players—Dave Gilbert and Greg Dyer—dominated Australia's batting averages after the seven-match tour of India in 1986–87:

	M	I	NO	R	HS	100s	Avge
D.R. Gilbert	5	4	2	152	117	1	76.00
G.C. Dyer	3	3	0	208	106	1	69.33

Both Gilbert and Dyer scored their maiden centuries in first-class cricket in the same match, against Delhi at Baroda.

•

When Jack Hobbs and Herbert Sutcliffe opened the batting for England their overall average in Test matches was a phenomenal 87.81. In 38 innings they shared 15 century opening stands, with a highest of 283 against Australia at Melbourne in 1924–25.

•

Mark Waugh topped both the batting and bowling averages on his first overseas Test tour—against the world champions, the West Indies—in 1990–91. With 367 runs at 61.17 in five Tests, his aggregate was second only to Mark Taylor's 441 runs at 49.00. With the ball he took eight wickets at 22.88, just ahead of Craig McDermott's 24 wickets at 23.50. He was also the leading fielder, taking 10 catches, a total equalled by the wicket-keeper Ian Healy.

•

In 1966 Jack Bailey, playing for the MCC, took 13 wickets in first-class matches at the record low average of 4.38.

•

On two occasions Australians have topped both the first-class batting and bowling averages in the same season in England:

1934	Don Bradman	2,020 runs at 84.16
	Bill O'Reilly	109 wickets at 17.04
1989	Dean Jones	1,510 runs at 88.82
	Terry Alderman	70 wickets at 15.64

Apart from Jones, another three Australian tourists made the top 10 in the 1989 first-class averages:

		M	I	NO	Runs	HS	100s	50s	Avge
1	Dean Jones	14	20	3	1,510	248	5	8	88.82
2	Steve Waugh	16	24	8	1,030	177*	4	3	64.37
6	Mark Taylor	17	30	1	1,669	219	3	10	57.55
8	David Boon	17	28	5	1,306	151	3	8	56.78
11	Allan Border	16	22	4	979	135	1	9	54.38

Jones' 88.82 tour average was the highest by any overseas batsmen in England since the freakish set of figures recorded by Australia's Bill Johnston in 1953—with the assistance of 16 not out innings, his average was 102.00.

•

In 1980 Geoff Boycott finished the first-class season in England with a batting average of over 50 for the 11th successive year, which beat Jack Hobbs' record of 10. His 50-plus average for every season throughout the 1970s is also a first-class record, and only twice in his last 20 seasons did he fail to achieve such high standards (38.87 in 1969 and 38.80 in 1981).

Season	Runs	Avge
1970	2,051	55.43
1971	2,503	100.12
1972	1,230	72.35
1973	1,527	63.62
1974	1,783	59.43
1975	1,915	73.65
1976	1,288	67.78
1977	1,701	68.04
1978	1,233	51.37
1979	1,538	102.53
1980	1,264	52.66
1981	1,009	38.80
1982	1,913	61.70
1983	1,941	55.45
1984	1,567	62.68
1985	1,657	75.31
1986	992	52.21

•

Between 1919 and 1936, 'Patsy' Hendren had an average of over 40 in every season.

•

During the 1980s, Mike Gatting averaged over 40 with the bat in each of the 10 seasons, exceeding 50 eight times.

Season	Runs	Avge
1980	880	41.90
1981	1,492	55.25
1982	1,651	58.96
1983	1,494	64.95
1984	2,257	68.39
1985	1,650	56.89
1986	1,091	54.55
1987	1,646	60.96
1988	1,469	47.38
1989	1,503	55.66

•

Two Smiths topped the respective batting averages in the 1983–84 Test series between New Zealand and England—Ian Smith with 198 runs at 99.00 and Chris Smith with 148 runs at 74.00.

•

•

Tony Lock's career batting average of 15.88 is the lowest by any player with 10,000 runs in first-class cricket.

•

K.S. Ranjitsinhji and C.B. Fry

C.B. Fry and K.S. Ranjitsinhji, two of England's specialist batsmen, finished the 1902 Test series against Australia with averages of 1.25 and 4.75 respectively.

•

Queensland all-rounder Ron Oxenham took 86 first-class wickets at an average of just 6.81 on Australia's 1935-36 tour of India and Sri Lanka.

•

In 1959-60 Bob Simpson had a phenomenal season with Western Australia, scoring close to 1,000 runs in just five matches. As an opening batsman he hit 902 runs at an average of 300.66—98, 230*, 236*, 79, 98 and 161*.

•

John Warr, who played in a couple of Tests for England in 1951, possesses one of the most disparate sets of batting and bowling averages of any player in Test cricket:

Batting					
M	*I*	*NO*	*Runs*	*HS*	*Avge*
2	4	0	4	4	1.00
Bowling					
		R	*W*	*Best*	*Avge*
		281	1	1-76	281.00

•

Harold Gilligan hit over 1,000 runs (1,186) for Sussex in 1923 and had an average of only 17.70. In the previous season Maurice Tate also hit 1,000 runs for Sussex, and he too earned an average of under 20—1,050 at 19.44.

•

Francis McHugh, who appeared in a total of 95 first-class matches between 1949 and 1956, had a first-class batting average of just 2.64. He batted 111 times during his career, for an aggregate of 179 runs with a highest score of 18 for Gloucestershire v Essex in 1953.

•

Peter Visser, a slow bowler who represented the New Zealand side Central Districts, had a career batting average of 0.91. In 17 first-class innings from 1983-84 to 1986-87 he managed to scrape together 11 runs, with a top score of 8.

•

In his 70 Tests, Dennis Lillee's 355 wickets were taken at an average of five per match. Richard Hadlee had a similar average for his 431 wickets in 86 tests.

•

The 1982-83 India-Pakistan Test series was rich in high averages, both positive and negative. Three Pakistan batsmen finished with a century average—Zaheer Abbas 130.00, Mudassar Nazar 126.83 and Javed Miandad 118.80. But five bowlers also came away with averages exceeding 100—Mohinder Amarnath 281.00, Ravi Shastri 176.00, Maninder Singh 148.00, Sikander Bakht 107.00 and Tahir Naqqash 105.50.

•

On seven occasions Essex bowler Ray Smith took 100 wickets in a season. Four times they were taken at an average in excess of 30, his 1947 haul of 125 wickets at 37.26 being the most expensive in English first-class cricket.

•

Steve Waugh finished the 1989 Test series against England with a century average with both bat and ball—506 runs at 126.50 and two wickets at 104.00.

•

Pakistan's Shoaib Mohammad achieved a rare milestone in 1990 when he recorded an average of over 100 in successive Test series: 103.00 v India in 1989-90 and 169.00 v New Zealand in 1990-91.

•

Stan McCabe had an average of 438.00 in Sheffield Shield matches for New South Wales in 1931-32. He scored three centuries in three innings, two not outs—229* and 106 & 103*.

•

Three batsmen had an average of over 100 in the 1975 World Cup—Glenn Turner 333 runs at 166.50, Sunil Gavaskar 113 runs at 113.00 and Deryck Murray 105 runs at 105.00.

•

Ken Barrington

In 1920 Jack Hobbs was placed in the top five of both the batting and the bowling averages in England. He came second with the bat scoring 2,827 runs at 58.89, and number one in the bowling averages, capturing 17 wickets at 11.82.

•

In Sydney club cricket, Bill O'Reilly eight times took 50 wickets in a season at an average below 10. In 1943–44, he claimed a record 147 wickets at 8.20.

Wkts	*Avge*	*Club*	*Season*
53	6.77	St George	1937–38
86	7.74	St George	1939–40
54	7.80	North Sydney	1931–32
147	8.20	St George	1943–44
51	8.30	St George	1944–45
109	8.60	St George	1942–43
108	9.00	St George	1941–42
52	9.11	St George	1934–35

•

Ken Barrington had the distinction of topping England's first-class batting averages on five successive overseas tours. On two of them, he headed the bowling averages as well:

1961–62	India & Pakistan	1,329 runs at 64.94
1962–63	Australia & New Zealand	1,763 runs at 80.13
1963–64	India	336 runs at 112.00
		7 wickets at 18.71
1964–65	South Africa	1,128 runs at 86.76
		24 wickets at 7.25
1965–66	Australia	946 runs at 67.57

•

On the 1991 Australian tour of the West Indies, Terry Alderman had a Test bowling average of 105.00 and a batting average of 0.00.

•

Graham Gooch, who compiled 2,746 runs in first-class cricket in 1990, finished the season with an average of 101.70. He became only the fourth player to achieve a century average in an English season:

Year	*Batsman*	*Teams*	*M*	*I*	*NO*	*Runs*	*HS*	*100s*	*Avge*
1938	Don Bradman	Australians	20	26	5	2,429	278	13	115.66
1953	Bill Johnston	Australians	16	17	16	102	28*	0	102.00
1971	Geoff Boycott	Yorkshire/England	21	30	5	2,503	233	13	100.12
1979	Geoff Boycott	Yorkshire/England	15	20	5	1,538	175*	6	102.53
1990	Graham Gooch	Essex/England	18	30	3	2,746	333	12	101.70

During the 1980s, overseas players dominated England's first-class batting and bowling averages. In 1981, Mike Gatting and Chris Tavaré were the only English players to appear in the top 10 batting averages—Zaheer Abbas 88.69, Javed Miandad 69.43, Allan Lamb 60.26, Viv Richards 57.26, Clive Rice 56.23, Peter Kirsten 55.34, Glenn Turner 55.28, *Mike Gatting 55.25*, Alvin Kallicharran 54.29, *Chris Tavaré 53.63.* In the bowling averages, it wasn't that much better, with only three Englishmen figuring in the top 10—Richard Hadlee 14.89, Sylvester Clarke 14.97, Joel Garner 15.32, Michael Holding 17.87, Ezra Mosely 18.11, *Arnie Sidebottom 19.12,* Clive Rice 19.20, *Ian Greig 19.32, Peter Hacker 19.39,* Malcolm Marshall 19.42.

•

Graham Yallop had an average of 113.20 in first-class cricket in 1983–84. He was the first Australian batsman to record a century average in Australia since Bob Simpson (300.66) in 1959–60. (South Africa's Barry Richards averaged 109.86 for South Australia in 1970–71; Pakistan's Hanif Mohammad had an average of 134.00 on their Australian tour in 1964–65).

•

Victoria's Sam Cosstick topped Australia's bowling averages a record five times during his brief first-class career, and did so each time with a sub-10 average:

Season	*O*	*M*	*R*	*W*	*BB*	*5wi*	*Avge*
1860–61	70.1	37	48	11	6–23	2	4.36
1868–69	99.3	64	65	12	6–1	1	5.42
1869–70	58.2	22	77	10	6–40	1	7.70
1870–71	69	41	64	11	8–21	1	5.82
1872–73	135.2	69	150	23	9–61	3	6.52

Another Victorian, Gideon Elliot, has the lowest average of all. In 1857–58 he took 21 wickets in first-class cricket at 2.90. The only bowler to take 50 wickets in a season at an average below 10 is Charlie Turner, whose 70 wickets in 1886–87 came at an average of 7.69.

•

21 Here, There and Everywhere

Allan Jones was the first English cricketer to play first-class cricket for four different counties—Sussex (1966–69), Somerset (1970–75), Middlesex (1976–79) and Glamorgan (1980–81). He also represented two teams in South Africa—Northern Transvaal (1972–73) and Orange Free State (1976–77).

•

Ian Watson had one of the most bizarre first-class careers known. He appeared in only three matches, each for a different county—Middlesex in 1969, Northamptonshire in 1971 and Hampshire in 1973.

•

Mike Macaulay, who played in one Test for South Africa, is the only player to have represented five provinces in the Currie Cup—Transvaal, Western Province, Orange Free State, North-Eastern Transvaal and Eastern Province.

•

The West Indian-born all-rounder Franklyn Stephenson made his first-class debut in 1981–82 for Tasmasnia v Victoria at Melbourne and took 10 wickets, including 6 for 19 in the second innings. Returning home he scored 165 as a night-watchman in his first match for Barbados, and then topped Gloucestershire's bowling average in 1982.

•

James Southerton, who played in the first-ever Test match, experienced an unusual summer in 1867 when he played first-class cricket for three different counties—Sussex, Hampshire and Surrey.

•

India's Vijay Manjrekar played for six teams in the Ranji Trophy—Bombay, Bengal, Andhra, Uttar Pradesh, Rajasthan and Maharashtra.

•

When Dirk Wellham made his first-class debut for Queensland in 1991–92, he became the fourth Australian Test cricketer to have played Sheffield Shield cricket for three states. Wellham had previously captained New South Wales and Tasmania; the others are Trevor Chappell (SA, WA, NSW), Gary Cosier (V, SA, Q) and Graeme Watson (V, WA, NSW).

•

C.S. Crawley had a distinctive first-class career of six matches for five different teams over seven years. He made his debut for Hampshire in 1923, then played for Free Foresters in 1924, Oxford University in 1924 and 1925, Harlequins in 1927 and Middlesex in 1929.

•

Kepler Wessels has played first-class cricket for eight different teams—Orange Free State, Western Province, Eastern Province, Northern Transvaal, Sussex, Queensland, Australia and South Africa.

Other well-known Test cricketers to have spread their wings and played for a number of sides include Michael Holding—Jamaica, Lancashire, Derbyshire, Tasmania, Canterbury and West Indies; Imran Khan—Lahore, PIA, Oxford University, Worcestershire, Sussex, New South Wales and Pakistan; Younis Ahmed—PIA, Surrey, Worcestershire, Glamorgan, South Australia and Pakistan.

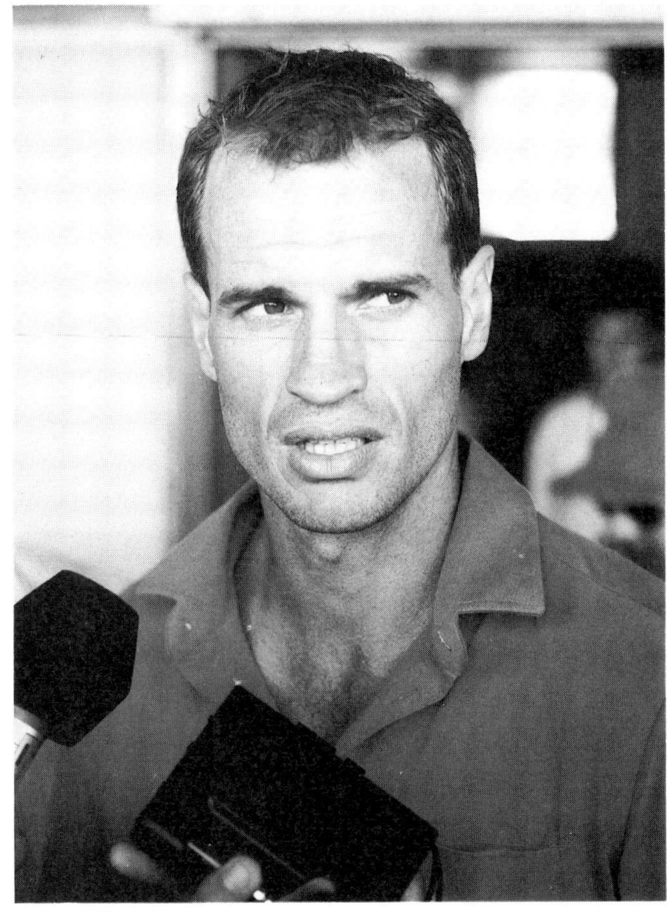

Kepler Wessels

22 Coincidentally

The first batsman to make identical three figure scores in each innings of a Test match was Sri Lanka's Duleep Mendis—105 & 105 v India at Madras in 1982–83.

•

In 1988 Franklyn Stephenson became the first player in over 80 years to score two centuries and take 10 wickets in the same match. George Hirst was the last man to achieve the feat in 1906, and coincidentally both players' scores were the same—111 and 117.

G.H. Hirst	Yorks v Somerset	111 & 117* and 6–70 & 5–45
F.D. Stephenson	Notts v Yorks	111 & 117 and 4–105 & 7–117

•

Playing at the MCG against the West Indies in 1968–69, Ian Chappell had the distinction of scoring the 1,000th century in Test match cricket. His 165 just happened to be the same score as that achieved by Charles Bannerman when he made the first Test century, also at the MCG in 1877.

•

On the 1971–72 West Indies tour, New Zealand batsman Glenn Turner scored 259 against Guyana at Georgetown. In his next innings he made the same score in the fourth Test on the same ground.

•

Only a handful of captains have been able to score over 600 runs in a Test series—England's Len Hutton and Australia's Bill Lawry are two of them. Both of these opening batsmen achieved the feat in a Test series against the West Indies and both did so in identical fashion.

	Season	*Tests*	*Inns*	*Runs*	*HS*
L. Hutton	1953–54	5	8	677	205
W.M. Lawry	1968–69	5	8	677	205

•

In the 1961 season in England a record number of batsmen—111—scored 1,000 runs and a record number of bowlers—31—took 100 wickets.

•

The four centuries recorded in the MCC Bicentenary Match at Lord's in 1987 were all scored by batsmen whose surnames began with the letter G—Graham Gooch 117, Mike Gatting 179, Sunil Gavaskar 188 and Gordon Greenidge 122.

•

During the Adelaide Test against England in 1990–91, four of Australia's top six batsmen were dismissed in identical fashion in each innings:

Geoff Marsh	(37 & 0)	c Gooch b Small
Mark Taylor	(5 & 4)	run out
Dean Jones	(0 & 8)	lbw DeFreitas
Mark Waugh	(138 & 23)	b Malcolm

•

South Africa was dismissed by England for 72 in the second innings of two successive Tests in 1956–57.

•

In Australia's first one-day international against Bangladesh, at Sharjah in 1990, Steve Waugh and Peter Taylor both returned bowling figures of 10–2–22–2.

•

When India was bowled out for 103 by the West Indies at Ahmedabad in 1983–84, no batsman made a duck, but six of them were dismissed for 1.

•

In 1982 Viv Richards, playing county cricket in England, recorded exactly the same batting figures as his Test captain Clive Lloyd had achieved the previous season:

	County	*Season*	*Inns*	*NO*	*Runs*	*Avge*
C.H. Lloyd	Lancashire	1981	31	2	1324	45.65
I.V.A. Richards	Somerset	1982	31	2	1324	45.65

•

Australia's Arthur Richardson finished the 1924–25 Test series against England with the identical batting and bowling average of 31.00. In eight innings he made 248 runs and with the ball took eight wickets for 248.

•

Nasser Hussain and Alec Stewart both made their England Test debuts in the same match, against the West Indies at Kingston in 1990. Both batsmen were caught off the bowling of Ian Bishop for 13, both faced 12 balls and both hit three boundaries.

•

In 1991 Mark Ramprakash and Graeme Hick made identical scores in each innings of their first Test appearance, against the West Indies at Leeds—Hick had a double failure on debut with scores of 6 and 6, while Ramprakash had innings of 27 and 27.

•

In 1973–74 Ian and Greg Chappell both appeared in two Sheffield Shield matches against Victoria. Both scored the same number of runs, and at the same average:

I.M. Chappell (SA)	83 & 95 at Melbourne 141* & 130 at Adelaide	449 runs at 149.66
G.S. Chappell (Q)	180 & 101 at Brisbane 115 & 53* at Melbourne	449 runs at 149.66

•

When Kent piled on 6 for 616 against Oxford in 1982, its first four batsmen contributed centuries, and all of them were dismissed in the 120s—Bob Woolmer 126, Neil Taylor 127, Chris Tavaré 125 and Mark Benson 120.

•

In 1953 New Zealand became the first side to make identical totals in both innings of a Test match—172 & 172 v South Africa at Wellington in 1952–53.

•

Australia was dismissed for 111 in two consecutive Tests, by England at Melbourne and Adelaide during the 1954–55 Ashes series.

•

In the third Test at Melbourne in 1977–78 India's B.S. Chandrasekhar returned identical figures in each innings with both bat and ball—0 & 0 and 6-52 & 6-52.

•

Ian and Greg Chappell both made the milestone of 2,000 runs against England in the same number of Tests (29) and during the same series (1979–80).

•

Steve Small, Trevor Bayliss and Mark O'Neill were each dismissed for 47 in the first innings of the New South Wales-Victoria match at Albury in 1989–90.

•

On the eighth day of the eighth month in 1988, Lancashire was reduced to 8 for 88 in its County Championship match with Middlesex at Manchester.

•

When Australia took on England in the third Test at Adelaide in 1982–83, both of the opening batsmen—Kepler Wessels and John Dyson—were dismissed in identical fashion, caught by the wicket-keeper Bob Taylor off the bowling of Ian Botham for 44.

•

On 28 July 1937 two batsmen scored 300 runs in a first-class match—322 by Eddie Paynter for Lancashire v Sussex at Hove and 316 by Hampshire's Richard Moore against Warwickshire at Bournemouth. Prior to 1937 the feat of 300 runs in a day had been achieved only nine times.

Geoff Lawson was the first New South Wales bowler to take 300 Sheffield Shield wickets. His first wicket in 1977–78 and his 300th, in 1989–90, were both taken at the SCG and both times the victim was West Australian opener Geoff Marsh.

•

Australia's 100th Test victory over England, at Manchester in 1989, was also Australia's 200th Test win overall.

•

When play was abandoned on the second day of the Australian XI-England match at Hobart in 1990–91, the score was none for 15 after 5 overs. Openers Peter Cantrell and David Boon had both made 5 and there were 5 extras—England's opening bowlers Devon Malcolm and Angus Fraser both had figures of 0 for 5.

•

Clive Lloyd's 100th Test—against Australia at Kingston in 1983–84—was also the 100th Test match in the West Indies.

•

England batsman Neil Fairbrother was caught by a substitute—Asif Mujtaba—in both innings of the third Test against Pakistan at Karachi in 1987–88.

Neil Fairbrother

The father-and-son combination of Hanif and Shoaib Mohammad had an affinity with scoring 203 not out in Test matches. This exact score was achieved by the pair on no fewer than three occasions:

203*	Hanif Mohammad	Pakistan v New Zealand	Lahore 1964-65
203*	Shoaib Mohammad	Pakistan v India	Lahore 1989-90
203*	Shoaib Mohammad	Pakistan v New Zealand	Karachi 1990-91

•

Viv Richards celebrated his 100th Test, against Australia at Brisbane in 1988-89, by taking his 100th Test catch. In his previous match on tour, against New South Wales, his score of 101 was the 100th century of his first-class career.

•

Allan Border's 125 at Perth in 1986-87 was the 200th century in Anglo-Australian Tests. It was his 20th Test century, in his 150th innings and took him past 2,000 runs in Tests against England.

•

The number three figured prominently in the efforts of Carl Rackemann in a first-class match at the county ground at Taunton in 1989. Bowling for the Australians against Somerset he took three wickets for 1 in 13 balls, and finished the first innings with the figures of 13-3-33-3.

•

Mark Taylor's first three hundreds in first-class cricket were all scored against South Australia—118 at Sydney and 100 at Adelaide in 1985-86 and 186 at Sydney in 1986-87.

•

On 20 August 1979 two Somerset batsmen scored 99 not out before lunch in different first-class matches—Viv Richards in a County Championship game against Middlesex at Lord's and Ian Botham in the third Test against India at Leeds.

•

During the first innings of the first Test against India at Colombo in 1985-86, two of Sri Lanka's batsmen, Ranjan Madugalle (103) and Arjuna Ranatunga (111), both scored their maiden centuries in Test cricket. The two had previously gained their maiden half-centuries (65 and 54) in the same innings, at Colombo in 1982, in Sri Lanka's inaugural Test, against England.

•

When England and the West Indies met in the second Test at Lord's in 1984, both scored exactly 119 runs on the second day—England 2-167 to 286 and West Indies 3-119.

•

In 1977 Geoff Boycott and John Edrich both scored their century of centuries in first-class cricket. On each occasion the batsman at the other end was Graham Roope.

•

Australia dismissed India for 136, 136 and 135 in successive Test innings, although in different series, in the late 1950s.

In consecutive Test matches against England at the Adelaide Oval, Greg Matthews had the highly unusual experience of taking part in a record 100-run stand for the sixth wicket—with Steve Waugh in 1986-87 and Mark Waugh in 1990-91:

146*	G.R.J. Matthews (73*) & S.R. Waugh (79*)
171	G.R.J. Matthews (65) & M.E. Waugh (138)

•

When England was dismissed for 225 and 252 by New Zealand at Leeds in 1983, all the wickets were taken by bowlers whose surnames began with the letter C. Lance Cairns took 10 for 144, Ewen Chatfield 6 for 162 and Jeremy Coney 4 for 51. All 20 wickets in a Test going in similar circumstances has occurred on only two other occasions—Billy Bates (14-102), Dick Barlow (4-76) and Sydney Barnes (2-36) for England v Australia at Melbourne in 1882-83; and Jim Laker (19-90) and Tony Lock (1-106) v Australia at Manchester in 1956.

•

Two Test matches got underway on 16 February 1973—New Zealand v Pakistan at Auckland and West Indies v Australia at Kingston. For only the third and fourth times in all Test cricket the first innings of both sides in both matches closed at the same total—402 by Pakistan and New Zealand and 7d-428 by Australia and 428 by West Indies.

•

When South Australia was out for 140 to Tasmania at Launceston in 1986-87, seven of its batsmen contributed to a near-perfect numerical sequence of scores:

Batsman	*Score*
J.T.W. Birchall	6
A.K. Zesers	5
D.W. Hookes	4
J.K. Pyke	3
A.S. Watson	2
W.B. Phillips	1
P.W. Gladigau	0*

•

In 1988 three batsmen finished the season in England with a batting average of 36.20—Rob Bailey of Northamptonshire, Andy Lloyd of Warwickshire and Duleep Mendis from Sri Lanka. Bailey and Lloyd both appeared in 24 matches during the season, and both scored exactly the same number of runs (1,448).

In 1990 there were six sets of batsmen with an identical total of runs and the same average:

David Ward	Surrey	2,072	76.74
Mark Waugh	Essex	2,072	76.74
Gordon Lord	Worcestershire	1,003	45.59
Nadeem Shahid	Essex	1,003	45.59
Robert Croft	Glamorgan	672	44.80
Steven Rhodes	Worcestershire	672	44.80
Phillip Cottey	Glamorgan	1,001	33.36
Tony Dodemaide	Sussex	1,001	33.36
Kiran Moré	Indians	295	32.77
Paul Romaines	Gloucestershire	295	32.77
John Childs	Essex	123	11.18
Darren Gough	Yorkshire	123	11.18

At the close of play on the first day of two successive Tests in India in 1986–87, the score was exactly the same—2 for 217 by Australia in the third Test at Bombay and by Sri Lanka in the first Test at Kanpur.

•

India's Mohinder Amarnath and Pakistan's Mudassar Nazar, whose fathers were also Test cricketers, both made their Test debuts on Christmas Eve against Australia. Amarnath at Madras in 1969–70 and Mudassar at Adelaide in 1976–77. Both batsmen scored their maiden Test centuries in the week before Christmas in 1977—Amarnath 100 v Australia at Perth and Mudassar 114 against England at Lahore. During the sixth Test at Karachi in 1982–83, both of them hit centuries and both passed the milestone of 2,000 Test runs. Both batsmen were the leading run-getters in the six-Test series—Amarnath hit 584 runs for India and Mudassar 761 for Pakistan.

•

In two consecutive Tests against India at Lord's—in 1936 and 1946—England lost its first two wickets in the first innings at the same score (16) both times. India experienced a similar pattern in each of the Tests, and both sides lost their first wicket in the second innings in 1936 at the same score.

First Test—England v India at Lord's 1936 Fall of wickets					First Test—England v India at Lord's 1946 Fall of wickets				
	I	*E*	*I*	*E*		*I*	*E*	*I*	*E*
Wkt	*1st*	*1st*	*2nd*	*2nd*	*Wkt*	*1st*	*1st*	*2nd*	*2nd*
1st	62	16	0	0	1st	15	16	67	–
2nd	62	16	18	–	2nd	15	16	117	–
3rd	64	30	22	–	3rd	44	61	126	–
4th	66	34	28	–	4th	74	70	129	–
5th	85	41	39	–	5th	86	252	174	–
6th	97	96	45	–	6th	87	284	185	–
7th	107	129	64	–	7th	144	344	190	–
8th	119	132	80	–	8th	147	416	249	–
9th	137	132	90	–	9th	157	421	263	–
10th	147	134	93	–	10th	200	428	275	–

•

During the third Test at Christchurch in 1981–82, Martin Crowe became Rod Marsh's 300th victim in Test cricket. His brother Jeff Crowe was Bob Willis' 300th Test victim, at Leeds in 1983, and Joel Garner's 250th, at Wellington in 1986–87.

•

Greg Chappell and David Gower both made scores of 3 and 98 not out in the second Test at Sydney in 1979–80.

•

Of the first 13 centuries scored by Mark Waugh in first-class cricket, five of them were exactly 100 not out:

New South Wales v Victoria	Melbourne 1987–88
New South Wales v Tasmania	Devonport 1988–89
Essex v Australians	Chelmsford 1989
New South Wales v Victoria	Albury 1989–90
New South Wales v Victoria	Melbourne 1989–90

Ian Botham appeared in his 100th Test and 100th one-day international on England's tour of New Zealand in 1992.

•

Only batsmen whose surnames began with the letter S opened the batting in the five-match Test series against Australia in 1991–92—Ravi Shastri and Kris Srikkanth (1st & 2nd Tests), Shastri and Navjot Sidhu (3rd Test), and Srikkanth and Sidhu (4th & 5th Tests).

•

When Allan Border picked up the bat and scored 9 against England at Brisbane in 1990–91, it was his 200th Test match innings. His 200th innings in one-day international cricket was also against England at Brisbane in 1990–91.

•

When England played Australia at Melbourne in 1878–79, both Australian openers made the same scores in each innings—Charles Bannerman 15 & 15* and Billy Murdoch 4 & 4*.

•

England's opening pair of Barry Wood and Dennis Amiss both scored 11 and 1 in the second Test against India at Calcutta in 1972–73.

•

In successive innings in the 1986 County Championship, the Middlesex batsman Roland Butcher had scores of 3, 3, 33, 3, 4 and 4.

•

The first four New Zealand batsmen to score a century on their Test debuts were all left-handers:

John Mills	117	v England	Wellington 1929–30
Bruce Taylor	105	v India	Calcutta 1964–65
Rodney Redmond	107	v Pakistan	Auckland 1972–73
Mark Greatbatch	107*	v England	Auckland 1987–88

•

When South Australia drew its Sheffield Shield match with Tasmania at Adelaide in 1991–92, it finished its second innings at 1 for 93. All three batsmen who made it to the middle made the same number of runs—Glenn Bishop 31, Greg Blewett 31* and Tim Nielsen 31*.

•

During the First Test against New Zealand at The Oval in 1983, both of England's openers hit centuries in the second innings—Kent's Chris Tavaré made 109, Lancashire's Graeme Fowler hit 105. Not since 1960 had England openers performed this feat, and again it was a Kent right-hander and a left-handed Lancashire batsman—Colin Cowdrey (155) and Geoff Pullar (175) against South Africa at The Oval.

•

Playing in a match for an Australian XI against the MCC at Brisbane in 1924–25, Ron Oxenham experienced an odd double in scoring a half-century and a duck. In the first innings he was stumped by Bert Strudwick off the bowling of 'Tich' Freeman, and stumped by Freeman off Strudwick in the second.

•

Three bowlers conceded exactly 100 runs in the Australia–Pakistan Test match at the MCG in 1972–73—Asif Masood 2–100, Sarfraz Nawaz 2–100 and Jeff Thomson 0–100.

•

In the Test series against South Africa in 1963–64, Australia's opening bowlers returned identical analyses in the second innings of two consecutive Tests—Ron Gaunt and Graham McKenzie 4–0–22–0 at Adelaide and McKenzie and Neil Hawke 4–0–16–0 at Sydney.

•

The English cricket club Lewes Priory made history in 1991 when its three teams all scored 222 on the same day. On 3 August its first XI made 6 for 222, its second XI 7 for 222, while their third team completed the hat-trick with a score of 6 for 222.

•

The Chappell brothers, Ian and Greg, were dismissed in identical fashion in three consecutive matches during the 1975 World Cup:

I.M. Chappell	c Murray b Boyce 25	Australia v West Indies at The Oval
G.S. Chappell	c Murray b Boyce 15	
I.M. Chappell	lbw b Snow 2	Australia v England at Leeds
G.S. Chappell	lbw b Snow 4	
I.M. Chappell	run out 62	Australia v West Indies at Lord's
G.S. Chappell	run out 15	

•

Jeff Thomson took exactly 200 Test wickets for Australia—100 of them against England.

When the MCC toured Pakistan in 1967 they came across two players by the name of Khalid Aziz in the match against North Zone. In the first innings both players were dismissed the same way—c Brearley b Hobbs.

•

In his first 23 Test matches for England, Derek Pringle had only ever taken five wickets in an innings three times. Although he'd played against most countries, each haul was taken against the West Indies, and in successive Test series at home—5–108 at Birmingham in 1984, 5–95 at Leeds in 1988 and 5–100 at Lord's in 1991.

•

In a first-class match at Sydney in 1913–14 between New South Wales and New Zealand, six different batsmen were dismissed for 7, including the first four in the tourists' second innings total of 105.

•

After three first-class matches in the 1991–92 season, both Steve and Mark Waugh had identical batting figures.

	M	*I*	*NO*	*Runs*	*100s*	*50s*	*Avge*
M.E. Waugh	3	4	0	215	1	1	53.75
S.R. Waugh	3	4	0	215	1	1	53.75

•

Australia and England began the second Test in 1977 on the seventh day of the seventh month on the 77th day of the Australians' tour.

•

Representing Victoria against the touring New Zealanders in 1973–74, Ray Bright had scores of 32 and 32, and with the ball returned the identical bowling figures of 7–3–20–0 in each innings.

23 Literary Connections

When Sidney Adams made his first-class debut for Northamptonshire in 1926, he picked up a wicket with his very first ball. His victim was Samuel Beckett, the Irish playwright of *Waiting for Godot* fame, who later won a Nobel Prize for Literature. A left-handed batsman and medium-pace bowler, Beckett appeared in two first-class matches in the mid-1920s.

THE FIRST-CLASS CAREER RECORD OF SAMUEL BECKETT
(Dublin University 1925–26)

Batting:

M	*I*	*NO*	*Runs*	*HS*	*Avge*
2	4	0	35	18	8.75

Bowling:

Runs	*W*	*BB*	*Avge*
64	0	–	–

•

The creator of Sherlock Holmes, Sir Arthur Conan Doyle, was a first-class cricketer who, on his debut for the MCC against London County in 1900, dismissed the great W.G. Grace.

THE FIRST-CLASS CAREER RECORD OF SIR ARTHUR CONAN DOYLE
(MCC 1900–07)

Batting:

M	*I*	*NO*	*Runs*	*HS*	*Avge*
10	18	6	231	43	19.25

Bowling:

Runs	*W*	*BB*	*Avge*
50	1	1–4	50.00

•

Rupert Brooke, the English poet, represented his school, Rugby, in a match at Lord's in 1906.

•

I became a bowler at school in the best of all possible ways. I used to bowl out the captains at the nets.

A.A. Milne

•

Gower is a goot captain, and is goot knowledge and literatured in the wars.

—William Shakespeare, *Henry V*

Joseph Wells, the first bowler to perform the feat of four wickets in four balls in a first-class match, was the father of novelist H.G. Wells. He gained his four wickets bowling for Kent against Sussex at Brighton in 1862, his second victim being one Spencer Leigh, a great-nephew of another famous English novelist, Jane Austen.

•

Reg Hargreaves, a slow bowler who played first-class cricket for Hampshire in the late 1800s, married Alice Liddell, the inspiration for Lewis Carroll's *Alice in Wonderland.*

•

John Snow, the feared English fast bowler, had a gentler side, with two volumes of his poetry published in the early 1970s—*Contrasts* and *Moments and Thoughts.*

•

J.M. Barrie, the author of *Peter Pan, The Admirable Crichton* and *Quality Street*, was a cricket fanatic, who had his own cricket team, known as The Allahakbarries.

I can bowl so slow, that if I don't like a ball I can run after it and bring it back.

—J.M. Barrie

•

Percy Jeeves, a bowler who played for Warwickshire in 1913/14, was the man immortalised by P.G. Wodehouse in the famous Bertie Wooster stories. Wodehouse was a member of the Dulwich College XI, a godfather to Mike Griffith who captained Sussex between 1968 and 1972, and also a vice-president of the Hollywood Cricket Club.

•

Although Max Walker never took a hat-trick in his first-class career, he was good enough to get one with his writing. In 1990, he was named Australia's best-selling author after three of his books—*How to Hypnotise Chooks* (1987), *How to Tame Lions* (1988) and *How to Kiss a Crocodile* (1989)—each sold over 150,000 copies.

•

I tend to believe that cricket is the greatest thing that God ever created, certainly better than sex, although sex isn't too bad either.

—Harold Pinter

Breathes there a man with soul so dead that he never heard of the Sydney Cricket Ground?

—'Banjo' Paterson

24 Extra Extras

Everton Weekes was a renowned international bridge player who once opposed actor Omar Sharif in the World Championship.

•

Peter Willey and Wayne Larkins received over 2,000 cans of beer from a Northampton brewery in appreciation of their efforts on England's 1978–79 tour of Australia.

•

Roddy Kinkead-Weekes, who kept wicket for Middlesex in a couple of first-class matches in 1976, was the boyfriend of Australian heiress Janie Shepherd when she was murdered near London in 1977.

•

Douglas Bader, the famous airman, was a keen cricketer who regularly played the game—in 1931 he represented the Royal Air Force against the Army, a match afforded first-class status, and top-scored with 65.

•

Mark Taylor set a bizarre and unwanted record in 1991 when he became the first batsman to be run out in both innings of a Test match more than once—against the West Indies at Adelaide in 1988–89 and against England, also at Adelaide, in 1990–91. These dismissals constituted four of his first six Test innings at the Adelaide Oval.

•

England opener John Jameson was run out three times in a row in his first four Test innings.

•

Mike Gatting and his brother Steve both won medals for ballroom dancing in 1968.

•

In the first innings of the Western Province-Transvaal match at Cape Town in 1980–81, Allan Lamb was the subject of a most unusual dismissal—Lamb c Cook b Rice.

•

Former Queensland premier Sir Joh Bjelke-Petersen once invented a rubber cricket bat. However, it was an idea that failed to excite any manufacturer and it remained just that, an idea.

•

New Zealand opening batsman Gordon Leggat had a varied beginning to his Test career, playing against different countries in his first four matches—West Indies (Auckland 1951–52), South Africa (Wellington 1952–53), England (Auckland 1954–55) and Pakistan (Karachi 1955–56). In 1992 Sri Lanka's Roshan Mahanama became the first batsman to appear against five different countries in consecutive Tests—Australia (Hobart 1989–90), India (Chandigarh 1990–91), New Zealand (Wellington 1990–91), England (Lord's 1991) and Pakistan (Gujranwala 1991–92).

•

Cricket came to London's Wembley Stadium in 1991, when it played host to a fund-raising limited-overs match between a Sports Celebrity XI and David English's Bunbury XI. The star of TV's *Minder*, Denis Waterman, played alongside first-class cricketers, such as John Morris and Chris Broad, in a match that aided disaster relief and the Lord's Taverners.

•

Jim Thomson, a slow left-arm bowler, had a rather forgettable, if not unusual, first-class career in which he gained selection just twice over a period of 22 years. He made his first-class debut for Scotland in 1962 and played in his next match in 1984.

THE LONGEST INTERVALS BETWEEN TWO APPEARANCES IN FIRST-CLASS CRICKET

32 years	R.H. Moss	Liverpool and District v Australians 1893 Worcestershire v Gloucestershire 1925
25 years	P.J. Kippax	Yorkshire v Pakistanis 1962 MCC v Yorkshire 1987
22 years	J. Thomson	Scotland v Ireland 1962 Scotland v Ireland 1984

•

During the 1982–83 season, a substitute player was permitted to bat in a Sheffield Shield match, a unique occurrence in Australian first-class cricket. Mike Maranta batted at number 11 for Queensland against New South Wales, in Brisbane, after John Maguire was selected midway through the match to represent Australia in a one-day international.

•

On the same day that Geoff Marsh was dropped from the Australian Test team in 1992, a horse called Marsh suffered a similar fate when it was scratched from the first race at the Werribee track in Victoria.

•

Rashid Patel attacks Raman Lamba with a stump during the 1990–91 Duleep Trophy final at Jamshedpur

Raman Lamba, who appeared in four Tests for India during the 1980s, found himself stumped, in a fashion not witnessed before in first-class cricket, during the final of the 1990–91 Duleep Trophy. Pace bowler Rashid Patel, playing for West Zone, hit Lamba with a stump after claiming the North Zone batsman had verbally abused him. Several other players, including Kiran Moré and Manoj Prabhakar were reported for 'irresponsible behaviour'. The match was abandoned in North Zone's favour and following a meeting of the Indian Cricket Board, Patel and Lamba were banned from playing first-class cricket for 14 and 11 months respectively. A few seasons earlier, Prabhakar had been involved in another on-field scuffle, during a club match in Delhi. Prabhakar and another Indian Test bowler Maninder Singh came to blows after an argument during play in the local Steel Trophy competition.

•

Among the shortest players in first-class cricket are former England wicket-keeper 'Tich' Cornford who was approximately 153 cm tall (5') and Surrey's Tom Gunn at 156.2 cm (5'1½"). One of the shortest Australian cricketers was Karl Schneider, who played for both Victoria and South Australia in the 1920s. He was 157.5 cm tall (5'2").

•

•

When fast bowler Phil Alley made his first-class debut in 1989–90, he became the tallest player in the history of Australian first-class cricket, and the second tallest in the world.

THE TALLEST-KNOWN FIRST-CLASS CRICKETERS

All First-class cricket		
Tony Allom	Surrey	209.5 cm (6'10½")
Phil Alley	South Australia/NSW	208.3 cm (6'10")
Paul Dunkels	Warwickshire/Sussex	205.8 cm (6'9")
Joel Garner	West Indies	203.2 cm (6'8")
Dallas Moir	Scotland/Derbyshire	203.2 cm (6'8")
Bruce Reid	Australia	203.2 cm (6'8")
John Larter	England	201.9 cm (6'7½")
Test Cricket		
Joel Garner	West Indies	203.2 cm (6'8")
Bruce Reid	Australia	203.2 cm (6'8")
John Larter	England	201.9 cm (6'7½")
Tony Greig	England	200.6 cm (6'7")
Curtly Ambrose	West Indies	200.6 cm (6'7")
Tom Moody	Australia	200.6 cm (6'7")
Jo Angel	Australia	200.6 cm (6'7")

•

In 1984 former England batsman Denis Compton, at the age of 66, became a father for the fifth time.

•

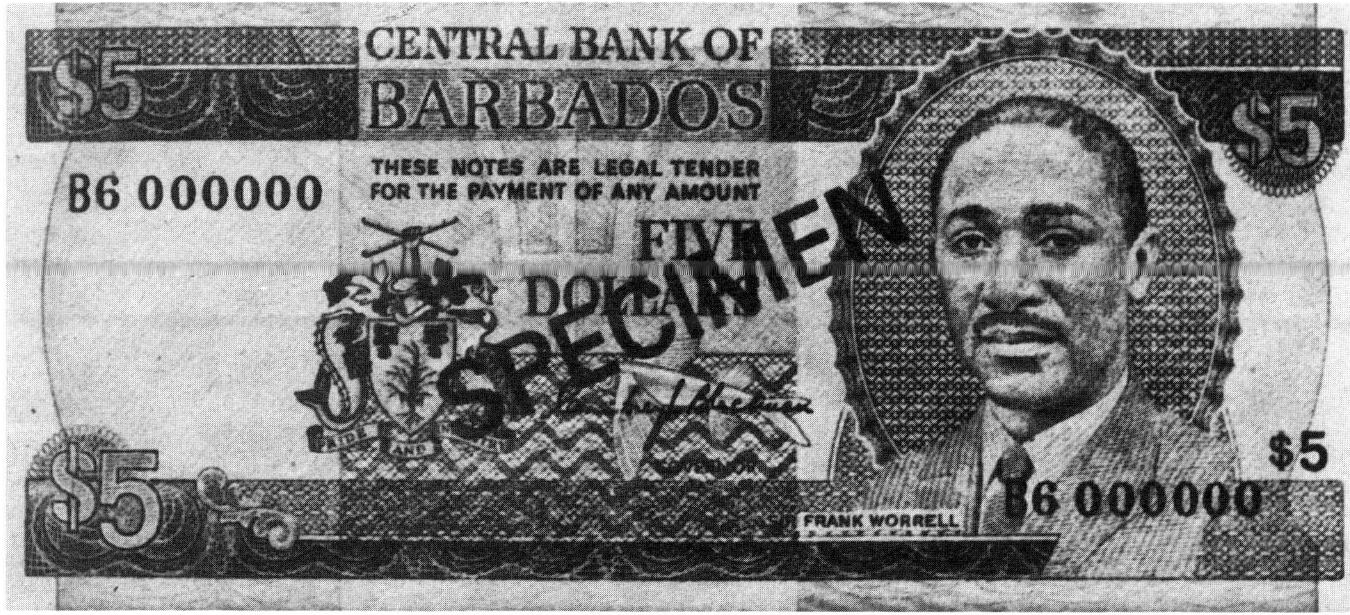

Barbados honoured one of its favourite sons in 1975 by issuing a $5 note containing the portrait of Frank Worrell.

•

Pakistan's Qasim Omar, who was banned from international cricket after accusing his team-mates of drug-dealing, is fluent in five languages—English, French, Swahili, Punjabi and Urdu.

•

Bobby Peel, a left-arm spinner who took over 1,000 wickets and scored over 10,000 runs in first-class cricket, was banned for life from playing for Yorkshire in 1897 when, under the influence of alcohol, he urinated on the pitch during a match at Bramall Lane.

•

When Omar Henry made his debut against India at Durban in 1992–93, he became the first non-white cricketer to represent South Africa in a Test.

•

Playing against Surrey at Cheltenham in 1928, Walter Hammond turned on an all-round performance without equal when he scored a century in each innings (139 & 143) and held 10 catches in the field, eight of them off the bowling of Charlie Parker. In his next match, which began the next day, again at Cheltenham, Hammond starred this time with the ball, taking 9 for 23 in the first innings against Worcestershire. As he also took a catch, Hammond had a hand in all 10 dismissals. In the next innings he took six wickets for a match return of 15 for 128 and in Gloucestershire's only innings scored 80.

•

Australia's first-Test victory over England at The Gabba in 1974–75 was played on a pitch that was prepared by the Lord Mayor of Brisbane. Alderman Clem Jones, a member of the ground's trust, did the job himself after sacking the curator who'd allegedly rolled the pitch incorrectly.

•

Indian cricket fans got a bit excited during a World Cup match in 1992, storming a power station after a cut in the electricity supply blackened TV screens while India was playing the West Indies in Wellington. Upset supporters broke every window at the station, injuring some of the staff. A week earlier, one fan's dedication resulted in six armed men robbing the Indian Overseas Bank in Calcutta of a million rupees. The bandits struck while the security guard, who'd taken the day off, was at home watching a live telecast of the India–Pakistan match being played in Sydney.

•

Mike Brearley once lectured philosophy at the University of California in Los Angeles.

•

Graham Cowdrey—brother of Chris and son of Colin—is a devotee of Van Morrison, having seen him in concert around a hundred times.

•

Bruce Francis, the former Australian Test batsman, stood unsuccessfully as a Liberal Party candidate for the New South Wales seat of Richmond in the 1993 federal election.

•

C.K. Nayudu made his first-class debut in 1916–17 and played his last match six decades later in 1963–64.

•

Henry Hyndman, who played first-class cricket for Sussex in the 1860s, was the founder of the Democratic Federation, England's first Marxist organisation.

•

South Africa's Clive Rice once posed nude for a women's magazine. England's Chris Lewis bared all for an American magazine in 1993.

•

England's Andy Lloyd, who was forced to retire hurt in his only appearance at Test level, is the only opening batsman never to have been dismissed in Test cricket. After accumulating 10 runs on his debut at Edgbaston in 1984, Lloyd was struck on the head by a ball from Malcolm Marshall and ended up in hospital suffering blurred vision. Lloyd's only taste of Test match cricket lasted a mere seven overs and 30 minutes.

•

In the third Test against Australia at The Oval in 1884, both W.G. Grace and Alfred Lyttelton opened England's batting, bowled and kept wicket.

•

Most of the streets in the Canberra suburb of Holt are named after famous Australian sports stars. Nineteen are named in honour of leading cricketers, cricket umpires and administrators—Armstrong Crescent, Bannerman Place, Bardsley Place, Blackham Street, Bonnor Close, Boyle Place, Crockett Place, Giffen Close, Grimmett Close, Grout Place, Kippax Place, McCabe Crescent, Moyes Crescent, Mullagh Place, Spofforth Street, Trott Place, Trumper Street, Wardill Close and Worrall Street.

At Menai, in southern Sydney, a similar collection of cricketing roads can be found—Barnes Crescent, Benaud Close, Bradman Road, Davidson Road, Grout Place, Harvey Place, Hassett Close, Kippax Place, Lindwall Close, McCabe Place, McKenzie Place, Meckiff Close, Miller Place, Morris Close, Noble Close, Oldfield Place, O'Neill Road, O'Reilly Close and Trumper Place.

In Wollongong, the suburb of Warilla contains as many as 35 streets named after cricketers. Included are Ponsford Street, Woodfull Street, Mailey Place, Walters Street and Toshack Street.

During the 1989–90 Currie Cup, Rodney Malamba made history by becoming the first black South African to play first-class cricket in the republic. A medium-fast bowler, Malamba took 20 wickets during the season for Natal and Natal B.

•

A letter to the editor of the *Bangkok Post* newspaper in Thailand in 1991 suggested a rather unusual approach to combatting the spread of the AIDS virus—'Safe alternatives to sex should be sought. A strong possibility is cricket. Cricket-playing nations are capable of only limited amounts of sexual activity.'

•

Trevor Hohns, who first played for Queensland in 1972–73, made his Test debut against the West Indies in 1988–89 after 122 appearances in first-class cricket. Only two others have played in 100 first-class matches before their first Test for Australia—Kepler Wessels 115 and Mark Waugh 100.

•

The Basin Reserve Test ground in Wellington was once a swamp, donated by Jeff and Martin Crowe's great-great-grandfather Edward Pearce.

•

Australian batsman Neil Harvey was once a Tupperware distributor.

•

Lala Amarnath and Mansur Ali Khan, both former Test captains, stood as rival candidates in India's 1971 general election.

•

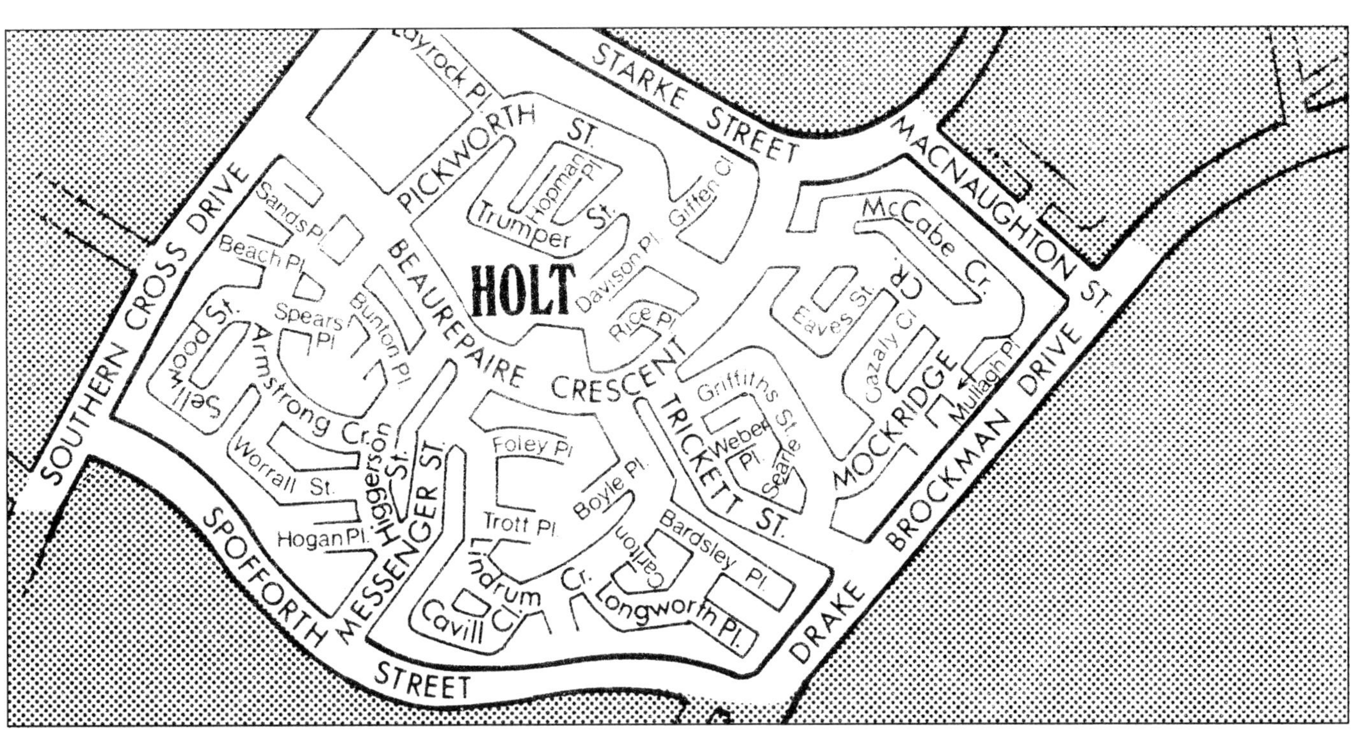

Three of Australia's brightest stars during the late 1980s and early '90s—Geoff Marsh, Bruce Reid and Merv Hughes—all made their Test debuts in the same match, against India at Adelaide in 1985–86.

•

The longest Test match played in Australia was the fifth Test against England at Melbourne in 1928–29—it lasted eight days.

•

Eric Edrich, a wicket-keeper who played for Lancashire during the 1940s, was Britain's champion chicken breeder in 1988.

•

The famous Test at Manchester in 1956 in which Jim Laker took his 19 wickets contained the first century in Test cricket by a priest. David Sheppard, who became Bishop of Liverpool in 1975, scored 113 for England as The Rev. D.S. Sheppard.

•

Former Queensland batsman Peter Cantrell represented The Netherlands in a one-day match against Pakistan at The Hague in 1992, and against England in 1993.

•

Fred Trueman's daughter, Rebecca, married Damon Welch, son of actress Raquel Welch.

•

Two of Australia's greatest pastimes—cricket and gambling—were brought together by the New South Wales Lotteries Office in 1990 with the release of an instant lottery ticket called 'Howzat!' The $2 game offered a first prize of $100,000.

On Australia's 1989 tour of England, Tom Moody developed a passion for things Scottish when he scored a century in the match against Scotland at Glasgow and broke the world record for haggis throwing. During a highland games festival, Moody threw the haggis a distance of 67 metres, an achievement which broke the previous record of 50 metres.

•

The one-day international against India at Port-of-Spain in 1982–83 contained an unscheduled break in play when a brief, but strong, earthquake struck during the afternoon. The tremor left a dozen spectators injured.

•

Prince Christian-Victor of Schleswig-Holstein, grandson of Queen Victoria, is the only member of the Royal Family to have played first-class cricket. In his only match he scored 35 and 0 for I Zingari v Gentlemen of England at Scarborough in 1887.

•

> **There is a widely held and quite erroneous belief that cricket is just another game.**
>
> **—HRH The Duke of Edinburgh**

•

Sir Alec Douglas-Home, the first-class cricketer who became British Prime Minister, is a third cousin once removed of Princess Diana.

•

Joseph Phillips, who played for Warwickshire, was the grandfather of Princess Anne's former husband Captain Mark Phillips.

•

The five 'Cricketers of the Year' in the 1949 *Wisden* were all Australians—Lindsay Hassett, Bill Johnston, Ray Lindwall, Arthur Morris and Don Tallon. It was five-out-of-five again in 1962, when Bill Alley, Richie Benaud, Alan Davidson, Bill Lawry and Norman O'Neill were named. Apart from Alley, who was playing for Somerset, the other nine were all members of Australian touring sides.

•

When John Traicos made his Test debut for Zimbabwe in 1992–93 he became the 14th cricketer to have represented two countries at Test level, having last played for South Africa 22 years earlier—a record gap between appearances by any Test player.

LONGEST INTERVALS BETWEEN TEST APPEARANCES

Years	*Days*	*Player*	*Country*	*Period*
22	222	John Traicos	SA/Z	10.3.70–18.10.92
17	316	George Gunn	E	1.3.12–11.1.30
17	111	Younis Ahmed	P	2.11.69–21.2.87
14	95	'Mick' Commaille	SA	14.3.10–17.6.24
14	28	Donald Cleverley	NZ	1.3.32–29.3.46

•

Cyril Perkins, a slow left-arm bowler, who appeared in a total of 57 first-class matches in England between 1934 and 1951, had the truly unfortunate experience of never playing in a winning side.

•

New Zealand all-rounder Dipak Patel never made it to the top in Test cricket, but in 1991–92 joined the select band of players to have scored a double century and taken 10 wickets in the same first-class match. Patel hit 204 in only 163 minutes off 155 balls and took 10 for 233 for Auckland against Northern Districts in a Shell Trophy match. He was the first New Zealander to achieve the rare double and the first since Johnny Douglas in 1921.

Dwight D. Eisenhower became the first president of the United States to watch Test cricket when he attended the fourth day's play of the third Test against Australia at Karachi in 1959–60. This, though, turned out to be one of the most boring days of Test cricket on record, with Pakistan scoring just 104 runs for the loss of five wickets. The only slower day's play in Test cricket was also between Pakistan and Australia, and on the same ground in 1956–57, when 95 runs were scored by both countries on the opening day.

•

Stephen Boock, a New Zealand spinner who appeared in 30 Tests, won a place on the Dunedin City Council in 1992, narrowly missing out on the position of mayor. Another who gained victory as a councillor in the election was Glenn Turner's wife Sukhi Turner.

•

The second Test between Zimbabwe and New Zealand at Harare in 1992–93 was the first Test to be interrupted by a one-day international. The limited-overs match was staged at the same venue after the first day's play in the Test.

•

Harold Heygate is the only batsman known to have been dismissed 'timed out' in first-class cricket. In 1919, representing Sussex against Somerset at Taunton, he was given out by umpire Alfred Street after failing to make his way to the crease in the required two-minute time. The umpire's decision caused great controversy, for not only was Heygate ill at the time, but the match also ended in a tie.

•

English bookmakers rated the sighting of the Loch Ness monster as more likely than England making a clean sweep of the 1993 Ashes series. The bookies had a Loch Ness monster sighting listed at 250 to 1 against odds of 300 to 1 for England beating Australia six-nil.

•

W.G. Grace	261 & 11–139 (5–62 & 6–77)	South v North at Prince's 1877
	221* & 11–120 (6–45 & 5–75)	Gloucestershire v Middlesex at Clifton 1885
George Giffen	237 & 12–192 (5–89 & 7–103)	South Australia v Victoria at Melbourne 1890–91
	271 & 16–166 (9–96 & 7–70)	South Australia v Victoria at Adelaide 1891–92
Ted Arnold	200* & 10–144 (3–70 & 7–44)	Worcestershire v Warwickshire at Birmingham 1909
Johnny Douglas	210* & 11–47 (9–47 & 2–0)	Essex v Derbyshire at Leyton 1921

25 Stop Press!

In only his second match for Australia, at Lord's in 1993, the young New South Wales opener Michael Slater scored his maiden Test hundred in his maiden first-class innings at the home of cricket. His knock of 152 was the highest of his first-class career to date, and the ninth highest by any Australian batsman in a Lord's Test. Having already posted a 100-run opening stand with Mark Taylor in the previous Test at Old Trafford, the two Wagga boys contributed 260 runs in partnership at Lord's, a record by Australia for any wicket at the ground beating the 231 for the second wicket by Bill Woodfull and Don Bradman in 1930. It was also Australia's third-highest opening stand in Tests against all countries.

> **It was an emotional moment for me to get a hundred at Lord's, especially being my first. With all the history at the ground and to do it on the hallowed turf, I was pretty out of control.**
>
> **—Michael Slater**

Slater's Man-of-the-Match performance in Australia's innings victory was not the only batting highlight. Taylor, with 111, completed back-to-back Test hundreds and passed the milestone of 1,000 Test runs in England in his 14th innings, a feat bettered only by Don Bradman in eight innings. Following the departure of Slater and Taylor the rich river of runs continued to flow with David Boon, at number 3, recording his first Test century (164*) in England, the fifth best score by an Australian at Lord's. Mark Waugh came in next and in his usual laidback style carved out an effortless 99 runs before being bowled going for what would have been his maiden three-figure score in a Test match in England. His dismissal was the 46th instance of a batsman out for 99 in a Test, and the 13th of an Australian. Had Waugh scored the extra run it would have been the first time in history that the first four batsmen in a Test line-up had all scored centuries in the same innings. Allan Border, at number 5, scored Australia's fifth consecutive half-century with a quick-fire 77, and became only the fifth overseas batsman to aggregate 500 runs in Test matches at Lord's.

HIGHEST TEST SCORES BY AUSTRALIAN BATSMEN AT LORD'S

Score	*Batsman*	*Test match*
254	Don Bradman	Australia v England 1930
206*	Bill Brown	Australia v England 1938
196	Allan Border	Australia v England 1985
193*	Warren Bardsley	Australia v England 1926
164*	David Boon	Australia v England 1993
164	Warren Bardsley	Australia v South Africa 1912
155	Bill Woodfull	Australia v England 1930
152*	Steve Waugh	Australia v England 1989
152	Michael Slater	Australia v England 1993

BATSMEN OUT FOR 99 IN A LORD'S TEST

Batsman	*Test match*
Charles Macartney	Australia v England 1912
Eddie Paynter	England v Australia 1938
Mike Smith	England v South Africa 1960
Ross Edwards	Australia v England 1975
Mark Waugh	Australia v England 1993
Michael Atherton	England v Australia 1993

INSTANCES OF THE FIRST THREE BATSMEN ALL SCORING CENTURIES IN THE SAME TEST INNINGS

Test match	*Batsmen*
England (2d-531) v South Africa at Lord's in 1924	Jack Hobbs (211), Herbert Sutcliffe (172), Frank Woolley (134*)
Australia (9d-600) v West Indies at Port-of-Spain in 1954–55	Colin McDonald (110), Arthur Morris (111), Neil Harvey (133)
Australia (6d-650) v West Indies at Bridgetown in 1964–65	Bill Lawry (210), Bob Simpson (201), Bob Cowper (102)
India (4d-600) v Australia at Sydney in 1985–86	Sunil Gavaskar (172), Kris Srikkanth (116), Mohinder Amarnath (138)
Australia (4d-632) v England at Lord's in 1993	Mark Taylor (111), Michael Slater (152), David Boon (164*)

•

> **I think we are all slightly down in the dumps after another loss. We may be in the wrong sign . . . Venus may be in the wrong juxtaposition with somewhere else.**
>
> **—England's chairman of selectors Ted Dexter, explaining away England's seventh successive Test loss, to Australia at Lord's in 1993**

Picture Credits

ABC, ACT Administration, ACT Cricket Association, Australia Post, Australian Foreign Affairs and Trade, Alec Bedser, Billy Birmingham (Little Digger Productions Pty Ltd), Bradman Museum, Channel 9, Channel 10, Ric Charlesworth, Derbyshire County Cricket Club, EMI Records, Fiji Ministry of Information, Phil Garlington, Gloucestershire County Cricket Club, Sir Richard Hadlee, Hampshire County Cricket Club, Lancashire County Cricket Club, Lord Home of the Hirsel, Lyndon Howe, Middlesex County Cricket Club, National Library of Australia, New South Wales Cricket Association, New South Wales State Lotteries Office, Nottinghamshire County Cricket Club, Pakistan Cricket Board, Somerset County Cricket Club, South Australian Cricket Association, South Sydney Rugby League Club, Sri Lankan Cricket Board, The Statesman Ltd, Surrey County Cricket Club, Tasmanian Cricket Association, Warwickshire County Cricket Club, West Australian Cricket Association, Worcestershire County Cricket Club.

Bibliography

Books

The Bradman Albums, Weldon, Sydney 1987

Robert Brooke, *The Collins Who's Who of English First-Class Cricketers 1945–1984*, Collins, London 1985

Philip Derriman and Ross Dundas, *The ABC Australian Cricket Almanac*, ABC, Sydney, various years

David Dobson, *Records of Australian First-Class Cricket 1851–1989*, David Dobson, Melbourne 1989

Bill Frindall, *Cricket Facts and Feats*, Guinness Superlatives Ltd, Enfield 1983

Bill Frindall, *The Wisden Book of Cricket Records*, Macdonald & Co, London 1986

Bill Frindall, *The Wisden Book of Test Cricket*, Macdonald and Jane's Publishers, London 1985

Bill Frindall, *The Wisden Book of One-Day International Cricket,* John Wisden & Co, London 1985

Christopher Martin-Jenkins, *The Complete Who's Who of Test Cricketers,* Macdonald & Co, London 1987

Allan Miller, *Allan's Australian Cricket Annual,* Allan Miller, Perth, various years

Jack Pollard, *Australian Cricket: The Game and The Players,* Angus & Robertson, Sydney 1988

Jack Pollard, *Highest, Most and Best – Australian Cricket Statistics 1850–1990,* Angus & Robertson, Sydney 1990

E.W. Swanton, *Barclays World of Cricket,* Collins, London 1986

Ray Webster and Allan Miller, *First-Class Cricket in Australia 1850–51 to 1941–42,* Ray Webster, Glen Waverley 1991

Wisden Cricketers' Almanack, John Wisden & Co, Guildford, various years

Peter Wynne-Thomas, *The Complete History of Cricket Tours,* Hamlyn, London 1989

Peter Wynne-Thomas, *The Hamlyn A–Z of Cricket Records,* Hamlyn, Twickenham 1985

Magazines

Australian Cricket

Cricketer

The Cricketer International

The Cricketer Quarterly

Wisden Cricket Monthly

Index

Page numbers in italics refer to photographs

Aaqib Javed, 51, 76, 115
Abdul Kardar, 84
  Qadir, 46–7, 90, *121*, 122
Acfield, David, 103
Adams, Don, 47
  Grantley, 53
  Sidney, 142
Adhikari, Hemu, 83
Afford, Andy, 114
Aftab Baloch, 50
Agnew, Jonathan, 59
Alderman, Bill, 105
  Terry, 9, 41–2, 44, 47, 59, 87, 105, 111, 118, 121–2, 132, 135
Alexander, 'Gerry', 83–4, 108
Alim-ud-Din, 51
Allbrook, Mark, 33
Allen, 'Gubby', 125
Alley, Bill, 100, 105, 149
  Phil, 145
Allom, Maurice, 49, 127
  Tony, 145
Amarnath, Lala, 147
  Mohinder, 10, 19, 21, 24, 34, 70, 112, 133, 140, 150
Ambrose, Curtly, 64, 119, 122, 145
Amerasinghe, Mudalige, 37
Ames, Les, 91
Amiss, Dennis, 10, 20, 69, 113, 140
Amm, Philip, 97
Andrew, Keith, 91
  Rob, 107
Angel, Jo, 145
Anne, Princess, 148
Antill, Tom, 111
Aran, Lal, 21
Archer, Ron, 14
Arlott, John, 89
Armstrong, Warwick, 20, 51
Arnold, Geoff, 45, 116
  Ted, 45, 149
Arnott, Kevin, 30
Arun, Bharat, 10
Asif Din, 17
  Masood, 141
  Mujtaba, 138
Asquith, Herbert, 53
Astill, Ewart, 51
Atherton, Michael, 9, 14, 26, 114, 150
Athey, Bill, 19, 93, 114, 120
Atkinson, Denis, 14
  Graham, 26
Austen, Jane, 142
Ayres, Warren, 114
Azharuddin, Mohammad, 14, 33, 71, 76, 82
Azmat Rana, 63

Bacchus, Faoud, 75
Badcock, 'Jack', 32
Baden-Powell, Lord, 57
Bader, Douglas, 144
Bailey, Jack, 132
  Rob, 139
  Trevor, 38, 116
Bairstow, David, 75, 93
Balderstone, Chris, 102
Baldwin, Stanley, 53
Balfour, Arthur, 55
  Leslie, 110
Banerjee, Shute, 38
Bannerman, Alec, 20–1
  Charles, 18, 20, 36, 125, 137, 140
Baporia, Esmail, 50
Baptiste, Eldine, 75
Barber, R.W., 45
Barclay, John, 126
Bardsley, Warren, 61, 103, 150
Barlow, Dick, 139
  Graham, 14
Barnato, J.W., 110
Barnes, Jimmy, 128
  Sid, 20, 61, 125
  Sydney, 41, 139
Barnett, Ben, 105
  Kim, 115
Barratt, Edward, 113
Barrie, J.M., 142
Barrington, Ken, 20, 23, 25, 126, *134*, 135
Bates, Billy, 139
Bavadra, Timoci, 56
Bayliss, Trevor, 138
Beck, John, 27
Beckett, Samuel, 142
Bedford, Peter, 109
Bedi, Bishen, 41
Bedser, Alec, 60
  Alec V., 41, 46, 48, 59, 65, 85
  Eric, 59, 65
Bell, Francis, 53
Benaud, Richie, 14, 29, 88, 129, 149
Benjamin, Winston, 26, 116
Benson, Mark, 138
Bernhardt, Sarah, 85
Berry, Darren, 91, 93
Bestwick, Bill, 64
  Bob, 64
Betancourt, Nelson, 83
Bettington, Reg, 67, 103
Bevan, Michael, 25
Bhaskar Pillai, Khishna, 39
Bignell, Guy, 120
Bilk, Acker, 127
Bill, O.W., 30
Binks, Jimmy, 91
Birchall, J.T.W., 139
Birmingham, Billy, 129
Bishop, Glenn, 36, 75, 100, 140
  Ian, 137
Bjelke-Petersen, Sir Joh, 144
Blackham, Jack, 21, 60, 83, 90, 92
Blackie, Don, 50
Blaker, Barbara, 62
  Joan, 62
  Richard, 62
Blewitt, Greg, 140
Blofeld, Henry, 60, 88
Blundell, Denis, 57
Bolger, Jim, 57
Bonham-Carter, Maurice, 53
Bonnor, George, 21
Boock, Stephen, 149
Boon, David, 22, 23, 27, 28, 71, 79, 106, 112–13, 121, 132, 138, 150
  Leslie, 106
Booth, Brian, 33, 104
  Roy, 91
Border, Allan, 9, 12, 15, 18, 22–4, 30, 57, 71, 83–4, 100, 109, 114–15, 131–2, 139–40, 150
Borwick, Peter, 107
Bosanquet, Bernard, 107
Botham, Ian, 29, 39, 44–6, 72, 83, 85, 97, 100, 106, 118, 126, 138–40
Bowes, Peter, 96
Boycott, Geoff, 19, 23–5, 29, 36, 38, 45, 76, 83, 98–9, 117, 122, 130, 132, 135, 139
Boyd, David, 70
Bracewell, Brendon, 58, 106, 117
  John, 26, 47, 58, 93, 117
Brady, Mike, 129
Bradley, 'Bill', 45
Bradman, Don, 10–11, 16, 18, 20, 22, 32, 35–6, 38, 48, 52, 55, 61, 79–81, 84–5, *103*, 104, 111, 113, 117, 119, 122, 127, *128*, 129–30, 132, 135, 150
  John, 120
Bradshaw, Keith, 100
Brathwaite, Nicholas, 55
Braund, Len, 116
Brearley, Horace, 64
  Mike, 14, 18, 64, 82–4, 146
Bremner, Colin, 90
  Rory, 129
Brice, Alfred, 108
Briggs, Johnny, 40–1
Bright, Ray, 141
Broad, Chris, 32, 114, 120, 144
Broadbridge, James, 28
Brooke, Rupert, 142
Brooke-Taylor, David, 88
  G.P., 88
  Tim, 88, *89*
Brotherhood, Rowland, 68
Brown, Alan, 107
  Bill, 16, 60, 150
  David, 46
  Freddie, 125
  George, 14
  William, 40
Bruce, William, 21, 125
Bryant, Dick, 62
  Frank, 62
Bucknall, Tony, 105
Bucknor, Steve, 104
Bula, I.L., 120
Bulger, Neil, *54*
Burge, Peter, 109
Burgess, Mark, 69
Burke, Jim, 125
Burn, Ken, 125
Burnett, Graham, 119
Burton, Fred, 104
Butcher, Alan, 59, 64
  Basil, 14, 46
  Gary, 64
  Mark, 59
  Roland, 14, 75, 140
Butt, Harry, 116
Butterfield, Leonard, 116

Caesar, William, 40
Cairns, Chris, 58–9, 63, 108
Lance, 31, 58–9, 63, 70, 139
Cakobau, Ratu Sir Edward, 53
Ratu Sir George, 57
Callaway, Sydney, 96
Calthorpe, the Hon. F.S.G., 60
Campbell, Greg, 9, 59
Campese, David, 107
Candler, John, 115
Cantrell, Peter, 138, 148
Capel, David, 114
Carew, 'Joey', 14
Cargill, Patrick, 88
Carmichael, Ian, 100
Carrol, Lewis, 142
Carter, Hanson, 125
Causby, Barry, 58
John, 58
Cazalet, Peter, 106
Chadwick, Derek, 30
Challenor, George, 30
Champion, Greg, 129
Chamundeswaranth, V., 120
Chandrasekhar, B.S., 45, 111–12, 138
Chapman, Percy, 67
Chappell, Greg, 9, 25, 30, 33, 38, *54*, 58–9, 61–2, 66–7, 71, 83, 86, *88*, 99, 138, 140–1
Ian, 14, 23, 30, 36, 54, 58–9, 61, 63, 66–7, *88*, 137–8, 141
Trevor, 29, 58, 66–7, 104, 136
Charlesworth, Ric, 110
Charlton, Michael, 89
Charma, Chetan, 71, 97
Chatfield, Ewan, 47, 139
Chauhan, Chetan, 28
Childs, John, 139
Chipp, Don, 55
Chowdhury, Nirode, 42
Christian-Victor, Prince, 148
Churchill, Winston, 53
Clapton, Eric, 127
Clark, Seymour, 114
Clarke, Sylvester, 135
Cleverley, Donald, 149
Clift, Paddy, 29
Close, Brian, 52
Cockett, John, 119
Collins, Herbie, 20, 106
Commaille, 'Mick', 149
Compton, Denis, 20, 24, 27, 30, 35–6, 85, 109, 119, 145
Leslie, 109
Coney, Jeremy, 12, 63, 139
Congdon, Bev, 73, 127
Coningham, Arthur, 45
Constantine, Learie, 39, 86
Cook, Geoff (G.), 60
Geoff, 116
Jimmy, 26, 35, 52, 98, 113
Cooper, William, 63, 125
Cornford, 'Tich', 145
Cosier, Gary, 54, 136
Cosstick, Sam, 135
Cotter, 'Tibby', 43
Cottey, Phillip, 139
Courtice, Andrew, 100
Cowans, Norman, 102
Cowdrey, Chris, 59, 83, 119, 146
Colin, 52, 54, 59, 82, 109, 140, 146
Graham, 119, 146
Cowper, Bob, 20, 24, 33, 150
Crawley, C.S., 136
Leonard, 104
Crippin, Ron, 69
Crisp, Bob, 112
Croft, Colin, 26, 33, 75, 120
Robert, 139
Croker, Lindsay, 119
Cromb, Ian, 107
Crowe, D.W., 63
Jeff, 12, 29, 58, 63, 65, 88, 101, 140, 147
Martin, 12, 19, 26, 35–6, 56, 63, 65, 84, 88, 140, 147
Russell, 88
Crump, Brian, 59
Curtin, John, 55
Curtis, Tim, 72, 96, 98

Dalton, Eric, 104
Daniel, Wayne, 14
Darling, Joe, 20, 112, 125
Rick, 27, 29, 69
Davidson, Alan, 41, 93, 149
Les, 106
Davies, Jack, 111
Davis, Ian, 27, 29, 54
Rodger, 104
Winston, 76
Davison, Brian, 97, 103
Dawson, Eddie, 45
DeFreitas, Phillip, 9, 125
Dell, Tony, 125
Denness, Mike, 69
Denton, Billy, 67
Jack, 67
Deodhar, Dinkar, 50
Depeiza, Clairmonte, 14
de Silva, Aravinda, 26
Devereaux, Louis, 107
Dewdney, Tom, 14
Dexter, Ted, 59, 108, 111, 150
Deyes, George, 112
Diana, Princess, 148
Dias, Roy, 71
Diesel, Johnny, 129
Dimattina, Michael, 105
Dipper, Alfred, 14
Disney, Walt, 85
Djura, Bronko, 105
Docker, Albert, 67
Cyril, 67
Ernest, 67
Keith, 67
Phillip, 67
Dodemaide, Tony, 70, 98, 100, 139
Dolman, Malcolm, 100
Donald, Allan, 69
Donnan, Harry, 68
Donnan, Nellie, 68
Donnelly, Martin, 20
Dooland, Bruce, 98
Douglas, Johnny, 14, 105, 149
Douglas-Home, Sir Alec, 53, 56, 148
Andrew, 53
Dowling, Graham, 82
Downton, George, 58
Paul, 14, 58, 121
Doyle, Sir Arthur Conan, 142
Ducat, Andy, 14, 104
Duckworth, George, 91
Duggan, Mary, 59
Dujon, Jeff, 26, 44, 62
Leroy, 62
Duleepsinhji, K.S., 62, 125
Duncan, Ross, 114
Dunkels, Paul, 145
Dunnell, Owen, 84
Durston, Jack, 14
Dwyer, E.B., 120
Dyer, Dennis, 45
Greg, 132
Dyson, John, 29, 70, 138
Eady, Charles, 47
East, Robert, 94
Ebeling, Hans, 119
Ede, George, 110
Edgar, A.J., 63
Bruce, 12, 37, 63, 111
Edinburgh, Duke of, 148
Edmonds, Phil, 14
Edrich, Bill, 30, 35
Eric, 148
John, 20, 69, 139
Edwards, Ross, 150
Egerton, Rob, 107
Eisenhower, Dwight D., 149
Ella, Mark, 104
Elliot, Gideon, 42, 45, 135
Ellison, Richard, 85, 116
Emburey, John, 14, 23, 26, 75, 83, 100, 116
Emerson, Denise, 59
Emery, Neville, 108
Phil, 108
Emmett, Tom, 44
English, David, 127, 144
Evans, Edwin, 48
Godfrey, 85, 91, 94
John, 14

Faber, Mark, 53
Fairbrother, Neil, 19, 28, 120, 138
Fairfax, Alan, 89
Falkinder, Bill, 54
Falkner, Nick, 30
Farnham, John, 129
Faulkner, Aubrey, 20
Peter, 100
Faull, Jo-Anne, 106
Martin, 106
Fazal Mahmood, 40, 60
Fee, Francis, 47
Fender, Percy, 14, 29
Fernandes, Maurice, 83
Ferris, J.J., 46, 100
Fields, Maurie, *87*
Fitzpatrick, Kate, 88
Fletcher, Duncan, 69
Keith, 83
Flint, B., 66
Derek, 66
K.R., 45
W.A., 66
Flower, Andy, 68
Grant, 30, 68
Foley, Geoff, 117
Forster of Lepe, Lord, 57
Foster, E.M., 89
Maurice, 105
Neil, 100
'Tip', 20, 66, 105, 116
Fowler, Graeme, 26, 29, 140
Francis, Bruce, 100, 146
Fraser, Angus, 43, 49, 138
Fraser, Malcolm, 55
Frawley, John, 109
Fredericks, Roy, 25, 30
Freeman, Eric, 107
Thomas, 57
'Tich', 41, 43, 46–7, 51, 141
French, Bruce, 71, 93
Dick, 105
Frost, A.R., 45
Fry, C.A., 63
C.B., 22, 63, 103, 111, 133
S., 63

Gaekwad, Anshuman, 9, 39
Gale, Terry, 107
Gallion, Jason, 96, 101

Gallop, Derek, 74
Gandhi, Mrs Indira, 55
Garlick, Paul, 113
Garner, Joel, 26, 49, 75, 99, 130, 135, 140, 145
Garrett, Tom, 21, 125
Gasnier, Reg, 108
Gatting, Mike, 14, 19, 29, 63, 75, 83, 100, 112, 114, 122, 132, 135, 137, 144
Steve, 144
Gaunt, Ron, 141
Gavaskar, Sunil, 20-1, 23-5, 31, 33, 45, 60, 76, 83, 116, 132-3, 137, 150
Geise, Greg, 100
Ghazali, Mohammad, 112
Ghulam Ahmed, 83
Gibbons, 'Doc', 23
Gibbs, Lance, 10, 46, 49, 60
Peter, 88
Giddy, Lennox, 107
Giffen, George, 149
Gifford, Norman, 52
Gilbert, Dave, 132
George, 62
Gill, Jim, 33
Gilligan, Harold, 66, 133
Gillingham, Frank, 87
Gilmour, Gary, 77
Giltinan, J.J., 108
Gladigau, P.W., 139
Gladstone, William, 55
Goddard, John, 28
Tom, 41
Trevor, 116
Gomes, Larry, 66, 75, 131
Sheldon, 66
Gooch, Graham, 9, 14, 18-19, 22, 24, 26-7, 34, 38, 42, 66, 73-4, 78, 82-4, 105, 110, 112, 116, 121-2, 135, 137
Gooden, N.L., 30
Goodman, Gary, 69
Gordon, Leslie, 87
Gore, Spencer, 102
Gough, Darren, 139
Gower, David, 14, 23-4, 29, 77, 83, 97-8, 105, 114, 116, 121, 129, 140
Grace, E.M., 102
Martha, 125
W.G., 18, 20-1, 47, 51, 62, 79, 82, 91, 102, 111, 123, 125, 130, 142, 147, 149
Grant, Cy, 127
'Jackie', 18
Rolph, 106
Graveney, David, 59
Ken, 59
Tom, 51, 52, 59, 83
Greatbatch, Mark, 28, 140
Green, David, 18
Greenidge, Gordon, 23, 25-6, 30, 33-4, 36, 51, 60, 71-3, 75, 97, 114, 137
Gregory, Arthur, 66
Charles S., 66
Charles W., 32, 66
David, 66, 84, 125
Jack, 66, 115
Ned, 60, 66, 68, 115
Syd, 20, 60, 66, 114-15, 125
Greig, Ian, 59, 135
Tony, 59, *88*, 99, 145
Greswell, Bill, 107
Griffith, Mike, 142
Griffiths, Jim, 113
Grimmett, Clarrie, 41-2, 46, 51, 91, 125
Grout, Nelma, 67
Wally, 67, 93
Gunjal, M.D., 130
Gunn, Billy, 10, 64
G.V., 64
George, 51, 64, 149
John, 64
Tom, 145
Gunnarsson, Jan, 109
Gurisinha, Asanka, 26, 36, 94

Hacker, Peter, 135
Hadlee, Barry, 62
Dayle, 58, 62, 66-7
Karen, 62
Walter, 63, 66
Richard, 10, 12, 18, 41, 46-7, 58, 62-3, 66-7, 116, 121, 133, 135
Hadlow, Patrick, 102
Hagan, Michael, 106
Haggett, Belinda, 37
Haig, Nigel, 14, 51
Hall, Wes, 97
Halliday, Simon, 107
Hallows, Charlie, 14
Hammond, Walter, 20-2, 32, 35, 52, 80, 90, 111, 130, 146
Hampshire, John, 90, 98
Hanif Mohammad, 20, 32, 59, 60-1, 63-7, 135, 139
Hanley, Rupert, 76
Hardcastle, Paul, 129
Hardie, Brian, 74
Hardinge, Wally, 14
Hardstaff, Joe, 33
Hargreaves, Reg, 142
Harper, Roger, 75
Roy, 127
Harris, Kim, 29
Tony, 105
Hartigan, Roger, 107
Harvey, Mervyn, 65
'Mick', 65
Neil, 14, 23, 31, 65, 106, 120, 149-50
Ray, 65
Robert, 106
Hassett, Lindsay, 16, 149
Hawke, Bob, 54-6
Lord, 82
Neil, 141
Hay, Harry, 42, 49
Hayden, Matthew, 22-3
Hayes, Frank, 119
Haynes, Desmond, 21, 25, 33-4, 44, 71-3, 75, 83, 111, 114, 130
Haysman, Michael, 96-7, 100
Hayward, Tom, 116
Hazare, Vijay, 24
Headley, Dean, 64
George, 31, 39, 64
Ron, 64
Healy, Ian, 46, 68, 83, 95, 106, 132
Ken, 68
Hearne, Alec, 60, 66
Frank, 66
George, 60, 66
George A., 45, 66
Jack, 60, 114
John, 14, 60, 66
Tom, 60
Walter, 60
Hegg, Warren, 93
Hemmings, Eddie, 47, 49
Henderson, Matthew, 45
Hendren, 'Patsy', 14, 18, 32, 51, 110, 112, 132
Henry, Omar, 52, 146
Heygate, Harold, 149
Heyoe Flint, Rachel, 66, 104
Hibbert, Paul, 28
Hick, Graeme, 9, 19, 27, 32, 38, 52, 97, 125, 137
Hickey, Denis, 100
Higgs, Jim, 45, 115
Ken, 19
Hilditch, Andrew, 19, 27, 83, 114
Hill, Arthur, 59
Clem, 19, 20, 24, 59, 62, 82, 87, 111, 114
Henry, 59
Les, 59, 62
Mark, 70
Percival, 59
Roland, 59
Stanley, 59, 62
Hirst, George, 137
Hirwani, Narendra, 41, 49
Hitch, John, 14
Hoad, Teddy, 83
Hobbs, Jack, 14, 20, 34, 57, 127, 132, 135, 150
Hodges, James, 125
Hogan, Paul, 86
Hogg, Rodney, 41, 42
Vincent, 118
Hohns, Trevor, 9, 147
Holding, Michael, 48, *54*, 75, 135-6
Holdsworth, Wayne, 43, 117
Holford, David, 14, 60
Holland, Bob, 12, 50, 97, 111
Hollies, Eric, 45, 117
Holmes, Percy, 14, 31
Holt, Harold, 54
Holyman, Joe, 92
Hookes, David, 9, 34, 36, 45, 61, 93, 114, 139
Hooman, Charles, 107
Hooper, Carl, 44
Horan, Tom, 83
Hornby, 'Monkey', 105, 130
Horne, Phil, 103
Houghton, David, 84, 108
Howard, Leslie, 86
Howarth, Dick, 45
Geoff, 10, 12, 58, 63
Hedley, 58
John, 112
Howell, Bill, 48
'Harry', 14
Hudson, Andrew, 118
Hughes, Billy, 56
Graeme, 108
Kim, 9, 18, 23-4, *54*, 83, 97, 112, 114
Merv, 9, 44, 48, 87, 100, 105, 148
Huish, Fred, 91
Human, Johnny, 49
Humpage, Geoff, 93
Hunte, Conrad, 31, 120
Hurst, Alan, 112
Geoff, 102, 127
Hussain, Dilawar, 90
Naser, 137
Hutton, Len, 20, 29, 32-3, 35, 52, 58, 85, 111-12, 137
Richard, 58
Hylton, Leslie, 125
Hyndman, Henry, 146

Ibrahim, K.C., 19
Ijaz Ahmed, 50
Faqih, 115
Illingworth, Ray, 51, 82
Richard, 9, 45
Imran Khan, 21, 40, 46, 60, 66, 75-6, 98, 116, 121, 126, 131, 136
Imtiaz Ahmed, 90
Indrajitsinhji, K.S., 62
Intikhab Alam, 45, 84
Inverarity, Alison, 104
John, 36, 104
Iqbal Qasim, 115
Ironmonger, Bert, 50
Irvine, Greg, 56

Isherwood, Ray, 105
Iverson, Jack, 125

Jackman, Robin, 88
Jackson, F.S., 53, 125
  Peter, 106
Jadeja, Ajay, 32, 63
Jahangir Khan, 66, 112
James, Kevan, 17
Jameson, John, 10, 144
  Tommy, 104
Jardine, Douglas, 64, 125
  Malcolm, 64
Jarman, Barry, 125
Jarvis, Affie, 40
  Kevin, 119
Javed Burki, 60, 66
  Miandad, 19–21, 23, 31, 76–7, 90, 121–2, 126, 130–1, 133, 135
Jayasuriya, Sanath, 35
Jeeves, Percy, 142
Jenkins, Roly, 126
Jennings, Ray, 90
Jerman, Lindsey, 26
Jessop, Gilbert, 107
John, Elton, 127
Johnson, Ian, *54*
  Laurence, 94
  Tyrell, 45
Johnston, Bill, 132, 135, 149
  Brian, 88
Jones, Alan, 64
  Allan, 136
  Andrew H., 26, 37, 71, 74
  Andrew, 64
  Clem Alderman, 146
  Dean, 10, 22, 29, 32, 36, *56*, 74–7, 87, 97, 114, 132, 137
  Sammy, 21, 118
Joshi, 'Nana', 93
Julien, Bernard, 69
Junor, Len, 51
Jupp, Henry, 20
  Vallance, 14

Kallicharran, Alvin, 10, 30, 74–5, 93, 130, 135
Kalyani, Shrikant, 10
Kambli, Vinod, 31–2, 50
Kanhai, Rohan, 10, 14, 95
Kapil Dev, 14, 21, 33, 40, 43, 45–7, 49, 69, 78, 83, 113
Karloff, Boris, 86
Karnain, Uvaisul, 70, 104
Keating, Paul, *56*, 57
Keeton, Walter, 45
Kelleway, Charles, 61
Kelly, James, 93, 125
  Paul, 129
Kemp-Welch, George, 53
Kendall, Francis, 114
  Tom, 125
Kent, Martin, 27
Kermode, Alex, 97
Kerr, Robbie, 100
Keshwala, Suresh, 10
Khalid Aziz, 141
Khan Mohammad, 40, 43
King, Frank, 14
  Ian, 69, 70
  John Barton, 130
Kinkead-Weekes, Roddy, 144
Kippax, P.J., 144
Kirmani, Syed, 18, 21, 90
Kirsten, Peter, 26, 78, 110, 135
Knight, Donald, 14
Knott, Alan, 18, 91, 94
Kripal Singh, Arjan, 35

Kuggeleijn, Chris, 120
Kuiper, Adrian, 72
Kuruppu, Brendon, 94, 95

Labrooy, Graeme, 28
Laird, Bruce, 9
Lamb, Allan, 9, 14, 22, 75, 83, 105, 114, 125, 135, 144
  Tim, 121
Lamba, Raman, 39, 145
Laker, Jim, 40–1, 85, 139, 148
Langer, Allan, 107
  Justin, 14
  Rob, 61
Langford, Brian, 76
Langley, Gil, 90
Langridge, Jim, 59, 63, 68
  John, 34, 59, 63, 68
Lara, Brian, 74
Larkins, Wayne, 144
Larter, John, 145
Larwood, Harold, 127
Lavender, Mark, 30
Laver, Frank, 45
Lawry, Bill, 14, 22, 24, 34, 36, 59, 69, *88*, 137, 149, 150
Lawson, Geoff, 9, 12, 46, 83, 93, 138
  R.J., 30
Lawton, Frank, 86
Leabeater, L.R., 30
Lee, Frank, 59, 63
  Harry, 59, 63
  Jack, 43
  Jack W., 59, 63
Legall, Ralph, 110
Leggat, Gordon, 144
Lehmann, Darren, 24, 50
Leigh, Spencer, 142
Le Mesurier, John, 87
Lennox, Charles, 57
Leonard, Art, 127
Leopold, Ward, 129
Lever, John, 45
Levy, Mark, 109
Lewis, Chris, 9, 49, 146
  Tony, 26, 82, 127
Leyland, Maurice, 33, 112
Lillee, Dennis, 9, 42–7, 50, 54, 69, 86, 90, 99, 113–14, 125, 133
Lillie, Dennis, 84
Lillywhite, James, 84
  William, 51
Lindwall, Ray, 14, 18, 103, 116, 149
Lindsay, Denis, 92
Linekar, Gary, 105
Lloyd, Andy, 139, 147
  Clive, 15, 30, 55, 60, 73, 75, 84, 119, 137–8
Lock, Tony, 41, 132, 139
Logie, Gus, 44
Lohmann, George, 116
Long, Arnold, 93, 126
Longfield, Tom, 59
Lord Beginner, 127
Lord, Graham, 139
Lovelace, Linda, 86
Lowry, Tom, 67, 84
Loxton, Sam, 56, 104
Luckhurst, Brian, 18, 58, 60
  Tim, 60
Lumsdaine, Jack, 127
Lycett, R., 109
Lyttelton, Alfred, 55, 91, 108, 147
  Charles, 57
  Spencer, 55

McCabe, Stan, 133
McCague, Martin, 99

McCool, Colin, 15, 59
  Russell, 59
McCorquodale, Alistair, 106
McCosker, Rick, 29, 61, 70, 116
McCurdy, Rod, 70–1, 97, 100
McDermott, Craig, 42, 108, 114, 132
McDonald, Colin, 14, 34, 45, 150
  Ted, 107
McDonnell, Percy, 18, 21, 125
McEwan, Ken, 33
McGilvray, Alan, 86
McGlew, 'Jackie', 43, 116
McHugh, Francis, 133
McKechnie, Brian, 104
McKenzie, Doug, 65, 106
  Eric, 65
  Graham, 14, 47, 50, 65, 96, 100, 106, 141
McKone, John, 42
McLachlan, Ian, 101
McLean, Ian, 29
McLeod, Eddie, 108
McMahon, John, 100
McPhee, Mark, 70
  Peter, 45
Macartney, Charles, 32, 51, 150
Macaulay, Mike, 136
Macauley, George, 45
MacDonald, Sir John, 55
Mackay, Ken 'Slasher', 25
MacKinnon, Francis, 44, 125
MacLaren, Archie, 32, 45, 50, 83–4
Maclean, John, 95
MacLeay, Ken, 44, 100
Macmillan, Harold, 53
Madal Lal, 21, 46
Maddocks, Len, 90
Madugalle, Ranjan, 139
Maguiness, Steve, 40
Maguire, John, 97, 99, 100
Mahamana, Roshan, 144
Maharaj Singh, Raja, 50
Majid Khan, 60, 66, 69, 97, 112, 155–16
Major, John, 55
Maka, Ebrahim, 93
Makepeace, Harry, 107
Malamba, Rodney, 147
Malcolm, Devon, 44, 47, 49, 125, 138
Malone, Mick, 40
Maninder Singh, 133, 145
Manjrekar, Sanjay, 59
  Vijay, 59, 136
Mankad, Vinoo, 34, 83
Manley, Michael, 56
Mann, Frank, 64, 67
  George, 64, 67
  Tony, 103
Mansoor Akhtar, 31
Mansur Ali Khan, 147
Maqsood Ahmed, 27
Mara, Ratu Sir Kamisese, 53
Maranta, Michael, 144
Marks, Hyam, 87
Marner, Peter, 69
Marriot, Charles, 45
Marsh, Geoff, 9, 27, 37, 54, 70–1, 78, 90, 100, 137–8, 144, 148
  Graham, 107
  Rod, 9, 12, 20, 38, 86, 92–5, 107, 114, 140
  Steve, 94
Marshall, John, 50
  Malcolm, 26, 41, 46, 75, 116, 121, 135, 147
Martin, 'Freddie', 30
  Ray, 87
Martyn, Damien, 96
Massie, Bob, 40
  Hugh, 83, 102
  Jack, 102

Matthews, Austin, 107
Chris, 96
Greg, 21, 44, 77, 87, 100, 116, 139
Jimmy, 104, 119
May, Dorothy, 87
Peter, 20, *54*, 66
Tim, 44
Mead, Phil, 14, 19, 32, 52
Measham, David, 127
Medlycott, Keith, 30
Meldrum, Molly, 129
Melly, George, 127
Melville, Alan, 30
Mendis, Duleep, 137, 139
Gehan, 126
Menzies, Sir Robert, 54, 56
Merchant, Vijay, 31, 79
Merrick, Tony, 113
Metcalfe, Ashley, 64
Midwinter, Billy, 91, 125
Miles, Tony, 129
Miller, Colin, 43
Geoff, 104
Keith, 14, 97, 104, 120
Mills, John, 140
Peter, 45
Milne, A.A., 142
Milton, Arthur, 103
Mitchell, Bruce, 30, 38
Mohammad Nazir, 60
Saeed, 60
Mohsin Khan, 21, 116, 122
Moin Khan, 51
Moir, Dallas, 145
Moles, Andy, 17, 31
Moody, Chris, 104
Tom, 34, 47, 70, 97-8, 145, 148
Moore, Bobby, 102
Richard, 138
Moré, Kiran, 139, 145
Morley, Robert, 85
Moroney, Jack, 116
Morris, Arthur, 14, 27, 33, 38, 48, 116, 149, 150
Hugh, 9
John, 117, 144
Sam, 21
Morrison, Danny, 112
John, 45
Van, 146
Mortensen, Michael, 109
Ole, 109
Morton, Frank, 116
Mosely, Ezra, 135
Moss, R.H., 144
Mott, Matthew, 77
Moyes, A.G., 30
Mudassar Nazar, 21, 36, 59, 116-17, 133, 140
Mulder, Brett, 100
Muldoon, Robert, 55
Munton, Tim, 71
Murdoch, Billy, 20, 83, *92*, 140
Murray, David, 75
Deryck, 10, 95, 133
John, 19, 91
Musgrove, Harry, 125
Mushtaq Mohammad, 50, 52, 63-5

Nadeem Shahid, 139
Nagel, Lisle, 63
Vernon, 63
Nanan, Ranjie, 48
Nash, Laurie, 107
Nawaz Sharif, 55
Nayudu, C.K., 84, 146
Nayyar, Manu, 39
Nazar Mohammad, 59
Nazir Ali, S., 36
Junior, 115
Nehru, Jawaharlal, 54
Newcombe, G., 120
John, 103
Newman, Betty, 63
Dawn, 63
Nicholas, Mark, 104
Nicholls, Paul, 38
Nielsen, Tim, 93, 140
Nimbalkar, B.B., 32
Niven, David, 86
Noble, Monty, 114
Noreiga, Jack, 46
Norman, Greg, 107
Nourse, 'Dave', 51, 63, 102
Dudley, 30, 50, 63
Nunes, Karl, 83-4
Nurse, Seymour, 20, 36
Nye, Lisa, 92

Oakes, Charles, 68
Jack, 68
O'Brien, Sir Timothy, 116
O'Donnell, Simon, 70, 87, 100, 104, 113, 117
O'Hagan, Jack, 127
O'Keefe, Kerry, 33
Old, Alan, 108
Chris, 49, 75, 108
Oldfield, Bert, 93
Olivier, Lawrence, 85, 88
O'Neill, Adam, 106
Gary, 56
Mark, 106, 118, 138
Norman, 33, 106, 149
O'Reilly, Bill, 116, 132, 135
Orwell, George, 89
Osborne, Mark, 117
O'Shaughnessy, Steve, 29
Ostler, Dominic, 17
Otto, Ralston, 64
Oxenham, Ron, 133, 140

Palairet, Henry, 105
Palmer, George, 21
Pandit, Chandra, 39, 130
Pandove, Dhruv, 50
Parfitt, P.H., 45
Parker, Charlie, 14, 29, 40, 146
Paul, 126
Parkes, Harry, 68
James, 68
Parkin, 'Ciss', 14
Parks, Bobby, 64, 93, 95
James, 64
Jim, 64
Parr, Francis, 127
Pascoe, Len, 54, 70
Pataudi, Nawab of, 110
jnr, Nawab of, 50
Patel, Dipak, 22, 46, 149
Rashid, 145
Paterson, 'Banjo', 143
Patil, Sandeep, 21
Patterson, Patrick, 101
Pavilion, Percy, 127
Pawson, Tony, 105
Payne, Alfred, 63
Arthur, 63
Paynter, Eddie, 45, 138, 150
Pearce, Edward, 147
Roland, 95
Peel, Bobby, 146
Pecci, Victor, 109
Penberthy, Tony, 45
Perkins, Cyril, 149
Perryman, Steve, 112
Pervez Akhtar, 11, 24
Phillips, Joseph, 148
Mark, Captain, 148
Ray, 90, 93
Wayne, 21, 29, 61, 71, 90, 93, 100, 139
Phillipson, Paul, 126
Pigott, Tony, 43
Pimple, Uday, 126
Pinter, Harold, 143
Pithey, David, 64
Tony, 64
Platts, John, 125
Pocock, Pat, 60, 113
Poidevin, Les, 97, 103
Pollock, Andrew, 62
Anthony, 62
Graeme, 20, 33, 62, 64
Peter, 62, 64
Shaun, 62
Ponsford, Bill, 23, 32, 35-6, 79, 106
Ponting, Rick, 59
Popplewell, Nigel, 29
Porter, Graeme, 77
Simon, 74
Potter, Dennis, 88
Laurie, 83
Sarah, 88
Prabhakar, Manoj, 39, 49, 145
Prideaux, Roger, 26, 67
Pringle, Chris, 120
Derek, 9, 64, 86, 120, 125, 141
Don, 64
Pressdee, Jim, 40
Procter, Mike, 29, 31, 121
Pullar, Geoff, 140
Pyke, J.K., 139

Qasim Feroze, 51
Omar, 19, 122, 146
Quaife, Bernard, 64
Willie, 64
Quilty, John, 42

Raees Mohammad, 63
Rao, J.S., 49
Rackemann, Carl, 70, 83, 93, 100, 139
Radley, Clive, 14
Rajindernath, V., 93
Rajput, Lalchand, 9, 10, 39
Raman, Venkat, 35
Ramaswami, Cota, 104
Ramiz Raja, 39, 73, 122
Ramprakash, Mark, 9, 25, 137-8
Ramshaw, Darrin, 38
Ranatunga, Arjuna, 39, 119, 139
Randall, Derek, 118
Ranjitsinhji, K.S., 20, 31, 62-3, 133
Ratnayake, Rumesh, 48
Ravi, 121
Redmond, Rodney, 140
Redpath, Ian, 24, 30, 33-4
Reid, Bruce, 60, 63, 104, 145, 148
John F., 60, 63
John R., 36, 82
Reiffel, Lou, 110
Paul, 100, 110
Ron, 110
Rhodes, 'Jonty', 105
Steven, 139
Wilfred, 14, 51, 60, 116
Rice, Clive, 26, 135, 146
Richards, Barry, 18, 31, 35, 52, 79, 98, 135
Malcolm, 59
Mervyn, 59, 103
Viv, 20, 23-4, 30, 44, 52, 59, 71, 75, 87, 103, 130, 135, 137, 139

Richardson, Arthur, 137
Peter, 90, 116
Richie, 109, 112
Tom, 40, 44
Vic, 66, 104, 116
Richmond, Tom, 14
Rimington, Stan, 126
Rippon, Albert, 67
Arthur, 67, 120
Ritchie, Greg, 21, 100
Rixon, Steve, 90, 93
Rizwan-uz-Zaman, 27, 118
Roberts, Andy, 60, 75, 130
Bruce, 26
Robins, Walter, 109
Robinson, Mark, 113–14, 131
Phillip, 114
Tim, 26, 37, 120
Roche, Tony, 109
Rock, Claude, 65
Harry, 22, 65
Norman, 65
Roebuck, Paul, 65
Peter, 65
Romaines, Paul, 139
Roope, Graham, 139
Rosendorff, Neil, 34
Rothwell, B.A., 45
Rowan, Eric, 51
Rowe, Gordon, 116
Lawrence, 20, 34
Rowell, Greg, 56
Roy, Pankaj, 34, 58, 113
Pranab, 58
Royle, Vernon, 44
Russell, Charles, 14
Jack, 9, 94
Rutherford, Ken, 19, 32, 38
Ryder, Jack, 20, 35

Sadiq Mohammad, 63, 65–7, 69, 115
Saeed Anwar, 73
Saldanha, Carlton, 10, 39
Salim Malik, 21, 52, 64, 131
Samarasekera, Matibage, 115
Sandham, Andy, 14
Sandhu, Balwindersingh, 21, 114
Sarfraz Nawaz, 60, 69, 118, 141
Sarwate, Chandu, 38
Saunders, Jack, 44
Stuart, 100
Saville, Graham, 66
Sealy, Derek, 39
Sellers, Peter, 86
Selvey, Mike, 14
Sen, Probir, 92–3
Schneider, Karl, 145
Scott, Chris, 46
Jack, 102
'Tup', 21
Verdun, 107
Shackleton, Derek, 47
Shafqat Rana, 63
Shafiq Ahmed, 115
Shakespeare, William, 142
Shakoor Rana, 63
Sharif, Omar, 144
Sharma, Ajay, 130
Sanjeev, 49
Yashpal, 21
Shastri, Ravi, 9, 14, 21, 30, 73, 76, 83, 118, 130, 133, 140
Shaw, Alfred, 131
Sheahan, Paul, 14, 63
Shepherd, Don, 40
Janie, 144
Sheppard, David, 148
Sherwell, Percy, 84, 95, 104
Shipperd, Greg, 28, 61
Shoaib Mahammad, 24, 38–9, 59–61, 64, 131, 133, 139
Shrewsbury, Arthur, 20
Siddons, Jamie, 84, 107, 114
Sidebottom, Arnie, 135
Sidhu, Navjot, 71, 140
Signal, Elizabeth, 63
Rosemary, 63
Sikander Bakht, 112, 133
Silva, Amal, 92
Simmons, Kennedy, 55
Phil, 45, 72
Simpson, Bob, 19–20, 22, 24, 32–4, 52, 59, 84, 119, 133, 135, 150
Sinfield, Reg, 118
Slack, Wilf, 114, 122
Slater, Michael, 150
Sleep, Peter, 99
Slinger, Sean, 77
Small, Gladstone, 40, 46, 100
Steve, 138
Smith, Alan, 92
C. Aubrey, 85–6
Chris, 17, 63, 93, 120, 132
'Collie', 14
Dave, 120
Horace, 45
Ian, 12, 92, 120, 131–2
Mike, 82, 103, 150
Neil, 120
Paul, 29, 31, 120
Ray, 133
Robin, 14, 22, 63, 109, 120, 125
Steve, 21, 33, 100, 120
Snedden, Andrew, 64
Colin, 64
Martin, 63–4, 73, 76
W.N., 63
Snook, Ian, 44
Snow, John, 19, 142
Sobers, Gary, 14, 19–20, 22, 60, 62, 96, 99, *103*, 116, 122–3, 130
Sofilas, Mark, 123
Sohail Mohammad, 64
Solomon, Joe, 35
Somers, Arthur, 57
Soule, Richard, 115
Southerton, James, 50, 136
Spofforth, Fred, 44, *45*
Srikkanth, Kris, 9, 39, 75, 83, 121, 140, 150
Stackpole, Keith, 14, 117
snr, Keith, 102
Stackpoole, John, 113
Statham, Brian, 55, 69, 112
Steele, David, 59
John, 59
Stephenson, Franklyn, 76, 100, 136–7
Stevenson, Graham, 75
Stewart, Alec, 93–4, 137
Stoddart, Andrew, 20
Stollmeyer, Jeffrey, 125
Street, Alfred, 149
Studd, Charles, 66, 68
George, 66, 68
Kynaston, 68
Peter, 68
Strudwick, Bert, 14, 140–1
Summers, George, 125
Surridge, Stuart, 125
Surti, Rusi, 27
Susskind, 'Fred', 45
Sutcliffe, Bert, 34–5
Herbert, 31–2, 34, 126, 132, 150
Simon, 29
Symons, Andrew, 77

Taber, Brian, 92
Tahir Naqqash, 133
Talat Ali, 45
Tallon, Don, 91, 125, 149
Tarrant, Frank, 96–7
Taslim Arif, 33, 90
Tate, Fred, 60
Maurice, 45, 60, 133
Tavaré, Chris, 114, 116, 135, 138, 140
Tayfield, Hugh, 40
Taylor, Bob, 51, 90, 93, 95, 138
Bruce, 140
Clare, 108
Mark, 9, 18, 22, 24, 33, 35, 45, 82, 102, 132, 137, 139, 144, 150
Mick, 10
Neil, 27, 138
Peter, 12, 137
Tendulkar, Sachin, 14, 50, 69, 76
Tennyson, Lionel, 14
Thatcher, Margaret, 57
Thomas, Dylan, 89
Graeme, 54
Thompson, George, 49
John, 107
Thomson, Jeff, 14, 70, 97, 141
Jim, 144
Shane, 71
Tillekeratne, Hashan, 94
Tindall, Dennis, 105
Eric, 105
Peter, 105
Titmus, Fred, 41, 126
Townley, Athol, 54
Townsend, Arthur, 64
Charlie, 64
David, 64
Frank, 64
Frank Norton, 64
Jonathan, 64
Leslie, 26
Traicos, John, 52, 149
Trenerry, Bill, 67
Ted, 67
Tribe, George, 97–8
Trim, John, 116
Trimble, Glenn, 100
Trimnell, S.C., 120
Trott, Albert, 46, 68, 96–7, 125, 130
Harry, 68
Trueman, Fred, 41, 112–13, 127, 148
Trumble, Hugh, 125
Trumper, Victor, 20, 45, 60, 102, 108, 111–12, 116, 123
jnr, Victor, 60
Tucker, Adrian, 34
Tufnell, Phil, 33, 42
Tufton, John, 121
Turnbull, O.G.N., 109
Turner, Alan, 27, 30, 116
Brian, 109
Charlie, 40, 41, 46, 135
Glenn, 26, 35, 52, 69, 109, 112, 133, 135, 137, 149
Greg, 109
Sukhi, 149
Tyldesley, Ernest, 14, 25, 32
G.E., 65
J.T., 65
Tylecote, Edmund, 90

Ulyett, George, 18, 20
Umrigar, Polly, 34, 83
Underwood, Derek, 44, 47–8, 16

Vance, Bert, 37
Varey, David, 66
  Jonathan, 66
Veletta, Mike, 30, 37, 60, 93, 100
Vengsarkar, Dilip, 21, 55, 83
Verity, Hedley, 41
Victoria, Queen, 148
Virgin, Roy, 26, 29
Visser, Peter, 40, 113, 133
Viswanath, Gundappa, 21, 60, 83
Vivian, Giff, 62
  Graham, 62

Waheed Mirza, 31
Walcott, Clyde, 14, 28, 31, 38, 119, 131
Walker, Alan, 104
  Charlie, 91
  Max, 48, 54, 142
  Willis, 126
Wall, Tim, 43, 113
Walsh, Courtney, 48, 78
  Lawrence, 63
  Norman, 63
Walters, Doug, 14, 25, 50
Waqar Younis, 43, 47, 51, 74
Ward, David, 139
  Tommy, 119
Warnapura, Badula, 84
Warne, Shane, 41
Warner, Jack, 85
  'Plum', 87
Warr, John, 133
Warren, Johnny, 109
Washbrook, Cyril, 85
Wasim Akram, 49, 51, 69, 77-8, 113, 121
  Bari, 60, 112
Waterman, Denis, 144
Watkin, Steve, 44, 125
Watson, A.S., 139
  Graeme, 70, 136
  Ian, 136
  John, 111
Watt, Lionel, 87
Waugh, Bev, 109
  Dean, 62
  Mark, 22, 25, 61-2, 65, 74-5, 87, 98, 100, 109, 112-13, 117, 132, 137, 139, 140-1, 147, 150
  Rodger, 109
  Steve, 9, 61-2, 65, 100, 104, 109, 117, 130, 132-3, 137, 139, 141, 150
Wazir Mohammad, 63-4, 67
Weekes, Everton, 14, 25, 30-1, 99, 111, 116, 120, 131, 143
Welch, Damon, 148
  Raquel, 148
Wellesley, the Hon. Captain, 53
Wellham, Dirk, 27, 83, 130, 136
Wells, Alan, 61, 119
  Colin, 61, 119
  H.G., 142
  Joseph, 142
Wesley, Colin, 112
Wessels, Kepler, 9, 18, 21, 33, 37, 49, 71, 76-7, 97, 105, 136, 138, 147
Westbrook, Ruth, 67
Wettimuny, Mithra, 66
  Sidath, 66
Wharton, Alan, 107
White, Jack, 14
Wickham, Archdale, 94
Wickremasinghe, Gamini, 38
Wijesuriya, Roger, 41
Wilkinson, Cyril, 107
Willey, Robin, 85
Willis, Bob, 10, 44, 83, 116, 130, 140
Wills, Tom, 108
Wilson, Harry, 115
  Jack, 104
Windaybank, Steve, 32
Winter, Graham, 107
Wisdom, Nick, 88
  Norman, 88
Wodehouse, P.G., 142
Wood, Barry, 140
  Graeme, 9, 21, 23, 27, 33, 60, 69, 71, 100, 111, 116
  Harry, 90
Woodfull, Bill, 116, 125, 150
Woods, Sammy, 109
Woolley, Claude, 59-60
  Frank, 14, 18, 32-3, 51-2, 59-60, 111, 131, 150
  Roger, 101, 121
Woolmer, Bob, 138
Woosnam, Max, 109
Worrell, Frank, 14, 20, 28, 31, 146
Wright, Alby, 111
  Charles, 116
  G.T., 63
  John, 10, 12, 22, 48, 63
Wyatt, Bob, 51

Yallop, Graham, 9, 12, 20, 83, 135
Yardley, Bruce, 9
  Norman, 27, 108
Yarnold, Hugo, 91
Yawar Saeed, 60
Young, Charles, 51
  Ken, 77
Younis Ahmed, 60, 136, 149

Zadow, Bob, 120
Zaheer Abbas, 20-1, 23, 95, 130, 133, 135
Zahid Fazal, 51
Zesers, Andrew, 120, 139
Zoehrer, Tim, 15, 93, 95, 120